THE LIMITS OF OPTIMISM

The Limits of Optimism

THOMAS JEFFERSON'S

DUALISTIC

ENLIGHTENMENT

Maurizio Valsania

UNIVERSITY OF VIRGINIA PRESS

CHARLOTTESVILLE AND LONDON

University of Virginia Press
© 2011 by the Rector and Visitors of the University of Virginia
All rights reserved
Printed in the United States of America on acid-free paper

First published 2011
First paperback edition published 2013
ISBN 978-0-8139-3445-7 (paper)

9 8 7 6 5 4 3 2 1

The Library of Congress has cataloged the hardcover edition as follows:

LIBRARY OF CONGRESS CATALOGING-IN-PUBLICATION DATA
Valsania, Maurizio, 1965–
    The limits of optimism : Thomas Jefferson's dualistic enlightenment / Maurizio Valsania.
        p.   cm.—(Jeffersonian America)
    Includes bibliographical references and index.
    ISBN 978-0-8139-3144-9 (cloth : alk. paper) — ISBN 978-0-8139-3151-7 (e-book)
    1. Jefferson, Thomas, 1743–1826. 2. United States—Intellectual life—18th century.
3. United States—Politics and government—1775–1783. 4. United States—Politics and
government—1783–1865. 5. Enlightenment—United States. I. Title.
    E332.2.V35 2011
    973.4'6092—dc22

                                                                    2010052849

Contents

Acknowledgments

I am indebted to many institutions and individuals for their generous support in the preparation of this book. The American Antiquarian Society, Worcester, Massachusetts (in particular, Paul Erickson and Caroline Sloat); the Library Company and the Historical Society of Pennsylvania, Philadelphia (in particular, James Green and Cornelia King); the McNeil Center, Philadelphia (in particular, Daniel Richter); the John D. Rockefeller Library, Williamsburg, Virginia (in particular, Inge Flester and James Horn).

My connection with the Robert H. Smith International Center for Jefferson Studies, Charlottesville, Virginia, deserves a special mention. Joan Hairfield and Andrew O'Shaughnessy have proved to be tremendously helpful and sympathetic.

A number of friends and colleagues have contributed in many ways to improve my project: Frank Cogliano, Jane Curran, Steven Edenbo, Dick Holway, Kenny Marotta, Morgan Myers, Peter Onuf, Eran Shalev, Hannah Spahn, Taylor Stoermer, Keith Thomson, Gaye Wilson, and Mike Zuckerman. I took their suggestions and criticisms very seriously. This is my way to express sincere gratitude.

This book would not have been possible without my lovely wife, Serenella Iovino.

THE LIMITS OF OPTIMISM

Introduction

As every biographer knows, Thomas Jefferson always coped with the challenges of life very valiantly. In spite of this, the conclusion that he was a gullible eighteenth-century optimistic humanist, although seemingly evident, is not really justified. Jefferson's humanistic message was in constant dialogue with an antihumanistic outlook. Likewise, his typical optimism always interacted with a pessimism, his sense of mission with a sense of failure, and his Enlightenment with a threatening darkness.

This book focuses on several examples of Jefferson's allowance for all that negated human hopes, despite his enduring commitment to the Enlightenment or, better, because of it. Jefferson referred to negativity in different ways throughout his life: ignorance, disillusionment, disorder, necessity, fate, death, barbarism, limits, nature, the course of time, and so forth. Casting a close look at Jefferson's letters and several other texts, I show that his optimism and assertiveness worked as compensatory devices to dispel the demons of negativity. Beneath the masculine overconfidence that Jefferson so often wielded, it is quite interesting to detect "differences." Tremors of reservation, a sense of the tragic and even blatant pessimism lie beneath Jefferson's famous rhetoric of optimism.

A fundamental tension thwarted Jefferson's peace of mind, and it was by no means occasional. The tension to which I am alluding is typical of the Enlightenment as a whole. Civilization, optimism, and especially Enlightenment are the correct catchwords under which to appraise Jefferson's ideas, interests, and activities. However, Enlightenment, as well as optimism and civilization, defy simple categorization. We have often been told that to be an Enlightenment devotee means to be unswerving in both fostering optimism and cultivating one's sense of innocence, self-confidence, and self-promotion. But the eighteenth-century Enlightenment, both in Europe and in the United States, represented a reaction against every form of precritical rationalism and against the allegation that human faculties could solve—or, at least, justify—all the flaws of existence.

As a consequence, the thesis that equates Enlightenment with a stubborn optimism is clearly insufficient. Enlightenment was, in fact, a form of dualism and represented an attempt, precarious and anxiety-ridden as every human attempt, to push back the boundaries of darkness. Jefferson's Enlightenment was an effort to spread light and virtue, and a risky struggle against negativity.

It is undeniable that Jefferson was unwilling to directly address the theme of negativity. He was not the prototypical existentialist philosopher. Nonetheless, negativity is always traceable beneath the surface of his optimistic discourse. It has been maintained that Jefferson had no tragic sense whatsoever. There are good reasons to disagree. Jefferson was an enlightened man, but one who habitually adopted a realistic outlook. His narrative of "getting on" made room for both a sense of vulnerability and a sense of failure and impossibility. Whereas he unquestionably promoted the human capacity to better things, he also shunned wishful thinking and boastful speculation by precisely targeting the very source of any shallow optimism: negativity was a basic presence in Jefferson's philosophy. He engaged necessity and fate; experienced despondency and acknowledged impossibility; and perceived a nonbenevolent nature and the ruinous course of time. Too often historians fail to acknowledge that a spirit of compromise was essential to the worldview of the Enlightenment itself, and of Jefferson especially. In just this spirit, Jefferson tried to resist the consoling myth that humans could attain complete dominion over the universe they inhabited.

To restate and adapt what Henry Vyverberg wrote some fifty years ago in his well-known study of the pessimism of the French Enlightenment, the present book tries to trace the disturbing uncertainties and intellectual reservations that entered the mind of even this master builder of the American experiment in the very moment he was planning the blueprints of the future. An enlightened realist, Jefferson maintained a very ambivalent relationship to modernization, progress, and world-redeeming ambitions. Since he found himself in the position of one who was planning optimistic blueprints of the future and since he was trying to build a dreamed-of future, he necessarily dealt in uncertainties, in objects not yet attained. In a sense, he was seeking to create what he promoted, and this is a condition that does not allow one to abide in exultation. In addition, while it is undeniable that he tried to offer himself in public as an unswerving master builder of hopeful narratives, it is probably also true that his belief in progress was neither the exclusive focus nor the logical consummation of his identity. Jefferson understood that the very historical course of American republic was far from manifest, and that its future might be death and ruin.[1]

It is undeniable that the positive aspect of the Enlightenment relied on imagination and the hope of progress. However, as Vyverberg put it, it is important to take seriously the insight that "the hope of progress need not involve a firm belief in the realization of that progress." Hope does not mean faith or certainty, as we will see. The Enlightenment's optimism was far from unshakable and did not signify a sense of achievement. "The most fervent expression of an ideal," Vyverberg went on, "might be accompanied by skepticism as to its practicality and even its final validity." The Enlightenment taught us to carefully sever the hope of progress from the delusion that progress was already at hand. As such, Enlightenment triggered a certain degree of tremor among its adepts.[2]

In the following chapters, I gather evidence from Jefferson's writings to prove that he was familiar with this twofold nature of the Enlightenment. Negativity loomed always large in Jefferson's philosophy, even though activism, assertiveness, optimism, faith in the future, self-confidence, exultation, and the rhetoric of "getting on" were important ingredients of his distinctive style of thought. He explicitly recognized that becoming an enlightened realist meant growing familiar with anxiety, disquiet, doubts, embarrassing compromises, and even impossibility. He was aware that future-oriented activism and self-confidence might have no solid basis, and that sooner or later fate might encroach upon "our best hopes." The hypothesis that I hope to turn into a theory is that Jefferson expressed that sense of dispersion and alienation that is typical of one who is deeply worried by the journey undertaken, rather than triumphantly at ease in it. Jefferson did not linger on triumphal myths. On the contrary, "limit yourself," "stay at home," "be prepared," and "guard against" were among the favorite metaphors of his narratives. My hypothesis is that by opposing every form of unshakable optimism, Jefferson's Enlightenment counteracted any blind confidence in human or American progress.[3]

All through his life Jefferson remained quite faithful to the Enlightenment and the implicit dualism between light and darkness, civilization and barbarism, positivity and negativity. In this respect, there was no significant development over time in his style and thought.

I am not suggesting, obviously, that his personality was monolithic and rigid. The issues of Jefferson's personality, his secrets, his inner life, his complexities, his impenetrability, lie well beyond the scope of the book. As a number of biographies and books built around chronological categories have made clear, the young man who drafted the Declaration of Independence, for instance, was in several ways a different man from the ex-president, fifty years later. Jefferson's body changed over time, the world around him underwent dramatic transformations, and there is no reason to believe that Jefferson's self, as a hypothetical metaphysical substance, was the sole element to remain untouched. Young Jefferson became a quite different person as the time went by. But even persons who become different from what they used to be can remain faithful to a specific style and an enduring commitment. The point is that all the Jeffersons who have fallen under the lens of countless biographies and essays on personality hardly ever relinquished the Enlightenment style of thought, and the dualistic rhythms connected to that philosophical tradition.[4]

The reader may draw a moral from this story. The account of Jefferson's life-long commitment to both Enlightenment and negativity not only teaches us about a late eighteenth-century champion of enlightened realism but also suggests a critique of the one-dimensional optimism that buoys up present-day capitalist societies. A study of Jefferson's awareness of negativity is a good way of educating our sense of the tragic, our humility, and our desire to further the best hopes of the Enlightenment. We desperately need to educate ourselves to see through the myth of unlimited possibilities.

Jefferson left us a number of written sources that enshrine authorial qualities. By "authorial" I mean those texts "taken over" by the private self, its processes of adjustment, and contradictions. An authorial text is a text in which the self is not watchful enough to prevent a leakage of its inner conceptual frameworks. Besides the declared purpose, the authorial text shows often a marginal content that is not public and formal, as it puts emphasis on personal voice, it chases unfamiliar experiences, and hence it is a potential threat to the status quo.

Before the advent of literary Romanticism, essays, narratives, treatises, sermons, dramas, and pamphlets were written by authors speaking publicly. "Publicly" means that the author was basically striving to summon his fellows through a call to conventions. Late eighteenth- and early nineteenth-century leaders qua leaders were hardly committed to the explicit recognition of negativity. To some extent, they were committed to uphold artificial distinctions between what is public, namely, didactical, instructional, and conventional— devoted to creating consensus, to teaching readers the virtue of becoming a better citizen—and what is "merely" aesthetic, private, unconventional and hence not admissible. The written texts those leaders bequeathed to posterity were often a one-dimensional story, highly selective, almost self-castigating in their aims and contents. They seldom were journals that kept realistic records of all the traveler's attempts to cope with the elements. On the contrary, the subordination of unconventional interests to the interests of the public was the very mark of a text's value.

However, today, like yesterday, the art of writing prompts a schizophrenic disposition. A written text is at once a communitarian instrument to summon the audience to pursue some kind of conventional vision and a means to keep note of personal feelings, fears, and unorthodox opinions. In the eighteenth century, this schizophrenic disorder was usually healed by subordinating the personal to the official goals, the unconventional to the conventional, the inner "author" to the public "officeholder," and anxieties to exultation. The national experience entailed in the art of writing almost always had a positive outcome in the period. "Public" texts enmeshed in civic overtones always forged an optimistic and one-dimensional sense of nationhood while rousing patriotic sentiments and communicating a sense of classical equilibrium. Through their texts, leaders built up pride and self-confidence as well as furthering the national experiment. Published texts never tried to figure out alternative pathways or to seriously uphold alternative worldviews. Their main purpose was to vindicate the decisions already made and to promote those decisions, often arbitrary ones, with the help of a national epic stressing "achievements." Public texts tried to instruct readers on the importance of fettering the self. They warned readers about the dangers of forsaking national responsibilities, discarding the established roles, refraining from institutional networks, and thwarting the sense of duty.

By and large, in letters or journals the author was more willing to confess inner feelings or to betray doubts and internal contradictions. We are not to expect, evidently, that even in the most personal letters would an eighteenth-century author tell all. Personal letters and journals contained a number of self-censorings, were highly selective, were written by officeholders supposedly in command of their personal dynamics, and adhered to the conventions of their time. On the other hand, there was a kind of tension in these texts that was lacking in more formal treatises and essays. Like other public texts, letters and journals were also intended to foster the official discourse, to depict emotional and intellectual swerving in a highly disapproving tone, to instruct readers on the importance of fettering the self and its negative stances, and to suggest that "achievements" were always more important than "attempts" and processes.

Nonetheless, letters and journals were to some extent full of "confusion." What Mildred Silver said about one of the most eminent champions of mid-nineteenth-century American optimism—the philosopher Ralph Waldo Emerson—is relevant to other optimist leaders who were active in the previous decades. If we are to look for Emerson's "reiterated denial of the possibility of progress for the race," Silver wrote, we should not forget his journals. In effect, the journals "seem much less hopeful of progress in the nineteenth-century acceptance of the word than the published works."[5]

Like Emerson, Jefferson was both an "author" (in the aforementioned sense) and a "representative man." He was sometimes unconventional but also quite often an insider, an unshakable nationalist, a policymaker, and a white male officeholder in a position of political power whose ideas and decisions mattered. "Representative" means that he was entitled to represent the official normative language; that he was quite successful in hiding from himself and from others his sense of negativity; and that he was influential on subsequent works and ideas. By focusing on this "representative" man and officeholder, this book intends, however, to be a nondeferential study of the concepts of whiteness and eighteenth-century maleness. It is a nondeferential study, as it emphasizes instances of failure, precarious attempts, negative languages, and incidental fractures in the official normative discourse. It traces weaknesses in a figure "expected" to be committed to exclusively uphold the official normative discourse. This book focuses on an officeholder who did not always succeed in meeting this high level of expectation. Jefferson did not succeed in both fettering himself and maintaining command of the process of his identity formation. He was a successful and influential white male, who sometimes downplayed the masculine "sense of mission" bestowed on him. Our protagonist was an insider who, at times, let down the expectations of the national apparatus, as he was supposed to do "good" by relating information in a slightly less realistic way than he actually did.[6]

This leader was a member of the economic elite, an element of the Virginia gentry. He had several economic and cultural affiliations and should be regarded as an agent of such forces. Of course, this is not tantamount to saying that he was just an unthoughtful instrument implementing the interests of his class. Jefferson was a human being, and human beings should be described dialectically as an array of contradictory motives, interests, and languages. They are "machines" that unremittingly attempt to cope with multifaceted reality. As a consequence, we can safely assume that a conflict existed between Jefferson's official role, position, place (and corresponding worldview), and other roles, positions, places (and corresponding worldviews) he experienced. The identity and the character of this leader should be interpreted as a process of identity formation and a struggle to try to gain coherence, consistency, and inner psychological conformity.[7]

Thomas Jefferson was a human being, not just the embodiment of *one* ideal, of *one* class interest, of *one* role, of *one* language, or an upholder of *the* official discourse. Individual identity exists in the very act of its own proclamation. To some extent, individual identity is a variable of the context where this proclamation is performed, not something that exists independently from it. Jefferson's attempt at gaining coherence was a struggle to conceal "confusion" by denying competing identities, languages, and illegitimate practices.

When such an attempt succeeds, these inner conflicts remain hidden. Taken at their face value, public proclamations of "unshakable optimism," for instance, seem to be the best refutation of their complementary double. Nevertheless, "confusion" is still traceable beneath the proclaimed identity, betrayed by texts that exhibit authorial qualities. Jefferson was not the personification of a clear-cut ideology that we can label by using the adjective "optimistic." He was not a character or an idea; he rather had characters, ideas, and identities, and this multiplicity invites us to focus on the interactions between these colliding ingredients, languages, and traits.

For the reasons just explained, this book must not be read as the attempt to prove that, notwithstanding a body of contrary evidence, Jefferson *was* pessimistic. It must be clear that the story I am telling is not concerned with Jefferson's *being* a despondent man. Rather, it is about his *dealing* with pessimism, with his *having* a sense of the tragic, with his *attempts* at coping with impossibility and the ocean of negativity. It is the story of a journey.

Herman Melville, at the end of chapter 58 of *Moby Dick*, provided a good portrayal of the kind of journey on which Jefferson set out and the prospect that traveling in general creates. "For as this appalling ocean surrounds the verdant land," Melville wrote, "so in the soul of man there lies an insular Tahiti, full of peace and joy, but encompassed by all the horrors of the half known life. God keep thee! Push not off from that isle, thou canst never return!"

The present book describes an audacious journey in the antihuman, in the half-formed, in impossibility, in dreams, and beyond the margins of conventionality. The recognition of the "appalling ocean" is the most important moment of enlightened travel. Fortunately, Jefferson did not comply with the advice of not leaving the island. He left it and bequeathed to posterity a detailed journal of what lay beyond. Even today, the "appalling ocean" lying beyond the verdant land has many facets and elicits different answers. At first, it triggers excitement and a certain compensatory boldness; otherwise one would never set out. It also produces anxiety, a sense of insignificance, and even despondency. When the traveler seizes upon the enormity of what exists beyond, it is too late to escape the fear that a shipwreck is inescapably approaching; at times, the traveler feels that the goal, the promised land, is but a cheerful dream evading reality. The traveler, like Jefferson, pushes off and senses that the ocean sweeps humans along and, also, that it exerts an irresistible fascination.

The overall structure of the book and the inherent connection between the chapters and their order should thus be clear.

Chapter 1 helps the readers to situate Jefferson in the context of the Enlightenment and the relevant literature. Readers have to wait a few pages before listening to Jefferson's own voice, but I am convinced that what is needed first and foremost is a detailed discussion of the notion of Enlightenment, a study of its priorities, and an adequate emphasis on the common platform shared by the different historical Enlightenments.

Chapter 2 considers Jefferson's unabated optimism and his bold certainty about the future. Sometimes, Jefferson tried to resist the burden of the Enlightenment. He wanted us to believe that he was a champion of self-confidence, a winner taken by full-fledged satisfaction, and a hero enthused by the faith that time looks benignly on the American cause. He wanted us to believe—or maybe he just wanted to convince himself—that the traveler has already arrived at the promised land. Occasionally, Jefferson tried to present himself that way: not an enlightened dualist and a traveler, but an ideal and a classical hero living in a metaphysical world. It was his way of evading the discomforts that the Enlightenment entailed.

Chapter 3 tells the story of the transformation of the heroic optimism-as-certainty into an anxiety-ridden worship of possibilities. Jefferson had a firsthand knowledge of both kinds of optimisms that I have identified, respectively, by the concepts of faith and hope. The two concepts must never be lumped together.

Chapter 4 emphasizes what lies beyond possibilities. It is clear that necessity is possibility's complementary double. I show that Jefferson, an enlightened and honest philosopher of *human* possibilities, took necessity into serious consideration. In effect, human possibility means possibility with a definite and limited range. Nature and time are introduced as the two most eloquent masks worn, as it were, by necessity.

Chapter 5 studies the despondency that unavoidably ensues when necessity is taken at face value. It tells what happens when necessity is internalized as a sense of impossibility.

Chapter 6 draws the conclusion that Jefferson, to some extent, distrusted his beloved ideals and imagination. Better: that he simultaneously trusted and distrusted ideals. A rich vein of realism is traceable beneath Jefferson's famous idealism. Such a duality is an unavoidable conclusion, as long as a truly enlightened philosopher can never be entirely satisfied with optimism, faith, and certainty but is asked to struggle with both necessity and impossibility.

1

Enlightenment & Dualism

THE QUESTION OF OPTIMISM

Late eighteenth-century American leaders have often been portrayed as prototypes of stubborn self-reliance and inescapable optimism. Over the years, philosophers, political scientists, historians, sociologists, journalists, and countless first- and second-rank intellectual figures have put considerable emphasis on tropes such as "heroic action," "Manifest Destiny," the "new Israel," and "world-redeeming ambitions." They have thus forced their audience to believe in the legitimacy of the automatic identification between these ambitions and a childish "unshakable optimism." The late eighteenth-century leader has often been portrayed as if he only saw the course of time as substantially complaisant to America's ultimate triumph.[1]

In particular, late eighteenth-century leaders, we have been told, were not just optimistic but had "the most extraordinary sense of optimism about the future of America." As Michael Kammen writes, "Jefferson's generation was exultant about the prospects for American civilization." By contrast, we "have developed serious reservations about the 'goodness' of American values and our own performance." Whereas we have our eyes "on the past, when not absolutely averted in shame," they had theirs on a compliant future. American leaders were unswerving in both fostering their "extraordinary" optimism and cultivating their sense of innocence, their self-affirmation, their self-promotion.[2]

There is something inadequate in such judgments that see in those hopes, desires, ambitions, and expectant declarations the simple expression of unshakable exultation and unswerving stubbornness. Optimism is not necessarily a synonym of stubbornness and can also be a signal of one's reliance on aspirations and hope. Optimism can easily become a form of desire. And since a desire should never be confused with its object, optimism is not per se the realization of its wished-for outcome. It is unquestionable that eighteenth-century leaders were full of desires. But their optimism-as-desire bespoke something they lacked, something they craved, something they imagined, not something they owned or celebrated. Optimism-as-desire did not make them exultant. As a consequence, we should dismiss any oppositional way of looking at "us" as yearning, skeptical, averting, shameful, frustrated, grimly complaining about missed opportunities, and fundamentally in a defensive mood, and "them" as living in a classical age of achieved equilibrium, satisfaction, and untottering self-assertion. Both "we" and "they" should be better portrayed as Janus headed, showing the face of Pollyanna while concealing the profile of Cassandra. We tend to portray eighteenth-century leaders, Jefferson in particular, as self-reliant persons speaking the language of exultation and classical equilibrium. In fact, even though they often told the story of their achievements, they were far from "convinced" about the message they proclaimed.

It is no doubt embarrassing to call attention to the Founding Fathers' sense of the negative. Dealing with their distrust of the journey undertaken amounts to confronting a still widespread American taboo. Since America has not happened yet, and since the future is the sole terrain of the "new Israel," any doctrine that calls into question the positive march of civilization seems automatically anti-American. It is not easy to raise the question of an American acknowledgment of negativity and failure even though, I believe, this is the only viable road to grasp the complexity of Jefferson's and his generation's worldviews. Because of its complexity, Jefferson's venture is highly disquieting to all those idealists who are unwilling to look askance at self-assuring myths, and who cannot accept Jefferson's assumption that human beings are peripheral and impermanent by their very constitution. All the interpreters who instinctively share a version of Americanism based on "unshakable optimism" and the conception that "man" shares the divine nature, that "man" stands secure at the very center of the universe, can hardly withstand the existential complexities, risks, and experiential ambiguities to which Jefferson's enlightened philosophy was accustomed.

"America has not happened yet" deserves further analysis. The United States was born of the most cheerful expectations of the Enlightenment: the primacy of reason, the reliability of human understanding, the value of individual freedom, confidence in method and education, and above all—the most "romantic" among the Enlightenment tenets—the belief in progress. Each of these tenets marked from the outset the stages of the process of national formation.

In the context of the Enlightenment, American citizens seemed to be expected to always advocate a developmental and dynamic sense of the country. "Dynamic sense" means that the ideas of progress, of having dominion over the land, cultivating the earth, bringing civilization, reason imposing harmony and order over darkness and wilderness, must always be joined to

a firm conviction of eventual success. National formation is seen as a necessarily everlasting process and a successful one at that, not limited to any
geographical or temporal boundary. In opposition to other communities that
founded their identity upon roots deeply sunk into the past—like genealogy,
homogeneous ethnicity, and defined geographic boundaries—we are told
that American founding leaders wanted to define themselves by reference
to the Revolution, to the process of cultural cohesion, and to a promised
optimistic future. The American nation should never be conceived either as a
"territorial definition," Sacvan Bercovitch warns, or as a temporal and, hence,
a transitory reality. It should be interpreted as something perennial, the very
defeat of death, "the symbol of an ideological consensus," and the land of
optimism, of imagination, and of promises fully realized.[3]

Such a myth of an unshakable optimism, still in effect in the twentieth
and twenty-first centuries, began to have large diffusion during the 1830s. It
was in that very romantic age that a new leading class made of "Manifest-des-
tiners" moved beyond eighteenth-century patterns. They seemed to eventually succeed in getting rid of Jeffersonian philosophy and its "embarrassing"
compromises and hesitation. The "Age of Laissez Nous Faire" seemed to di-
vest itself of any tie and any republican responsibility.

We could naturally question whether that generation really succeeded in
this project of simplification, but some historians insist that in the 1830s the
United States ceased to perceive itself as a temporary balance between negative and positive forces and dependent on checks and balances. According to
William Appleman Williams, for instance, the national history turned into
a vision of an absolute expansion, a list of successes without setbacks. Success became the only criterion to certify ex post facto the moral and political
rightness of an undertaking, and even its historical necessity. The idea was
that those leaders who win and thrive have always the right to win and thrive.
The eighteenth-century "encompassing view, based upon a sense of interrelated wholeness and community and defined by a system of equity and balance, failed to withstand the forces it had done so much to create." The new
"forces" signified an expansion without contractions, the supreme right of the
winner, and gave good reason for an optimism without despair. This new approach to the national history sounded attractive to Van Buren, to President
Jackson and other "War Hawk" men like Henry Clay and John C. Calhoun.
Williams emphasized that the worship of those expansive forces was deeply
at variance with the eighteenth-century "sense of interrelated wholeness" and
with the Enlightenment sensibility of Jefferson's generation.[4]

By the 1830s new leaders arose, and a new romantic acquisitiveness took
hold. Subtler analysis would be required to demonstrate the pervasiveness

of the myth in the period, but when we today speak of an American optimism without pessimism or when we uncritically approve of the idea that
despondency and fatalism are deeply un-American, we show we are still vic-
tims of that same acquisitive stance. Those myths were alien to Jefferson and
his generation. Whether or not hawkish leaders were completely taken by the
acquisitive spirit, it is undeniable that at the closing of the eighteenth century
we would have found instead unbearable degrees of "confusion": stronger
commitments to the past, to republican models, to nature, to the ideas of necessity, fate and impermanence, and a stronger "sense of interrelated wholeness," to use Williams's happy expression. Late eighteenth-century intellectual
journeys were philosophically more complex and multifaceted than their romantic replacement. Complex and often contradictory tenets, a mixture of
past and future, of old and new, of nature and culture, were intermingled in
old leaders' discourses, and the simultaneous presence of these contradictory
"laws" may turn those figures into quasi-tragic characters.

Eighteenth-century American leaders never learned to speak one language exclusively, and certainly not the language of unhampered expansion
and ideological consensus. They continued to speak their dialects and work
with more than one set of ideas. Historians keep casting synthesizing gazes on
eighteenth-century America and hope to determine "the" operative code—be
it some form of Lockean liberalism, or some version of classical republicanism. Nevertheless, reality is far more complex. There is nothing pathological,
as Daniel Walker Howe also stresses, in the fact that early Americans, Jefferson included, "subscribed to both republican and liberal ideas and drew upon
them both freely when they wanted to make a point. The distinction between
the two philosophies is more one of our making than of theirs." Historians
long to coalesce their discourses around a single organizing theme in order
to portray both past events and past lives as a coherent whole. But the organizing theme is often an abstraction. Eighteenth-century American leaders
were prey to, and at once buttressed by, discourses that, as Carroll Smith-
Rosenberg says, "contested one another, layering political rhetoric and beliefs
with diverse meanings and values, molding perceptions and behaviors."[5]

Eighteenth-century leaders considered it normal to float among what we
today would call republicanism, liberalism, democratic and egalitarian ideals,
aristocratic visions, traditionalism, modernism, and so on. Within Jefferson's
philosophy, for instance, a particular discourse existed that was clearly caught
in a backward-looking "Roman" or, alternatively, "Saxon" republicanism,
centered on vanishing virtue, on nostalgia, and quite at odds with advancing
modernity. At the same time, another discourse existed that clearly offset the
first: a progressive, forward-looking, liberal philosophy advocating Lockean
politics and Smithian economics, aiming at a complete rejection of the past,

and wholeheartedly embracing capitalism. Jefferson's philosophy never came to a decision between these two (or manifold) options. Jefferson's Americanism was typical of a traveler who kept on "looking both ways," as Peter Onuf writes, "toward an idealized Saxon past and toward a progressively enlightened future." Jefferson invites "wildly contradictory characterizations of his political thought" and, we should also say, of his Americanism.[6]

The dialectic between backward- and forward-looking discourses does not amount to an either/or perspective, in which, when the past-oriented discourse is present, the future-oriented one must be absent. Jefferson was a good example in this regard. The optimist philosopher who quite often celebrated the detachment from the dark ages of the past and who in the mid-1820s still rejoiced for the march of civilization advancing from the sea coast, coexisted with another quite pessimistic philosopher who asserted that "the human mind," hopefully, "will some day get back to the freedom it enjoyed 2000 years ago" during the Roman Empire. Despite the fact that Jefferson celebrated the triumph over unfavorable circumstances as a clear signal that there was good reason to trust the things to come, other discourses existed that were locked in the past, lingering on a vague nostalgia about what was passing and missing. The commitment to modernity, future, and innovation did not loosen an enduring attachment to the classical world. Nor, more generally, were eighteenth-century leaders, Jefferson included, particularly troubled by the problems posed by their backward-looking Americanism and, as Carl Richard recognizes, "by their attempt to live in both intellectual worlds simultaneously."[7]

One of the reasons why "War Hawk" nineteenth-century leaders looked askance at their fathers was probably because the old version of Americanism was perceived as unbearably nostalgic or even aristocratic. I am not maintaining that Jefferson's contemporaries were backward-looking and hostile to modernity, but those leaders had to painfully attain a new whole set of values. If often they seemed quite thrilled to live in the New World, other times they appeared bewildered and had to put as good a face as they could on a society urging them to quickly adopt new operative tools. They were struggling to adjust themselves to a new social order whose sinews were commerce, corporations, banks, paper money, consumerism, a growing population, politics turned into a profession, a higher level of participation, and ordinary people conducting, for the first time, genuine American business.[8]

"Most American revolutionary leaders," Gordon Wood writes, "adhered to and spoke the language of what we have called civic humanism or classical republicanism. However much this republican ideology contributed to America's future culture, it was essentially backward-looking. It was rooted in a traditional aristocratic aversion to commerce and remained committed to communal goals at the expense of private desires." Whether or not they really adhered to republicanism, it is undeniable that in their plea for innovation eighteenth-century leaders were definitely not in a position to overlook the forces of tradition and the values of family, patronage, disinterestedness, self-effacement, and gentility in which they had been reared. Especially for the leaders who were born in the South, it was a painful task to deal with those contradictory visions. We should not downplay the Founding Fathers' sincere commitment to emergent industrialism, capitalism, free trade, and liberalism. However, we cannot ignore that the conflict between the old and new dimensions was altogether harsh, and that it never came to an easy synthesis.[9]

Eighteenth-century Americanism was much more multifaceted than any reduction of Americanism to a straight version of "unshakable optimism." During the age of Jefferson, the new nation was not gripped by ideological consensus or by the myth of progress as unhampered expansion. As Onuf observes, "there is something alien and inaccessible about Jefferson—something attributable not simply to temporal and cultural distance." This eighteenth-century Virginian leader was alien and inaccessible because he was a "figure of contradiction" and a "man of many faces," as Merrill Peterson also put it, who never yielded to a unique, synthetic, clear-cut, and consolatory vision of both human life and American history.[10]

Just like his contemporaries, Jefferson was never faithful to a precise ideology, be it so-called classical republicanism, a transitional liberalism, or a full-fledged capitalism. He cast no simplistic or ideological visions on reality and, accordingly, his philosophy does not deserve to be interpreted in a simplistic or ideological way. Jefferson was to some extent inaccessible because his philosophy overflowed with all those typical permanent dialectical tensions and unsolvable antonyms of the "national character" that have long since been surveyed by scholars. In fact, he was idealist and materialist; he was an individualist with a strong sense of community; he was tough-minded and impressionable; he was a creature of imagination and a ruthless operator; he worshipped his native woods and fields while lusting for innovation and cosmopolitanism; he was at once religious and secular; he quested after the highest moral standards without forsaking the opportunistic ethos of the market; he was a free-thinker permeated by anxiety, and an optimist permeated by grief. If, as Michael Zuckerman recognizes, "we have always been an antinomian nation," Jefferson was definitely the most typical exponent of a down-to-earth version of Americanism and optimism, the best man of many faces for a challenging nation of many faces.[11]

ENLIGHTENMENT AND DUALISM

The true prototype of the eighteenth-century traveler, Jefferson had the kind of wavering optimism that is typical of those who know that no victories are possible, just temporary truces. Jefferson was, thus, a man of many faces not because he was pathological, but because he was aware of dwelling in a fluid and unfolding world. It was as a traveler that he embraced a number of situations, spoke several languages, and had no chance to arrive at unqualified self-assertion, unswerving faith, and the rhetoric of unhampered expansion. It is travel as such that triggers answers and attitudes that change over time and that only the superficial scholar might label incoherent. I am telling the story of Jefferson as a traveler of sorts, but I am not primarily concerned with his geographical travels. The travel I am considering is a deeper experience that sensitive human beings, not just a handful of eighteenth-century leaders, sometimes undergo when they meet the unknown, when they face barbarism and negativity. I am quite convinced that Jefferson was not unique as a traveler, but his travel certainly was. Few human beings have had the chance to live through the moment when a nation was being born, when two revolutions broke out, and when both European and American societies began their laborious march toward a new capitalist order.

As a traveler in time, Jefferson remained unsystematic. His philosophy was in turn unsystematic and a matter of adjustment. "Circumstances forced him to remain an incidental scientist and philosopher," Malone argued. "I have tried to show the central figure as a living man and growing mind in a changing world, not as a statue in a niche or a portrait on the wall. Jefferson was never static, and in this period of his life he had to adjust himself to momentous changes in external circumstances. This part of the story of his mind [his years in Paris] is essentially one of adjustment." Malone's comments stressing adjustment suggest that Jefferson was, in an essential way, the philosopher of the incidental. "Adjustment" is probably the most important key to enter Jefferson's unconventional mind, certainly not limited to his years in Paris. All through his life, he acknowledged the role of circumstances and perceived ingenuity as a provisional tool to better cope with an ever-changing world.[12]

When in the Advertisement of the *Notes on the State of Virginia,* for example, Jefferson warned the reader that "the subjects are all treated imperfectly," he was communicating something deeper than a formulaic disclaimer about his book. He was speaking as a traveler must. He was disclosing his most secret way of dwelling in the world, characterized by a keen sense of the temporality of existence, a sense of imperfection, and an incessant call to the circumstances. Jefferson was anti-systematic and had no problem in admitting intrinsic limits, for instance, even of his descriptive project on Virginia. In 1814, Jefferson the traveler wrote to John Melish that "the work itself indeed is nothing more than the measure of a shadow, never stationary, but lengthening as the sun advances, and to be taken anew from hour to hour. It must remain, therefore, for some other hand to sketch its appearance at another epoch, to furnish another element for calculating the course and motion of this member of our federal system."[13]

That passage is probably the best abridgment of Jefferson's enlightened and realistic philosophy. The underlying general idea was that human works and ventures would be temporal and imperfect and could not rise above their limits. The acknowledgment that error and limits were "incident to our imperfect nature," as he once philosophized, makes the story of Jefferson's commitment to optimism much more interesting. Jefferson's optimism was complicated by the fact that he perceived himself as a traveler, that he portrayed himself as a fading character in the broad *affresco* of the passing generations ("the earth belongs to the living") or, which is the same, by the fact that he was one of the most important representatives of Enlightenment culture in America.[14]

Just like optimism, enlightenment is a puzzling notion that means many different things. The historical Enlightenment, as it actually existed, was primarily "an event" or, better, a set of unrepeatable historical processes, of books, institutions, and authors located at a precise moment in the course of eighteenth-century transatlantic history. As a historical and geographical set of phenomena, the Enlightenment was so complex and multifaceted—there were too many Enlightenments—that an all-encompassing discussion of its particularities is an impossibility. As to its contents, themes, and priorities, we are also compelled to acknowledge that they were treated with different emphases according to the places and the moments taken into consideration. The Enlightenment was not a school or a coherent corpus of doctrines, and almost every protagonist had a personal and unique way of interpreting it.[15]

We cannot arrive at a characterization of the Enlightenment, let alone at an adequate definition. However, insofar as those different historical Enlightenments reacted against earlier philosophical approaches and beliefs, some basic ingredients and a common platform must be identifiable. It is an either/or option: either "enlightenment" is a useful operative tool, and hence its adepts share a common and somehow identifiable style, or "enlightenment" is too generic a term, something we should dismiss altogether. I leave readers the burden to judge for themselves, but I cannot help thinking that the common platform can be identified. In a positive way, all the Enlightenments prompted an analogous trust in the law of nature, a very similar faith in the sufficiency of human reason, in the desirability of individual freedom, in the reliability of human understanding, and in self-government. The historical Enlightenments also encouraged reliance on method and faith in education; they laid a precise emphasis on the technical and operative character of philosophy, on the skillful management of resources, and on the reasons why one should cherish hope in achievements and progress. The Enlightenments were a form of desire that purported optimism, another form of desire. As a correlate, this desire claimed utilitarianism, activism, assertiveness, entrepreneurship, and anti-traditionalism.

The devotees of the Enlightenments, in other words, shared a common goal—the moralization and humanization of the world—which was something more than a generic humanism. It was not a generic humanism because the Enlightenments, by means of specific instruments and concepts (education, science, freedom, self-government, and so on), tried to bring about a new and hopeful society. Enlightenment philosophers shared more than just a common target. For the first time in human history, they widely agreed on the use of common instruments. They identified a goal and delved extensively into the best instruments to realize it. It is the character of being something *specifically* practical, communal, and self-conscious that allows us to differentiate the Enlightenments from a generic humanistic bias.[16]

Jefferson's optimism was complicated by the fact that this traveler perceived himself as a man of the Enlightenment. Why a complication? The goal of moralization and humanization of the world, the emphasis on instruments, this specific style we are examining, entailed something ominous. The sense of venture, of fighting against enemies, and the fear of being defeated were also, undeniably, ingredients of the Enlightenment. By its very nature, the Enlightenment also elicited important negative factors. In the same way the traveler is asked to be aware of the hazards associated with the unknown land, being an Enlightenment devotee meant to commit oneself to realism, to forbearance, and to intellectual humility. The Enlightenment recognized that human knowledge is always contingent, that "truth advances, and error recedes, step by step only," as Jefferson said. Experience, however fluctuating, was envisioned as the only reliable source of wisdom, more than any metaphysical or consoling religious idea. Enlightenment was a mode of traveling and explicitly averted once-and-for-all principles, idealism, spiritualism, rationalism, abstract reasoning, and all-encompassing systems.[17]

In general terms, being an Enlightenment devotee meant to accept a culture of limits: in this context, the narrative of optimism, expansion, success, and "getting on" always took into consideration both the risk of being exposed to failure and a sense of impossibility. Enlightenment was at once a spur to action and a device to nurture the sense of human limitation. Just like traveling, the Enlightenment also breached one's provincialism and childish dreams. To borrow from Jefferson's words, it "makes men wiser, but less happy."[18]

Gordon Wood once wrote that Jefferson "had no tragic sense whatsoever." However, any disciple of the Enlightenment was asked to develop a strong sense of the negative. A tragic sense is tantamount to the awareness that the self's enlightened goals, values, and instruments are besieged and often beleaguered by "uncanny" powers of which the self does not, could not, approve. Whoever brings light into darkness must acknowledge that darkness is a reality, not just a hypothesis. Like all the other exponents of the Enlightenment, Jefferson incessantly moved in such a dualistic framework, in which hope and despair, "rational" and "irrational" energy, relentlessly faced each other. The goal that the Enlightenment upheld would have made no sense outside a world conceived in strict dualistic terms.[19]

Dualism can designate several tenets taken from different fields, from religion to metaphysics, from epistemology to logic. There is a mind/body dualism, a god-of-the-light/god-of-the-night dualism, an appearance/reality dualism, a concept/intuition dualism, a conscious/unconscious dualism, and so forth. In general, "dualism" designates any view that draws on two separate explanatory principles.

Quite often dualism indicates a vision of civilization, namely, of "rational" energy and light, as surrounded by barbarism and darkness, namely, by "irrational" energy. The dialectic of "rational" and "irrational" moments has been recognized by a number of thinkers over the centuries. A tragic conflict between the Apollonian and the Dionysian moments, as the two principles have also been called, persists in most human mythologies. It was Friedrich Nietzsche who proposed a philosophy that wound human existence around the Greek myths of Apollo and Dionysus. While Apollo is the power that fixes the limits through form, Dionysus, on the other hand, represents the "irrational" activity that Appollonian form strives to control and clarify. There is no way out of this conflict.[20]

Dualism is relevant to Jefferson insofar as his enlightenment took into serious account a tension and at times an open struggle between the two principles. Moreover, I believe Jefferson's binary rhetoric has not been adequately analyzed by historians, despite the fact that it is an exceedingly important phenomenon. Also, Jefferson's version of the Enlightenment accepted a dualism that polarized both life and history between the principles of light and darkness. The idea, for instance, of an "American experiment," which he articulated in his typical vocabulary, was embedded in the awareness of an imminent struggle, and maybe defeat: America was repeatedly defined as a little thing encircled by overwhelming powers. The American republic that Jefferson the man of the Enlightenment upheld throughout his entire life did not arise from a sense of fulfillment and the belief that the mission was accomplished.[21]

Jefferson was acquainted with the struggle between Apollo and Dionysus, although not because he ever explicitly mentioned the Greek gods or because he was the improbable American forerunner of Nietzsche. More simply, the vision of a never-ending conflict between the two principles gave the basic rhythm to Jefferson's philosophy. Often caught in the struggle, unable to rescue himself from the conflict, capable of thinking only in those dualistic terms, Jefferson developed a strong sense of the tragic. Several examples could be provided to show that Jefferson adopted dualistic patterns as a rule. More examples are discussed in the following chapters, but let me remark on one.

In 1763, as a young man, Jefferson wrote John Page a letter that offers a good illustration of his typical dualism:

> Perfect happiness I beleive was never intended by the deity to be the lot of any one of his creatures in this world; . . . The most fortunate of us all in our journey through life frequently meet with calamities and misfortunes which may greatly afflict us: and to fortify our minds against the attacks of these calamities and misfortunes should be one of the principal studies and endeavors of our lives. The only method of doing this is to assume a perfect resignation to the divine will, to consider that whatever does happen, must happen, and that by our uneasiness we cannot prevent the blow before it does fall, but we may add to it's force after it has fallen. These considerations and others such as these may enable us in some measure to surmount the difficulties thrown in our way, to bear up with a tolerable degree of patience under this burthen of life, and to proceed with a pious and unshaken resignation till we arrive at our journey's end, where we may deliver up our trust into the hands of him who gave it, and receive such reward as to him shall seem proportioned to our merit.[22]

In this letter, as in other letters of the same period, we come across ideas that are conventional and stolen from the classics, Greek, Roman, and English. The degree of originality is quite irrelevant. What is startling is that the young Jefferson felt compelled to wholeheartedly identify with those conventional tropes and with the worldview that they convey: that happiness and human wishes, namely, "rational" energy, are always crushed by an "irrational" power manifesting itself through calamities and misfortunes; that our mind, at best, could grow fortified against the attacks that are thrown at us, in perfect resignation to a condition that our mind faces, but that cannot be changed; that life is a burden because by definition beleaguered by a power that is divergent from life; that life is a journey, and hence intrinsically temporal, short, precarious, while the dimension that begins beyond the journey's end is a land of eternal reward and punishment. The dualism between the feebleness of human aspirations and a cosmic necessity attained an eloquent expression, that "whatever does happen, must happen."[23]

That letter to Page is far from unique. In his *Literary Commonplace Book,* one of the few documents from his early years, Jefferson copied very divergent passages from a number of authors. The *Literary Commonplace Book* is an interesting document because most of the 407 passages were entered when Jefferson was between the ages of fifteen and thirty, wax to be molded.

By glancing through this extraordinary document, the modern reader can easily get the impression that young Jefferson exhibited singular attention toward the conventional theme—entrenched in several cultures and places—of the never-ending struggle between the two principles: between human desires, happiness, fulfillment, all the energy that could be deemed "rational," and the antihuman, "irrational" powers that undermine the former. Young Jefferson, quite expectedly, copied from Horace's hymn to youth and to thoughtless joy: "Reap the harvest of to-day, putting as little trust as may be in the morrow." But he did not forget Euripides: "Lie still, be brave, so wilt thou find thy sickness easier to bear; suffering for mortals is nature's iron law." It has been noted that there is no reason to believe that Jefferson agreed with everything he selected. It is true that Jefferson's thought is not Euripides's thought. What matters is not his agreement, however, but the question of what struck his mind the most, whether he liked it or not, what he acknowledged as worth copying, and what he considered appropriate to describe in a realistic way the several facets of human existence. The words and passages that he chose reveal that joy and sickness, today and tomorrow, thoughtlessness and forbearance, once again "rational" and "irrational" energy, form the thesis-antithesis according to which Jefferson's dualistic philosophy was evolving.[24]

Dualism was the constant rhythm of Jefferson's philosophy throughout its development over the years. The words changed, the classic authors were often forgotten or left in the background, but when a mature Jefferson chose to express himself through his own more personal voice, the impression of a fundamental dual *tempo* is intact. "I still dare to use the word philosophy," Jefferson wrote in 1801, "notwithstanding the war waged against it by bigotry & despotism."[25]

Analogous to Jefferson's habit of recording passages in his *Literary Commonplace Book* was his habit of keeping scrapbooks. Four books of clippings still survive in which the president, from 1801 to 1808, cut and pasted hundreds of poems and prose extracts. The scope of the scrapbooks is wide, as Jefferson went from patriotism, marriage, romantic love, courtship, friendship, women, domestic tranquility, and humor to the more customary opposition between life and death. The impression of dealing with a mind that worked according to a binary rhetoric is as strong as it was in the case of the *Literary Commonplace Book,* or in the juvenile letter to Page. The extracts still tell the reader that life is opposed to death, just as the day faces the night, and just as hope always fights against despair. In particular, on the theme of hope and despair, Jonathan Gross, the editor of Jefferson's scrapbooks, makes an interesting comment. We know that Jefferson wrote an original poem on hope, which was always one of his favorite subjects. On the same page of the scrapbook where that poem was pasted, Jefferson also arranged "The Grave," which, as Gross puts it, "perhaps shows Jefferson's taste for antithesis and complementarity." Jefferson had a very strong taste for antitheses and complementarities because his mind was used to casting attention to the "rational" as well as to the "irrational" principle.[26]

The "rational" and the "irrational" principles turn up on several occasions, disguised under different shapes. Take the dualisms, for example, between British "corruption" and American "health" or, more generally, between France and England. Take also the dualism between Roman virtue and Gothic barbarism or between "wise" men and "whimsical" women. Take the division between Whig and Tory as "founded in the nature of men," the Tory being the prototype of the wimpy man beset with his absurd fears, a slave to his qualms who did not trust his fellows' rationality. Take, of course, the dualism between republican virtue and monarchic vice, between union and factions, between the federalist and the republican parties, between rural "simplicity" and moneyed power, between tradition and innovation, between white "ingenuity" and black "stupidity," as discussed in the *Notes.*[27]

Jefferson's dualism was not a generic dualism, but it has to be interpreted as a corollary of the Enlightenment. I have already noted that the Enlightenment was dualistic and that it was a culture of the limits. It is now the appropriate time to discuss this hypothesis in detail.

Jefferson is usually regarded as the national hero in the struggle for enlightenment. The "pursuit of reason" and the commitment to "civilization" are two typical lenses through which that hero is seen. Quite correctly, reason and civilization are deemed to be the essential axioms of the whole Enlightenment culture. Commemorating the bicentennial of Jefferson's birth,

Charles Beard eloquently said: "I make bold to assert before this tribunal that the world-view, civilization, is the just formula under which to appraise Mr. Jefferson's ideas, interests, and activities. . . . As I am given to see things, all other views and phrases attached to Mr. Jefferson's name or asserted as characterizations are too partial or too narrow." There is no doubt that Jefferson, like every exponent of the Enlightenment, was deeply committed to civilization and optimism, but this is just a starting point. The real problems to sort out are what is the relationship between the Enlightenment and civilization and, probably most important, what does civilization mean in this context?[28]

A good characterization of the Enlightenment, not limited to Thomas Jefferson, is given by Robert Pogue Harrison. That characterization helps us to clarify the terms in which the Enlightenment understood civilization. It is a good portrayal because it discounts the dogma that the Enlightenment was tantamount to faith in achievements, unrestricted by any tragic sense. In its place the idea of a hazardous experiment once again takes the stage: "Enlightenment is a projective detachment from the past—a way of thinking which detaches the present from tradition and projects it forward into an ideal secular future ideally governed by the law of reason. The future remains Enlightenment's true heritage, while the present lags behind its republic of reason. Since the present has yet to accomplish all the social and political reforms dictated by reason, Enlightenment relates to its present age critically. . . . Enlightenment is always underway. It is an unending labor to come of age."[29]

In Harrison's view, Enlightenment was a refusal of the world-as-it-is and, accordingly, it was an "unending labor" to build a better society, the only one we could legitimately call civilized. Only in that world would the forces of reason eventually thrive and the struggle with negativity disappear. Harrison's view is a good starting point for a critical appraisal because it calls explicit attention to the fact that the Enlightenment was charged with tensions. In particular, Harrison sees civilization as something-to-be-realized and casts a lucid gaze onto the dualistic structure of the Enlightenment's worldview: the light is always brought into the night. Even though complex and multifaceted, the various versions of the Enlightenment fostered a specific style of thought, an ethos, a mode of existential dissatisfaction that directly demanded practical reactions, labor, and a persistent criticism of the present.

The Enlightenment never fully consented to a celebration of civilization and of the results already attained. The "unending labor" repudiated and subverted the dark present in the name of a luminous future. In this regard, Immanuel Kant's distinction is still of paramount importance. In *An Answer to the Question: What Is Enlightenment* (1784), Kant made clear that eighteenth-century philosophers, who prided themselves on the title of Enlightenment devotees, were conscious they were not living in an enlightened age where night and darkness were defeated; they knew perfectly they lived in an age of enlightenment, which is something very different.

As Gordon Wood correctly argues, "the eighteenth-century Enlightenment represented the pushing back the boundaries of darkness and what was called Gothic barbarism and the spreading of light and knowledge." Since darkness has always been an encumbering presence, Enlightenment can be defined as a culture of tension or, in other words, as a form of philosophical dualism. It is true that the Enlightenment was a worship of light and reason, but if it was so, it is only because darkness was perceived as acutely real. A good portrayal of the Enlightenment would be one (like Harrison's or Wood's) that puts adequate emphasis on the fact that Enlightenment did not deal with reason and light as if those elements constituted the very substance of the universe around as well as inside of us. Descartes, Spinoza, and Leibniz, among other European seventeenth-century rationalist philosophers, had a specific frame of mind that was openly contested by the majority of the exponents of Enlightenment culture. Those philosophers often found a shelter in the childish credence that this was the best among the possible worlds: a perfect, completed, un-evolving, closed universe, unalterable by human ingenuity, both by revolutions or reforms. "God," Gottfried Leibniz wrote in the *Theodicy* (1710), "having chosen the most perfect of all possible worlds, had been prompted by his wisdom to permit the evil which was bound up with it, but which still did not prevent this world from being, all things considered, the best that could be chosen."[30]

It is false that "the Enlightenment family was composed of rationalists." The Enlightenment reacted precisely to seventeenth-century rationalism and to the quietism that rationalism entailed. Quietism was the stance typical of those philosophers and theologians from the seventeenth century, and also from the medieval world, who were sure they were affiliated with something greater than their finitude, and greater than their mere circumstantial role in the history of human events. It is, of course, legitimate to consider seventeenth-century rationalism as the source of the Enlightenment, but only when ample allowance is made for the fact that the philosophers of the Enlightenment rose up against their fathers to find their own way in the world. Enlightenment represented the "pushing back" of the boundaries of darkness, a process, as Wood correctly points out, and not a final accomplishment to be celebrated. Dualism and tension are the very betrayal of the fathers' message. In a way the seventeenth-century "contemplators" would never have tolerated, the Enlightenment dealt with desires, with frustrations, with unsolved tensions, with disharmonies, with ideals-to-be-realized, with fears and, consequently, with a "romantic" heart and passions, with the bodily dimension of existence, and with reason as a simple temper and an attitude of this body. Enlightenment dealt with a darkness, call it the negative or the "irrational" moment, which is something fatally and acutely real. Quietism was no longer an alternative.[31]

Darkness was always presupposed by every philosopher of the Enlightenment. It was the first and foremost postulate, but, as stated, it needs to be envisaged as something fatally and acutely real. While in rationalistic philosophies, such as those of Spinoza, Leibniz, or Hegel, the negative was in the last analysis unreal, not an enemy but rather a stage of the process, the Enlightenment gave the negative an enormous importance. Every Enlightenment devotee knew that darkness was ready to put shackles on human ventures. Alexander Pope, maybe the most renowned prophet of the Enlightenment despite the fact that he sometimes flirted with rationalism, depicted this dualism in very eloquent terms:

> Lo! Thy dread Empire, CHAOS! is restor'd;
> Light dies before thy uncreating word:
> Thy hand, great Anarch! Lets the curtain fall;
> And Universal Darkness buries All.[32]

Since "Universal Darkness" was perceived as an ever-present reality, Enlightenment was mainly a question of enhancing the desire and fostering the passionate impetus to defeat it. Only from the heart might spring the good, hopeful, "rational" energy that allows humans to fight against such a powerful enemy. Interpreters establish criteria to divide the Enlightenment into periods and are quite right in locating that phenomenon in national and geographic contexts. However, in a certain sense, all the Enlightenment, both in Europe and in America, both in the 1750s and in the 1820s, was by its very nature sentimental and full of inspirational images. "I behold you," Helvétius wrote in a famous letter to Montesquieu commenting *The Spirit of Laws* (1748), "like the hero of Milton, after having traversed the immensity of chaos, rising illustrious out of darkness." In several senses, the Enlightenment was a reaction against rationalism and against the quietism and the contemplative stance that rationalism entailed. To find the good energy to boost the hope that something could and should be done to change human life for the better, French as well as British, and German as well as American, philosophers relied heavily on the heart. Passions, sentiments, feelings, the heart, and in particular the body were the keywords of the Enlightenment culture.[33]

A number of prejudices are usually associated with the understanding of the Enlightenment. The one just mentioned is that the Enlightenment was a form of optimistic rationalism. Another is that we have to wait for the advent of the nineteenth-century literary Romanticism if we want to find authors eager to extol, if not to "invent," the sentimental and bodily dimension of human existence. Nothing can be further from the truth. The Enlightenment was an effort, a desire, and a *métier,* as Diderot and D'Alembert would say, that only bodily creatures could undertake. From the very outset, those philosophers toiled away over something extremely corporeal. The bodily dimension of human existence was clearly revealed to them. The Enlightenment called forcefully for the body, and, accordingly, it explicitly acknowledged mortality. Transience, finitude, a "this-worldly-dimension," were increasingly deemed to be the only conditions actually suitable for real human beings.

Bodies reappeared on the scene after two centuries of theological dominion and spiritualistic prejudices. They had the chance to regain those qualities that the Italian Renaissance had formerly bestowed on them. The development of modern physiology, physical anthropology, and comparative anatomy was not the cause of this rediscovery, but part of a moment of a general awakening of materialism. Modern sciences of life could begin their course because a general materialistic climate was propitious.

For their part, Enlightenment thinkers eventually succeeded in dismissing theological and rationalistic biases that endorsed an anti-materialistic prejudice. A new transatlantic climate was favorable to the rejection of the idea that matter *must* be inert and dead, that it *must* be a *minus* when compared to that spiritual *plus* that could link humans to the deity and this world to the other. A culture of corporeal limits, the Enlightenment was materialistic in a way that no seventeenth-century mechanicism could ever have been. René Descartes, the French rationalist philosopher, had reduced matter to an abstraction, a caricature of itself. In this way, he had met the predominant theological standards of his time: that matter *must* be simple extension; that spirit *had* to be the true substance; that matter, as neo-Platonic mystics would put the question, *must* be the principle opposed to life. The Enlightenment challenged all those prejudices.

When eighteenth-century philosophers criticized classic mechanicism (Descartes's doctrine that matter is mere extension, that is moved, but is not a spring of movement), they did so in the only possible way, by openly subverting theological censures. They often advocated a vitalism, namely, the doctrine that organized matter has an inherent vital force and therefore should be distinguished from an inorganic substrate that requires divinity and "Spirit" to be vivified. "Seemingly paradoxically," Roy Porter has written in an influential book on the British Enlightenment, "vitalism was thereby recruited to bolster materialism: having banished belief in the natural qualities and manifestations of the soul and other spiritual power ('anima'), enlightened thinkers such as Erasmus Darwin then found the mechanical philosophy inadequate to explain those special features of living matter (such as generation) which the 'animists' had highlighted; hence they extended the power of self-organization to all matter, by analogy with such phenomena as crystal growth." The theology-acquiescent distinction between matter and spirit eventually dissolved. In the *Disquisitions Relating to Matter and Spirit* (1777), Joseph Priestley, a friend of both Erasmus Darwin and Thomas Jefferson, made extremely clear that all matter must be spiritualized, or vice versa, and that the mysteries of mind/body relationship have to be deleted as a false problem. Bodies reappeared, but vivified and rehabilitated.[34]

Like several other men of the Enlightenment, Jefferson was exposed to a resurgent materialism. During Jefferson's lifetime, materialism dethroned human beings from their supposed spiritual exceptionalism, from their hypothetical likeliness to God, and from an alleged dominion over the natural world. Humans were relocated in a living nature.

"We are veritable moles in the field of nature," La Mettrie wrote as a conclusion to his famous *Man a Machine* (1747), and as a consequence "we achieve little more than the mole's journey and it is our pride which prescribes limits to the limitless." Erasmus Darwin agreed, and stated clearly that the real philosopher "should eye with tenderness all living forms, / his brother-emmets, and his sister-worms." Whether British or French, the Enlightenment gave several lessons of intellectual humility, and materialism was the main rhetorical instrument deployed to this purpose. "Too small for such an immensity," the great naturalist Buffon wrote, "overwhelmed by the number of wonders, the human mind succumbs" (Trop petit pour cette immensité, accablé par le nombre des merveilles, l'esprit humain succombe). Effaced by the scenario of "a perpetuity of destructions and renewals" (une perpétuité de destructions & de renouvellemens), human beings should come to terms with the fact that they are but lesser parts of an all-powerful, not fully understandable nature. This antihumanistic message—that humans live in a powerhouse that they cannot fully understand, let alone control—was what Buffon had clearly in mind and tried to spell out in all of his writings: "The first truth that comes out of this serious examination of Nature, is a truth perhaps humiliating for man; it is that he ought to list himself in the class of animals, which he resembles through all that he has of material properties, and even their instinct would appear to him possibly more sure than his reason, and their industry more admirable than his arts."[35]

The goal of the Enlightenment was the public exposure of pretensions and self-righteousness, and a direct attack on "know-alls," on metaphysicians who thought they could fathom all the secrets of the world. Humility and a spirit of compromise sanctioned Enlightenment's firm refusal of the myth of systematic and metaphysical knowledge. In their personal language, each of the eighteenth-century enlightened philosophers embodied, as Porter has put it, "Enlightenment's hatred of a priori scholiasts, logic-choppers, pedants, know-alls and other dunces." They all launched warnings to humans to heed their limits, to acknowledge the powers of circumstances, and to also realize that the seemingly greatest human ideal, being human, is in reality contingent, tentative, an evolutionary strategy: humans were no longer the proprietors of the world.[36]

Diderot stated the matter clearly: "And, indeed, how is it possible that our knowledge should not be uncertain and circumscribed? Our organs are so feeble, and our means so insufficient, our studies so much interrupted, our life so much agitated, and the object of our inquiries is of so immense an extent!" The truly enlightened philosopher, César Chesneau Dumarsais wrote in the *Encyclopédie* (1751–72), under the famous entry "Philosophe," is not an all-knower; he just "walks the night," like every other ordinary human being, "but he is preceded by a flaming torch" (il marche la nuit, mais il est précédé d'un flambeau). From Voltaire to Buffon, from Pope to Macpherson, from Destutt de Tracy to Sterne, from England to France and America, the Enlightenments were very coherent in their project of disclaiming the dream of determining the "first principle" and the secret telos of all things, and of reducing everything to order and clear form. "This is the aim of metaphysics," wrote Destutt de Tracy, one of the greatest living authors according to Jefferson's judgment. "We would rank it among the arts of imagination intended for our satisfaction, and not for our instruction."[37]

As Montesquieu made clear in all his writings, there are excellent reasons to conclude that human beings are radically dependent on the environment. By the same token, as David Hartley taught in his *Observations on Man* (1749), there are still better reasons to presume that they are a sheer combination of matter. The consequence is that humans' expectations should be attuned to the actual position that these beings hold in an infinite universe, allowing for several kinds of inhabitants, for different peoples of diverse "races" and tribes. Montesquieu's *Persian Letters* (translated and published in London in 1722) together with Swift's *Gulliver's Travels* (1726) proclaimed the principle of cultural relativism that is the side effect of humility and the spirit of compromise. Living in an age of comparative appreciation of multiple civilizations, including the extra-terrestrial ones as depicted by Voltaire's *Micromegas* (1752), probably the most famous experiment in perspective, Jefferson must have been well acquainted with these relativistic insights and appreciations of varieties.[38]

The proof is that in his *Literary Commonplace Book* he entered a very eloquent passage, from Bolingbroke, that might be considered a manifesto of enlightened humility: "I combat the pride and presumption of metaphysicians in a most flagrant instance, in the assumption by which man is made the final cause of the whole creation; . . . That noble scene of the universe, which modern philosophy has opened, gives ample room for all the planetary inhabitants." When childish presumptions are disregarded, a pragmatic and enlightened "spirit of compromise" is thus inevitably encouraged. Darren Staloff rightly observes that this spirit, and not an alleged rationalism, was truly "emblematic of the worldview of the Enlightenment itself." Compromise means the acknowledgment of passing time, of human transience, of the fact that the land could only be given in usufruct to the living, of the fact that the greatest universal ideal is in reality a "little thing," that being faithful to every form of purism, starting from language observance, is plain nonsense and the signal of an arrogance unfit to transient beings.[39]

Jefferson was affected by these Enlightenment lessons of humility and materialism, not only because he read and confronted Buffon, because he was "influenced" by Locke, or because at the College of William and Mary he attended lectures in natural philosophy by William Small, a friend of both Erasmus Darwin's and Joseph Priestley's. It is true that in his *Autobiography* the old Jefferson declared that those lectures fixed the destiny of his life. It is also true that in the *Notes* Buffon was ever-present. But the analysis of Jefferson's early reading habits or associations is not the only or the principal means to unveil his commitments and allegiances. From Adrienne Koch to Allen Jayne, historians have tried to ascertain Jefferson's philosophical sources, what he read and when. They have shown that Jefferson was "indebted" to Buffon, Bolingbroke, Locke, Kames, Hume, Reid, Shaftesbury, and many others, although it is somewhat difficult to say to what extent he was and, furthermore, quite unclear what is meant by "indebted." Jefferson also drew elements from Destutt de Tracy and other ideologists, while Voltaire and Rousseau seem to have remained quite marginal.[40]

As a matter of fact, the fire that destroyed Shadwell, Jefferson's mother's house, destroyed most of his personal papers, maybe the most important repository to ascertain his "debts." But over-emphasizing the role of the sources might be deceptive. The sweeping conclusion we reach by following that line—that Jefferson was an eclectic (who is not?), and that many thinkers contributed to his worldview—could conceal the more important fact that Jefferson was immersed in a specific culture: he internalized Enlightenment's priorities, style, concepts, and anxieties. As a consequence, it might not be so crucial to demonstrate whether or not he actually read some authors. To shed light on Jefferson's dualistic philosophy, it is also useful to focus on the Enlightenment's values and priorities, not just on the authors who happened to endorse them. Because the Enlightenment was hegemonic, and because its "message" still resounds very clearly in our time as it must have during Jefferson's lifetime, we could safely argue that the loss at Shadwell was not so dire for the historian. Commitments and allegiances stem from taking active part in a culture, namely, from educating oneself by the attempts one makes to translate those values into practice and a life conduct. Likewise, for example, we should not expect that when late twentieth-century writers put emphasis on "constructedness" and show they are influenced by "postmodern" philosophy, they must do so because they have actually read Foucault, Jameson, or Rorty.[41]

* * *

Arguing that humans are part of a living nature, that they are bodies striving to achieve a possible goal, also means emphasizing that they are mortal. Once again, a specific climate existed that put a clear emphasis on that link. Jefferson could easily have breathed a materialistic cultural atmosphere in which death and life were strictly mingled. I have already called attention to Jefferson's allowance for the "ripeness of time for death" and the theme of "passing generations." In their personal and unique way, Buffon, La Mettrie, d'Holbach, Helvétius, Condillac, Voltaire, Diderot, Bolingbroke, Locke, Kames, Hume, Reid, Shaftesbury, Priestley, and many other philosophers have also underscored human mortality. Both their allegiance to materialism and their discourses on human possibilities are demonstrations of that. What was common to *all* the philosophers of the Enlightenment, whether or not they formally endorsed materialism, was the tenet that only mortals have possibilities, that only mortals could hope, struggle, succeed, while overpowerful gods would instantaneously transform into reality everything they willed. A discourse on possibilities and civilization is per se a discourse on risks taken, on limits, on mortality and human transience. A number of texts and authors prepared that climate. Throughout the eighteenth century, in literature as well as in philosophy, wide allowance was made for mortality.

Quite often, the emphasis on mortality also took the very romantic form of a worship of death. James Macpherson, one of Jefferson's favorite poets, was but one among many others to have deepened a phenomenology of death. Horace Walpole's *The Castle of Otranto* (1764), Joseph Warton's *The Enthusiast* (1744), Thomas Gray's odes and sonnets, Samuel Richardson's *Pamela* (1740), Edward Young's *Night Thoughts* (1742), William Collins's *Persian Ec-*

logues (1742), and James Thomson's *Seasons* (1726–30), to name just a few, all worshipped death or, at least, cultivated sadness to increase pleasure. It would be wrong to claim that these texts gave voice to an anti-Enlightenment literary movement. Quite the opposite. They were a specific version of the ethos of the Enlightenment, just like Macpherson's poems, in which mortality was analyzed in a way that mostly struck the imagination by an examination of the terrible, of the unknown and the uncanny associated with death and dying. Also these proto-romantic examples had a role in the Enlightenment's battle against seventeenth-century theology and rationalism, which defined human beings' most real part as an immaterial and immortal "soul." The fact that Jefferson refused to flirt with mist-shrouded castles, demons, phantoms, and Satan is not so decisive. Like more formal philosophical texts written by more academic authors such as Buffon, Hume, or Locke, those literary texts have contributed to create a climate centered on temporality and transience with which Jefferson was compelled to resonate.[42]

Jefferson was forced to vibrate with the rhythms those texts raised, whether or not he had actually read them, and whether or not he agreed with or repudiated them. The Enlightenment as a whole was a culture of transience and temporality (and hence of *human* possibilities), of real life and real death, and it is no wonder that it also created some very romantic modes of figuring the dying body. In its battle to forsake the consolation of rationalism and theology, the Enlightenment took advantage of all the texts, including Sterne's *Tristram Shandy* (1760–67)—another author of whom Jefferson was fond—that used literary imagination to pay tribute to the imperfection of bodily existence. Texts like *Tristram Shandy* are so important because they praised the incomplete over the Aristotelian form, and the capricious over the constant. It does not matter that Jefferson preferred Palladio or Jacques-Louis David to more "romantic" artists, and the "Roman" style to the "Gothic." Like other enlightened philosophers, Jefferson was awakened to materiality and human imperfection; to the idea that humans eat, drink, and are placed in this world; that they have to be treated anatomically, like other animals; and that humans are not essentially immortal, but may be so, as Priestley maintained in his treatise on matter and spirit, just because God might choose to resurrect their bodies.[43]

Enlightenment's true pitfalls were not Macpherson's cemeteries or Walpole's apparitions. The real hindrance to the process of enlightenment and hence to civilization was not the ghost per se, but rather seventeenth-century quietism, rationalism, the denial of mortality, and every form of religious bigotry associated with them. Ghosts and darkness, dying bodies and Gothic cemeteries, gave visible representation to the "other" side of bodily life and were thus potential allies to the modern science of anatomy. Just as Walpole and Macpherson did, the Enlightenment proposed a dialectical conception of life in which death—and all the images usually associated with it, like failure, fate, necessity, impossibility, and so on—was a fundamental component. The real enemy to the painful process of enlightenment was the antipragmatic attitude fostered by those contemplative minds who believed that the world was divine and rational (not that rationality was a simple option among others); that it was the best among the possible ones; that time and becoming were mere illusions; that humans did not actually die, because their immaterial soul shared the divine nature.

An enlightened man who "walked the night," Jefferson became a malleable, changeable, curious, many-sided and antisystematic philosopher. Certainly, this philosopher widely employed buoyant rhetoric, as he sought to moralize and humanize society. But since the Enlightenment was a culture of limits, it is no surprise that he also utilized less positive languages. As Adrienne Koch wrote, "His lack of philosophic system, with which some charge Jefferson, he considered an accomplishment." In the same way, the alleged lack of a coherent character (the famous "man of many faces") should also be considered in highly appreciative terms by historians. Jefferson's philosophy must be regarded as the evidence that he succeeded in converting the Enlightenment's forbearance and anti-metaphysical approach into a rule of life. Enlightenment philosophers came to a versatile definition of human identity because the universe they inhabited was dualistically portrayed as a work in progress threatened by darkness ("Thy dread Empire, CHAOS! is restor'd"), and a momentary product of the never-ending struggle between "rational" and "irrational" energy. Jefferson could thus easily become a humanitarian, a liberal, a republican, an elitist, an optimist, a pessimist, a pragmatist, a dreamer, with no particular qualms about adapting himself to the changing times.[44]

2

Optimism as Certainty

Before entering the world of the dualist philosopher, we need to examine Jefferson's unabated optimism. It might seem paradoxical, after all the arguments made in the previous chapter, but Jefferson often championed unabated optimism. The Enlightenment and all its tensions were periodically belied by this type of optimism, unabated, unshakable, and unswerving. It had little in common with the kind of optimism we encounter in the following chapter.

As a man of the Enlightenment, Jefferson was never at rest. He was always trying, tinkering, and experimenting. Pulling up and tearing down became customary habits of this enlightened Virginian, not limited to the renovations he undertook at Monticello for years on end. The world in which this man lived, *as a man of the Enlightenment,* was characterized by a supreme impermanence. Nevertheless, it is quite common to run into some of Jefferson's discourses where he expressed a dogged faith in the course of American history and a sense of complete satisfaction. Despite his enlightenment, we should say, Jefferson often presented himself as if he was convinced that, in America at least, there was only rational energy. Jefferson's Enlightenment was not able to completely wipe away attitudes such as satisfaction, self-righteousness, and a sense of imminent victory. Seventeenth-century rationalism was a sharp enough weapon to still assail Jefferson's Enlightenment. As a consequence, it is far from surprising that interpreters could be deceived and argue that Jefferson "had no trace of skepticism in his nature," for instance, or that he "had no tragic sense whatsoever."[1]

It is undeniable that Jefferson, quite often, voiced a strong sense of achievement and an unswerving faith in the errand. There are several explanations for indulging in such loud expressions of satisfaction.

Putting on this kind of optimism, I surmise, is a good way to efface a deep sense of insecurity and to resist, at least momentarily, the distress associated with the real process of enlightenment. But just as bravado and defiance are often signs of insecurity, the need to show in public one's boldness reveals the presence of consuming doubts. Eighteenth-century Enlightenment was a culture of performance, but it was not an easy task to perform. It is natural that Jefferson tried to resist the Enlightenment by focusing exclusively on selected positive elements. It would not be a mistake to argue that Jefferson was at times childishly optimistic *because* as an enlightened man he strongly sensed the negative, and because a tension, at times unbearable, thwarted his peace of mind. Optimism can easily become a way of compensating for one's insecurity, and there is no doubt that the Enlightenment enhanced insecurity. Human beings were becoming wiser, as we have noted, but less content with their erstwhile illusions. A dose of "compensatory consecration" was probably needed. However, speculating on the secret reasons why Jefferson employed the idiom of unabated optimism is a waste of time. The story to tell is that, not why, Jefferson was committed to this type of optimism, and that he often spoke that language, in spite of his enlightenment and all the questions the Enlightenment raised.[2]

Like other leaders, at the closing of the Revolution Jefferson was thrilled by the new rosy prospect. He was not just excited; he was satisfied. From Yorktown until well into the nineteenth century, he had time to collect evidence to bolster his confidence that the successful Revolution, as Gordon Wood writes, "had created a society fundamentally different from the colonial society of the eighteenth century. It was in fact a new society unlike any that had ever existed anywhere in the world." Revolutionaries succeeded in creating a new society, but the novelties that mesmerized Jefferson were not just mere novelties. They were the realization of a dream. All the hopes of the Enlightenment seemed to coalesce in the new historical reality, and Jefferson had the frequent impression that the dreamed-of future was, as we see shortly, within reach. All the desires and trembling aspirations of the previous decade appeared to give way to the acknowledgment that the new republic was clearly on the verge of accomplishing, and to some extent had already accomplished, all the social and political reforms dictated by reason.[3]

To some extent, the detachment from the dark ages of the past was perceived as an accomplished fact. Just as the novelties were not mere novelties, so the past was not simply past. The past was seen as essentially wrong: it was a minus from which revolutionaries had successfully broken. The new republic was, thus, *qualitatively* new: it was better than all the societies that had ever existed, and it was a rational one.

The novelty of a rational society having "ever existed anywhere" urged Jefferson to the practical use of history. This is to say that, to a large extent, he valued history not because past ages and past civilizations were something worthy in themselves, but because they had ushered in the American republican present.

Throughout his life, Jefferson read widely in history. He collected man-

uscripts and, of course, books. He read the major historians of the seventeenth and eighteenth century, including Rapin, Gibbon, Hume, Robertson,
Bolingbroke, Montesquieu, and Voltaire. However, despite his uncommon
emphasis on primary sources and accuracy in historical studies, he always
adopted these writers' utilitarian view of history. "In part," Trevor Colbourn
wrote, Jefferson "studied history as an extension of political experience and
as a guide to the perfectible future through the errors of the blemished past."
In this way, he found the subject of history not only a diversion and an academic exercise, but a guide to the present and a lesson for the future. As a
public man and an American patriot, Jefferson never felt entitled to study the
past for the sake of the past, or to look at the past with the nostalgic eye of an
antiquarian. He desired both to learn from the past and to exploit the past.
More precisely, history was read "comparatively," with the intent to let the
present emerge as something better than the former ages. Perhaps as a form
of self-assurance and emotional compensation, quite often Jefferson wanted
to convert the age of the Enlightenment into an already enlightened age.[4]

The success of the Revolution demonstrated to Jefferson that the past was
somehow always "wrong" when compared to the new present. He felt he had
good reasons to refuse to move backward in a search for improvement. It is
a contemptible platitude, Jefferson declared to Elbridge Gerry, "to believe
that government, religion, morality, & every other science were in the highest perfection in ages of the darkest ignorance, and that nothing can ever be
devised more perfect than what was established by our forefathers." Jefferson's
main desire was never to swerve from this forthright doctrine. Corresponding with the broad-minded philosopher and theologian Joseph Priestley, Jefferson became still more talkative. That "we are to look backwards instead of
forwards for the improvement of the human mind, and to recur to the annals
of our ancestors for what is most perfect in government, in religion & in
learning, is worthy of those bigots in religion & government, by whom it has
been recommended, & whose purposes it would answer, but it is not an idea
which this country will endure." Jefferson was unwilling to look backward. It
was the prospect already open before his eyes what most captivated him.[5]

Going backward was far from suitable to postrevolutionary Americans.
Jefferson celebrated, through the American victory, both the uniqueness of
the American character and the benign alliance between the new republic
and its success. "It is a part of the American character," he wrote in his forties,
"to consider nothing as desperate; to surmount every difficulty by resolution
and contrivance."[6]

This "surmounting" man did not ground his expectations in a rationalistic belief that the world in general would be the best among the possible

ones. Leibniz, the German philosopher, expressed such an idealist tenet, but Jefferson customarily hung on to a more pragmatic framework. The enlightened age that Americans would begin to enjoy was the outcome of the audacious and clever choices made to avert George Grenville's and Lord North's fetters. Colonists achieved a better world through the exercise of their will. Jefferson expressed to William Green Munford his ardent wish to comply with the dictates of the French *philosophe* Condorcet, whose doctrine was that the human mind "is perfectible to a degree of which we cannot as yet form any conception." In this context, perfectibility did not refer to speculating about a universe without flaws. Perfectibility was a proof of the American character.[7]

There was no significant development in Jefferson's thought and character as far as unabated optimism is concerned. I leave to readers the task of judging for themselves whether in a given instance Thomas Jefferson had this type of optimism because he was convinced, because he wanted to convince his contemporaries, because he wanted to convince posterity, because he was looking for a momentary solace, or because of a certain combination among these elements. Suffice it to say that he had optimism: he had optimism at the closing of the Revolution and still had the idiom of optimism at his deathbed.

In 1801, President Jefferson embraced a cheerful vision of the American future. Not content with what had taken place already, Jefferson was looking forward to distant times when the whole continent would be inhabited by "a people speaking the same language, governed in similar forms, & by similar laws." He insisted that he was not going to lose confidence in future generations. "When I contemplate the immense advance in science and discoveries in the arts which have been made within the period of my life," the Sage of Monticello declared to Benjamin Waterhouse, "I look forward with confidence to equal advances by the present generation, and have no doubt that they will consequently be as much wiser than we have been as we than our fathers were, and they than the burners of witches." Jefferson had "no doubt." The better instincts of humanity would ultimately prevail, and had already prevailed to a large extent, in the American continent if not elsewhere. Satisfied by the way things went, the march of civilization was for Jefferson a reality. At eighty-one years of age, Jefferson still rejoiced for "this march of civilization advancing from the sea coast." Progress seemed firmly established, and "where this progress will stop no one can say. . . . Barbarism has, in the meantime, been receding before the steady step of amelioration; and will in time, I trust, disappear from the earth."[8]

Tropes such as "I am confident," "I am sure," and "I trust" return over and over again. In the famous letter written on 24 June 1826, Jefferson gathered his dwindling mental energies to still depict images of "arousing men" who "burst the chains under which monkish ignorance and superstition had persuaded them to bind themselves," and who "assume the blessings and security of self-government." He felt he had strength enough to avow publicly and loudly his abiding satisfaction in "the general spread of the light of science," which "*has already laid open* to every view the palpable truth, that the mass of mankind has not been born with saddles on their backs."[9]

Democratic-minded revolutionaries like Jefferson, more than Federalists and conservative leaders, were keen on discovering "evidence" to sustain their trust in human capacities. Jefferson explicitly ascribed the doctrine of indefinite improvability of the human mind in science, ethics, and government to his fellow democrats, "those who advocated reformation of institutions." Understandably, Jefferson allotted a spirit contrary to progress and a backward-looking stance to the "enemies of reform," those Federalists like Pickering, Wolcott, Tracy, and Sedgwick, who "advocated steady adherence to the principles, practices and institutions of our fathers, which they represented as the consummation of wisdom, and akmé of excellence, beyond which the human mind could never advance." Jefferson depicted Federalists as if they lacked a present; as if they did not appreciate living in an enlightened age because they were still prisoners of the past.[10]

Though hesitant about common people's worth, less democratic-minded leaders would have refused Jefferson's indictment of antiprogressivism, emptiness, and nostalgia. It is no wonder that Federalists, in turn, perceived themselves as optimists and as successful heroes in the national battle against the constraints posed by aristocratic lineages, cosmological necessity, feudal hierarchies, wildness, gloomy destiny, and the past. Anti-Jeffersonian leaders placed the source of their optimism in God's wisdom more than in human capacity, but they did not renounce the mission of looking at the world with confidence. The only difference was that God, more than a surmounting American character, was seen as the real power that blessed the new republic with the gift of a new present. Less democratic-minded leaders were thrilled by improvability because they were often animated by a firm confidence that God had given, in the victory, the mark of his approval of the new nation.

More than Jeffersonians did, Federalists read the victory at Yorktown as the harbinger of the advent of the Christ of republican America. Thanks to God, the forces of morality and revelation had ultimately triumphed over iniquity. This American Christ, son of an American God, had none of the traits described by Jonathan Edwards's *Sinners in the Hands of an Angry God* (1741). The American, postrevolutionary God was not angry anymore and

had an infinitely satisfying divine love for the American man. Edward's ago-
nizing sense of moral blame and vileness before God was eventually dimin-
ished by a religious universalism, the doctrine that in the long run the "God
of love" would prove stronger than the "God of justice," and the final res-
toration of all souls would be granted. The all-loving God would work to
establish the perfection of humankind under the banner of the victorious
American nation. The vista of a "Manifest Destiny" was not yet invented,
but postrevolutionary Americans, both Jeffersonians and anti-Jeffersonians,
could well agree with its content and argue that they were entitled by God to
lay claims that transcended other people's rights, laws, and traditions and to
rule the whole continent. John Adams, among many others, asserted a strong
sense of American destiny under God. He never envisioned God as a mere
distant watchmaker who wound up the universe and then let events take
their course. His benevolent and providential God, as a proxy for the trust in
common people, was closely caught up in the events of American history.[11]

Providence was also appealing to Jefferson. The fact that the national economic endeavors were swiftly and steadily thriving disclosed God's approval
of the American experiment. The old Jefferson liked to philosophize about
the consoling idea of a "march of civilization." Jefferson wrote to William
Ludlow, for instance, that "a journey from the savages of the Rocky Mountains, eastwardly towards our sea-coast . . . is equivalent to a survey, in time,
of the progress of man from the infancy of creation to the present day." He
never seriously suggested that struggles were over, or that the epic dimension
of human events was but a memory. But the rhetoric of the march of civilization stretching up to the "present day" implies that such a march has a sense
and a direction, that it is presided over by a sort of providential hand, and
that the United States occupies the final stage of this successful development.
Since the time preceding his election to the presidency, Jefferson seemed to
be allured by the idea of an existing link between his nation's march and
God's plan. Not that troubles were over, Jefferson wrote to Benjamin Rush,
but even "when great evils happen, I am in the habit of looking out for what
good may arise from them as consolations to us: and Providence has in fact so
established the order of things as that most evils are the means of producing
some good."[12]

Occasionally a pre-Enlightenment and quite Leibnizian philosopher,
Jefferson was disposed to interpret evils as instruments chosen by God to
implement further good. Those Americans who had the chance to listen to
the president deliver his first inaugural address must have surely been both
edified and puzzled by a direct appeal to such an "overruling providence"
turning evils into instruments to realize his plan. Despite Jefferson's fame as

a modern atheist and Jacobin, the president had many things to teach about his blessed America, a nation dear to God and "advancing rapidly to destinies beyond the reach of mortal eye."[13]

Theological conundrums apart, Jefferson's unswerving optimism was more frequently voiced by means of the language of technological improvement. It was Jefferson's approval of technology that seems to better reveal his satisfaction about both the American experiment and civilization at large. As the old Jefferson said in the letter to Waterhouse just recalled, by contemplating "the immense advance in science and discoveries" he felt the urge to "look forward with confidence." In May 1786, after he returned to Paris from his two-month trip to England, a much younger Jefferson extolled the English for their being in command of the "mechanical arts" and stated clearly that in that country technology has been carried "to a wonderful perfection." Jefferson himself invented or had a role in the invention of several useful instruments. He designed a simple and efficient moldboard plow that drew attention throughout the Association of Agricultural Societies in America and within England's Board of Agriculture. He also invented a writing desk, a swivel chair, and a walking cane that converted to a chair, and he was no less than amazed by a copying machine that duplicated letters as they were being written. With enthusiasm he supported a number of other inventions, including the hot-air balloon, dry docks for ships, fireproofing for houses, telescopes, the camera obscura, carriage odometers, and personal pedometers.[14]

The proof that the nation's present and future were no less than cheerful was drawn from the spreading of technological discoveries. Of course, Jefferson was not alone in his appreciative attitude. Both Yankees and southern leaders responded favorably to technology. A buttress to national expansion and a dynamic agent of change, technology became the official American *verbum* and conveyed a wide-ranging sense of unlimited possibility.

Needless to say, to the northern Yankee the mere hypothesis of relying on the importation of articles manufactured abroad that could be produced at home was tantamount to a subjugation, and was thus perceived as contrary to the very ideals of the Revolution. Yankee leaders were confident they would prevent shortcomings like England's urbanism and moral degradation by means of the decentralization of production. For their part, southern "agrarians" like Jefferson saw in technology and industry a general improvement of national destiny. "Men from all walks of life," Jennifer Clark writes, "saw technological development as indicative of America's national future, and perceived this change in accordance with their particular expectations and hopes for America." Technology became the foremost buttress to the widely held belief in a hopeful future, both the cause and the effect of America's glorious expansion. Leaders boasted of having eventually become "lord of creation," as if through technology nature became a yielding being, submissive and womanly vis-à-vis a resolute manly dominion. The rhetoric of technology was used with increased confidence to point out both that rosy expectations were well founded, and that the American nation had already secured noteworthy assets. As the nineteenth century wore on, "the notion of progress became palpable," Leo Marx wrote, and "'improvements' were visible to everyone."[15]

It is not uncommon to hear about a "long-lasting" tradition of American anti-urbanism, to be interpreted as a latent anti-industrialist prejudice and an anti-technological bias. American anti-urbanism is often presented as a persistent trait of the leaders' *mentalité* that was nourished by a mixture of fear of mobs, concern for social order as prerequisite of economic development, and dread of anti-national radicalism. However, anti-urbanism is a more complex issue than it might first appear. Taken at face value, condemnations of "begrimed" cities seem to clearly reveal an absolute hatred. Jefferson's admonition about the mobs of great cities, made in the Query 19 of the *Notes,* is probably the best-known example. A republic with "an immensity of land courting the industry of the husbandman" does not need to develop another form of "industry." In particular, such a republic does not need its laborer to be concentrated in urban areas. Therefore, are cities really necessary to the American republic? "The mobs of great cities," Jefferson answered with some irony, "add just so much to the support of pure government, as sores do to the strength of the human body." Speaking about "sores," the physician Benjamin Rush can also be quoted as an eloquent testimony. "I consider them [cities] in the same light that I do abscesses on the human body," he declared to Jefferson in 1800, "viz., as reservoirs of all the impurities of a community."[16]

Clear-cut though these opinions are, we should not deduce from similar statements that cities in general were perceived as symptoms of a lethal malady. Rush, Jefferson, and many other leaders disliked cities *each time* they could identify the urban space as a site for corruption and impurity. Their moral revulsion was directed against some of the characteristics of life in the city, European in particular. At the closing of the eighteenth century, the cities that better stirred the visions of moral corruption, irreligion, and political radicalism, and that could better have been portrayed as an obsolete, quasi-feudal institution, were with no exceptions European. American cities were more agreeable when compared to those beyond the ocean. But even the European cities, when seen from a different angle, seemed to lose their dismal appearance. In the same period he was denouncing cities as "sores" of the social body, Jefferson had eyes to appreciate their potentiality and beauty. In the letter to John Page written right after he returned to Paris from his trip to England, he put emphasis on the fact that "the city of London, tho' handsomer than Paris, is not so handsome as Philadelphia." And he added the favorable judgment I recall a few paragraphs above, that "the mechanical arts in London are carried to a wonderful perfection." To condemn cities *as such* would be tantamount to censuring modernity or even to scorning the best examples of human order and beauty imposed over wild nature.[17]

In this regard, Peter Onuf is quite correct in maintaining that "Jefferson may not have had much good to say about cities, but this was because these were the prime sites for old regime corruption, not because he rejected urbanity itself or the progress of commercial civilization."[18]

Neither Rush nor Jefferson ever seriously rejected urbanity itself or the advance of technology. At the beginning of the nineteenth century, industrious Philadelphia, former national capital and the domain of Ben Franklin, still stood for the best values and ideas of the Enlightenment culture. Jefferson hoped to develop American cities following Philadelphia's example without the shortcomings of European cities. Just as we should not equate European and American circumstances, we should not project the patrician anti-urbanism of Ralph Waldo Emerson and Thomas Carlyle, for instance, onto the late eighteenth-century leaders. During Jefferson's lifetime, American cities had not yet developed those qualities that came to characterize them in the late nineteenth century. Immigration, class struggle, and filthy outskirts had not yet turned the American cities into copies of a Dickensian London. It is one thing to play the role of the yeoman, which Jefferson quite often did, overtly praising simplicity of manners, innocence, and orderliness. It is quite another thing to link such a posture of anti-urbanism with an actual refusal of technology, industry, and modernity. Technology *was* at the time the most obvious symbol of success. Only a scant number of mountain men, voyageurs, and marginalized people were so daringly "un-American" as to seriously question that technology had quickened the transformation of wilderness into a garden and a firm, and American cities into better places than their European counterparts. Those who actually reverted to the simple, static, "natural," and primitive were but unrepresentative exceptions.[19]

The American "renunciation" of the city was hardly a renunciation; nor was that kind of rhetoric an actual withdrawal from technology. Cities were widely perceived as the places where technological progress was made visible. When Jefferson and other leaders happened to speak against cities, industry, technology, and modern life in general, we should keep in mind that often they were expressing concern at unsupervised growth, not disapproval of the ideal of progress per se. Jefferson never seriously advocated pastoralism or ruralism, nor did he crave a pre-technological world. His very optimism would have prevented him from doing that. Even though he put emphasis on the need of vigilance to forestall the unwanted consequences of growth (corporations, banks, paper money, consumerism, and a Jacksonian society of common men), he never rejected technological innovation. On the contrary, technology was seen as an instrument to enhance the leaders' sense of control.

We should also reject the seemingly commonsensical opinion that southern agrarianism entailed a commitment to a defined, well-structured, and specific worldview, admittedly anti-industrial and inconsistent with technology. It would be better to emphasize the urban-rural, industrial-agrarian continuum. Southern leaders were not constitutionally committed to the doctrine of "simple life," and any oppositional representation of agrarianism versus industrialism is too simplistic. Every American leader would have agreed that nature must turn, had turned, into a garden for the good will and industry of the American citizens, in the same way the past had turned into the craved-for future.[20]

Nature was never seriously conceived as a leisure park for a slothful aristocracy. Everybody, Jefferson included, expected to manipulate nature in accordance with the needs of an emergent entrepreneurial class. The American southerner pledged unequivocal loyalty to progress, even though his images of what a hopeful technological future should be did not necessarily match with the Yankee's. The southerner basically opposed the European landlord, even though he liked to mimic some of his outer traits. Jefferson had some of the postures of the medieval Cavalier, as he celebrated the elegant verandas and ordered landscapes, as he enjoyed being acknowledged as the master of his "country," Albemarle County. He could well pretend to be like an English squire, in "an effort," as Theodore Marmor wrote, "to idealize plantations as American equivalents of feudal manors." However, the southerner had been fighting aristocratic ideals. Like the Yankee, the southerner lived in a future that was going to be realized, and that was already significantly realized thanks to technology. As to more substantial traits, such as the disdain for work, advocacy of hereditary political offices in rural areas, contempt for trade, and bias toward the principle that progress is neither necessary nor desirable, the southerner appears to be the very prototype of the optimistic, future-oriented leader. The American southern planter owned and ran his agricultural firm while experimenting with the best ways to increase the productivity of the soil and achieving agricultural improvements.[21]

Even though Jefferson flaunted anti-urbanism or paid lip service to the "simple and natural" way of life, he was in all his deeds as pro-technology as every other man in an analogous position of dominance. Jefferson is often approvingly recognized by environmentalists for his advocacy of a static, almost "Virgilian" agricultural pattern, but his language of rural self-sufficiency is seriously deceitful. In the *Notes* he allowed that "those who labour in the earth are the chosen people of God." "Corruption of morals in the mass of cultivators," Jefferson averred, "is a phaenomenon of which no age nor nation has furnished an example." Given these premises, the conclusion was drawn, and "let our work-shops remain in Europe." According to Leo Marx, Jefferson would refuse to advocate "farms as productive units." He would reject productivity and large-scale agriculture. Jefferson's husbandman would be "the good shepherd of the old pastoral dressed in American homespun." The accent on the "happy rustic" and "the contained self-sufficiency of the pastoral community" would end up in the blatant scorn of technology-oriented policies. Marx's conclusion was that Jefferson's main goal was "sufficiency, not economic growth—a virtual stasis that is a counterpart of the desired psychic balance or peace."[22]

The irony, however, is that despite the images of "peace" between farmers and nature, Jefferson was an unwavering optimistic foe of the "Virgilian pattern" and a man who lived in a quickly growing, quickly changing society. Jefferson's farmer had never been a subsistence farmer but rather an industrious, surplus-producing entrepreneur. Despite the undeniable language of rural self-sufficiency, Jefferson's notion of an independent farmer never spoke against using technology and dominating the environment by machines and inventions. Jefferson viewed the country as a worked and improved territory, thriving by means of roads, canals, and bridges.

Starting from his diplomatic work in Europe and ending with his presidency, Jefferson behaved optimistically like a first-rate expansionist hardly distinguishable from Alexander Hamilton, the paramount American modernist.

Therefore, it is hard to differ with Richard Slotkin's judgment of Jefferson "as a representative philosopher of the operative ideology of American capitalism, whose doctrines are not logically inconsistent with the development of industrial entrepreneurship." When he was elected to the presidency of the United States, Jefferson helped America's transition to the Hamiltonian order. He regarded even the new Bank of the United States as having its potential benefits. He also wholeheartedly approved of labor-saving devices and embraced an increasingly machine-enhanced industrialization. American southern leaders may have clung in imagination to an "agrarian myth," a romantic myth of little farmers targeting self-sufficiency. However, they never produced, even in theory, a design to implement some form of nostalgic agrarianism. Agriculture, commerce, manufacture, and industry were expected to boost each other's efficacy. In 1798, Jefferson had already expressed serious doubts about the United States as remaining "merely agricultural." It is a question "yet to be solved," he wrote to Horatio Gates, "how far that state is more friendly to principles of virtue & liberty." Jeffersonian "agrarian" democracy, as Richard Hofstadter wrote, "accepted fundamental economic premises which elsewhere served magnificently to rationalize the capitalist order."[23]

As a man who lived in an enlightened age, who enjoyed successes, who was fond of technology, and who perceived himself as rescued from the dark past, Jefferson could not have behaved in a more optimistic way than he often did. After the Peace of Paris, American leaders became progressively familiar with the "acknowledgment" that the victorious nation already dwelt in the abode of realized aspirations: the nation was right when it wisely decided to avow its faith in "man's perfectibility," in a supportive God, and in particular in technology. After he entered the presidency and accomplished the "Revolution of 1800," Jefferson retrieved his erstwhile conviction that "the storm we have passed through proves our vessel indestructible." He tried his best to publicize the fact that he never seriously mistrusted the solidity of the American vessel.[24]

In 1816, Jefferson still felt he had good reasons to agree with John Adams, "that it is a good world on the whole." Those who disagree, he maintained on that occasion, must suffer from some sort of pathology: "There are indeed (who might say Nay) gloomy and hypochondriac minds, inhabitants of diseased bodies, disgusted with the present, and despairing of the future; always counting that the worst will happen, because it may happen." Contradicting a number of more pessimistic statements, Jefferson declared his temperament "sanguine." "I steer my bark with Hope in the head, leaving Fear astern. My hopes indeed sometimes fail; but not oftener than the forebodings of the gloomy." In letters such as this, despair, doubts and forebodings were portrayed as accidents, transitory drawbacks, and as momentary "terrible convulsions" happening "even in the happiest life." Jefferson's idea was that whoever is unsatisfied with the tack made so far by the American vessel must be an hypochondriac victim of "sensations of Grief." Pessimistic stances, hence, should be cured by a pathologist: "I wish the pathologists then would tell us what is the use of grief in the economy, and of what good it is the cause, proximate or remote."[25]

American leaders were often happy to live in their present. Jefferson was no exception. Several quotations could be provided to corroborate the claim. To William Ludlow, for instance, Jefferson wrote that "*this* march of civilization" is "advancing from the sea coast." I have to emphasize the pronoun "this" because it betrays the feeling of a man who was sincerely happy to be where he was, and who wished to be remembered for his staunch support of the doctrine of optimism. "Here" and "this" are magical words that highlight the importance of the present moment. Progress was clearly a reality in America, and "where *this* progress will stop no one can say." A satisfied Jefferson boasted about the achievements and the indestructibility of his vessel.[26]

To the "brothers" of the Choctaw Nation, President Jefferson communicated that sense of pride that is typical of a man who likes to linger over the wealth he possesses. He smugly declared that "compared with you, we are but as of yesterday in this land. Yet see how much more we have multiplied by industry, and the exercise of that reason which you possess in common with us. Follow then our example, brethren, and we will aid you with great pleasure." In his forties as well as in his eighties, Jefferson desired to convey the impression that Americans were right when they decided to be self-confident about the prospect that sooner or later the errand would be fulfilled, that sooner or later the correct pathway to the "good things to come" would be secured, that every backward step from that accomplishment and every betrayal of the dream would eventually be prevented. To future generations Jefferson desired to bequeath the vision that such a realm had come into being, and that it was the fulfillment of the country's history, not what would abrogate the secular history in the name of the sacred one.[27]

The view that through the Revolution, to a large extent, such a realm had become a reality did not imply that a final destination had been reached. American leaders, Jefferson included, were satisfied by what they had attained, but they did not renounce further aspirations. They were certain that the American success had just begun. Since Americans had the chance to savor the taste of the awaiting future, their appetite grew exponentially.

Americans were convinced, in other words, that their present was an invitation to leap forward. "Unlike the Roman myth," Richard Lewis wrote, "—which envisaged life within a long, dense corridor of meaningful history—the American myth saw life and history as just beginning. It described the world as starting up again under fresh initiative, in a divinely granted second chance for the human race, after the first chance had been so disastrously fumbled in the darkening Old World." The American myth told that things had just begun: we are not slaves of our past, American leaders used to repeat; we are new, we decide the course of our history, and we are the hidden force of events. Americans seemed to succeed in seeing history as a tool for development, a means to break the cycles of the past, to prevent tyranny, and to further the human desire of self-edification through *exempla virtutis* of antiquity.[28]

Jefferson, in particular, dispensed advice to relatives, friends, and younger men, insisting that history should be a basic subject in every course of reading. He was not driven by submissive reverence to authorities, however. Both the American and the French revolutions had explicitly shed the authority of the past. By shedding the past or, which is the same, by reducing it to a repository of cases from which one may select the most interesting exempla, American leaders rejected the belief that the past was the principal—let alone the unique—source of information about human society. Jefferson and his peers found intellectual and material resources to look askance at the wisdom of the ages. If the past is a repository of wisdom, they believed, it is only because the past gives some material to work with, but one is free to avoid previous mistakes. Those men who won the Revolution imagined a future far different from the dreary past already known. To some extent, it was not a new idea, as Thucydides had already held that the past does not bind future generations, and that knowledge of the past can prevent its repetition.[29]

Each time Jefferson rejoiced for "this march of civilization" and for the fact that "where this progress will stop no one can say," each time he contemplated "the immense advance in science" that took place during his lifetime, he made such success clearly dependent on "the good sense of man," and on the power of human reason when "left free to exert her force." The discourse on the "efficacy of man," which Jefferson on several occasions endorsed, meant in this case that humans have defeated the past through their choices, and that they have freed themselves from necessity and precedents. Jefferson built a resolute language of will and masculine control that asserted the importance of individual and communal initiative. The basic idea was that the fate of nations would depend on moral causes, which means on choices, and human beings would have the major part in determining the course of events. The death and the fortune of a nation were no longer supposed to be embedded in a historical necessity but were made dependent on the level of licentiousness and immorality or of frugality and morality of those who make history.[30]

Jefferson and his optimistic peers had faith that new principles and new scenarios, to draw on Samuel Stanhope Smith, "could be created and nurtured by republican laws, and that these principles, together with the power of the mind, could give man's 'ideas and motives a new direction.'" The idea of the "power of the mind" was, of course, alluring to Jefferson and was repeated over and over again on almost every page of Thomas Paine's *Common Sense* (1776): "A new Era for politics is struck; a new method of thinking hath arisen. All plans, proposals, &c. prior to the nineteenth of April, i.e. to the commencement of hostilities, are like the almanacks of the last year; which, though proper then, are superceded and useless now." What was particularly striking was not just the negative side of the thesis, namely, that the past has no bearing on future generations; it was the positive assertion that excited Jeffersonians. "We have it in our power to begin the world over again," Paine said.[31]

The new visions pointing so expectantly toward the future found solid support in another chain of arguments. As Richard Price put it, the United States was "the hope, and likely soon to be the refuge of mankind." It was not infrequent to see enthusiastic European writers hailing the American Revolution as something that possessed a universal character. The hope of the whole world depended upon the maintenance and development of the American experiment. The American republic would thus play a stellar role in the history of freedom. Even in *Common Sense* Paine had urged Americans to think of themselves not as if they were merely a people among other people. To find a source of always new strength, Paine had stressed the need for Americans to think of themselves as a particular and a universal people simultaneously. The impression conveyed by similar messages was that of a sincere internationalism that stemmed from the very local interests of former colonists. It was, obviously, a rhetorical expedient designed to prompt optimism. Such an expedient encouraged ex-colonists by compensating for the impression of being peripheral with the empowering notion of being at the center of the world.[32]

By 1800, interpretations of the Revolution that were current in America justified the Revolutionary War by claiming that the colonists fought not just for their political independence but for the rights of humanity. Those "universalistic" interpretations tried to rescue the American cause from the dimension of mere localism and to consign it to another superior dimension. American nationalism, James Loewenberg wrote, "paradoxically, was an internationalism. It was rooted in humanity not in geography."[33]

Jefferson the unabated optimist was a follower of universalism and internationalism. With Richard Rush, for instance, the Sage of Monticello insisted that Americans had to be conceived not simply as colonists but as "members . . . of the universal society of mankind, and standing in high and responsible relation with them." These members yearned to become an avant-garde of the free world. As a consequence, "were we to break to pieces," as Jefferson also said to Rush, "it would damp the hopes and the efforts of the good, and give triumph to those of the bad through the whole enslaved world." The unlikely failure of the republic could only be bemoaned in terms of a "treason against the hopes of the world," as he powerfully wrote to John Holmes. Not that the cause of the new republic could really fail. While other civilizations were organisms waiting in life for their own destruction, America seemed to have many more chances to succeed and thrive. Jefferson saw the American republic as the embodiment of the universal and godly principles of reason, freedom, and right. A "metaphysical" and superior dimension began where the realm of mere particularity and geography ended.[34]

Jefferson looked optimistically toward the future because, like Paine or Price, he was convinced that the United States was the proof that realities beyond the local could exist in history. The American republic had a universal import, and its citizens stood in such a "high and responsible relation" with the whole of humanity because by winning the Revolution colonists had revealed that ideals could become concrete, realizing themselves in history. With this notion of a concrete ideal we reach the core of Jefferson's unabated optimism—let me use the adjective "precritical"—before it has been awakened to the painful process of enlightenment.

A number of instances of concrete ideals have been discussed by historians. The philosophical language of universalism centered on ideals of self-evidence, moral sense, reason, truth, laws of nature, natural rights, natural law, and so on is analyzed in an extensive literature. However, historians have not always drawn sufficient attention to the fact that the concrete ideal can provide a very effective spur to optimism. What is particularly relevant here is that, by the late eighteenth century, the faith in a future that was altogether novel and that could potentially embrace the entire human race benefited from a clear proof of its strength. The best proof that such a faith was well founded was the very realization of the colonists' project: since those ideals had realized themselves, Americans had demonstrated to the world the capacity of human beings to develop constructively under "metaphysical" conditions, not just geographical, local, and particular ones. A completely new outlook on the question of universals and "abstract" principles was thus legitimized. In this sense, commenting on the "success" of the Constitution, Benjamin Rush declared that "Justice has descended from heaven to dwell in our land."[35]

Jefferson, not surprisingly, was among the paramount supporters of concrete ideals—ideals that would exist in "our land" and that would exert a strong positive influence on human affairs.

Take, for instance, his view of the moral sense as a basis on which to develop a universalistic and naturalistic ethics. Jefferson's letter to Thomas

Law of 13 June 1814 is widely recognized and quoted in this regard. The true foundation of morality, Jefferson maintained on that occasion, is something unconditioned and not dependent on any reasoning about God, truth, or utility and self-interest. An instinct implanted in our breast stimulates us to "irresistibly" feel and succor others' distresses. It is the adverb "irresistibly" that characterizes morality as a true universal disposition, not depending on habits, cultures, or geographical variables. Jefferson was not original from a strict doctrinaire point of view. The notion of a "moral sense" developed in an extended cultural environment that, from the mid-seventeenth century on, was repeatedly trying to resist both the Calvinistic and the Hobbesian depreciation of human nature. While pessimist Thomas Hobbes set the selfish principle as the only motive that would prompt human action, a number of optimist authors, from Henry More to George Turnbull, from Malebranche to Shaftesbury, from Wollaston to Hutcheson, from Joseph Butler to Thomas Reid, acknowledged compassion as a natural affection acting before *cogitatio* and calculation could make their way.[36]

Optimism can evidently avail itself of the doctrine that God and nature have determined our predisposition to feel love for others through an instinct universally implanted in humanity, and not dependent on acquired habits. The doctrine of the moral sense averred that it was not choice, deliberation, or conformity with locally established norms that turned an action into a moral behavior; it was the rapidity, spontaneity, and naturalness of the reaction to external factors that really mattered. This was a naturalistic ethics of unconscious response, of plain feeling, of independence from particular cultures and places that seemed to Jefferson and other optimistic philosophers to achieve levels of universality that no doctrine based on calculus could reach. While calculus and reasoning, like habits and customs, are linear sequences that need time to develop and become widely acknowledged, a response based on the moral instinct is not subject to any social or psychological trial. Those responses are accepted and acknowledged from the start because they are natural and, so to speak, always a priori. Instinctual responses do not need to pass any exam, nor comply with any established norm; they do not need to *become* the norm because they form norms and standards. An instinct, including a moral instinct, is thus universal by reason of its essential meta-historicity.

The doctrine of the moral sense was a variation on the broader naturalist canon. Nature can become a powerful instrument to wipe out irrational habits and the tyranny of traditions. The clearest example of a universal breaking the veil of particularity, natural moral sense provided a formidable support to every doctrine of optimism. Nature manifested itself in the moral instinct and, for a rather overconfident Jefferson, was the best concrete ideal that rational human beings could ever experience. By freeing their moral instincts from acquired habits and the limits of culture and geography, nature was capable of rescuing humans from the miseries of particularity. To cut the political bonds with England and to get rid of British arbitrary prerogatives and privileges, revolutionaries needed only to put themselves in a state of nature. In this context, "state of nature" meant that a metaphysical guide existed that could teach lessons of both morality and politics. Revolutionaries were sure, in other words, that the realms of morality and politics were founded in nature as a meta-historical dimension.[37]

In *A Summary View of the Rights of British America,* as well as in the Declaration and a number of other texts, nature was portrayed as if it was the main character of the drama. Nature provided the best direction to human choices. This version of ethical naturalism was upheld by Jefferson, the unconditional optimist, and by several other no less optimistic American revolutionaries.

This "classical nature," as we could appropriately label it, allowed Jefferson to understand the secret source of the law, both moral and political. Classical nature was the source of the moral sense and was law, norm, and order among phenomena, no link of which could ever be lost. The adjective "classical" highlights nature's essential meta-historicity. Classical nature should always be preferred to tradition, because tradition is but ignorance, superstition, and a chain of mistakes made in the past. The study of history and traditions, as Charles Miller writes, "may be indispensable for knowing what to avoid, but the study of nature is required in order to know what to embrace. If the laws of nature, just as the forces of history, seem to bind us down, for Jefferson there was an important difference between them. Nature binds us only to what is true and good." As classical, nature is always supportive, always a prop to morality, always the best method to free the moral sense, and always the best *magistra* in politics. While history and traditions bind us down, it is nature that drives us up to the main road to unswerving faith and optimism.[38]

Universals pierced into existence in several other cases and incited Jefferson to look optimistically toward the future. Take his discourse on the "will of the nation." Writing in 1792 to the then minister to England Thomas Pinckney and commenting on the newly established French Republic, Jefferson was far from daunted by the occasional bloodshed. Accidents should not hide the importance of the goals that the French Revolution was attaining: "We certainly cannot deny to other nations that principle whereon our own government is founded, that every nation has a right to govern itself internally under what forms it pleases, and to change these forms at *it's own will:* and externally to transact business with other nations thro' whatever organ it chuses, whether that be a king, convention, assembly, committee, president,

or whatever it be. *The only thing essential is the will of the nation.* Taking this
as your polar star, you can hardly err."[39]

What was such a "will" for Jefferson? And why should it work like a polar
star despite the fact that in the ordinary sense "will" is often synonymous
to "arbitrariness"? The best answer is perhaps to be found in a letter written a few days later by Jefferson to his son-in-law, Thomas Mann Randolph.
That short letter gives us the opportunity to realize that the "will" that Jefferson was endorsing by wishing France could be put under its banner was
the principle of "a government of laws addressed to the reason of the people,
and not to their weaknesses." The "will" was analogous to the moral sense
because it also was "essential," as opposed to "local" or "particular"; a meta-
historical and universal principle speaking to a superior faculty and pointing
to a metaphysical dimension. The will of the nation qua "government of laws
addressed to the reason" was a source of force, not of weakness, because it
did not stem from the country's blind egotism, from the barbarian desire
of growing increasingly effective, or from the mere outpouring of one's life
drive. Unconventionally enough, the word "will" was selected by Jefferson
as a "polar star" because it foiled prejudices rooted in ancient traditions that
became calcified as time went by. That "will" did not stand in behalf of mere
particular and arbitrary interests and was something fresh, new, outside acquired habits and conventions, that spoke directly to people's minds.[40]

Given the equality of will and reason, we understand why Jefferson may
have claimed that some innocent blood is acceptable when at stake is nothing less than the contest between weakness, prejudices, traditions, despotism,
particularism, and the "conditioned" on the one side and human liberty, reason, law, universalism, and the "unconditioned" on the other. It is true that,
at the beginning of 1793, Jefferson was not acquainted with the horrors that
were going on in France; but even if he were, his judgment would not have
been much different.

"The liberty of the whole earth," Jefferson wrote William Short at the
same period, depended on the issue of the contest between despotism and
the human liberty, between the reasons of the particular and the reasons of
the universal, and "was ever such a prize won with so little innocent blood?
My own affections have been deeply wounded by some of the martyrs to this
cause, but rather than it should have failed, I would have seen half the earth
desolated. Were there but an Adam and an Eve left in every country, and left
free, it would be better than as it now is." Jefferson was obviously speaking in
hyperbole to emphasize the importance he attached to the cause of republican France. He was clearly not advocating a holocaust. What he was advocating, however, was the cause of the universal Adam and Eve, prototypes of a

meta-historical humanity able to take inspiration from the unconditioned, such as moral sense or the "will of the nation."[41]

Jefferson was confident about the high probability that human beings could let their lives be guided by metaphysical universals, and France drew all his sympathies. Not that he was of the "French party." France was not embraced by Jefferson for its own sake, as a particular team to join. It was rather an analogue of the similar American venture and, hence, another concrete ideal. France was transfigured into the very symbol of the best human hopes. "I have so much confidence on the good sense of man, and his qualifications for self-government," he wrote to Diodati in 1789, "that I am never afraid of the issue where reason is left free to exert her force; and I will agree to be stoned as a false prophet if all does not end well in this country." It is ironic, but Jefferson should actually be stoned, at least as France is concerned. Jefferson's call to "good sense," however, is essential to grasp the kind of unswerving optimism that was implicit in many of his discourses and writings. Just like "moral sense" or "reason," "good sense" was not simply a faculty. It was what activated, in human beings, the opportunity of becoming citizens of another world, whether or not Jefferson used the phrase. In 1789, France was the beginning, as America was fifteen years earlier, "of the history of European liberty."[42]

The "history of liberty" is quite a paradoxical expression, given that free human beings—when they are fostered by reason, moral sense, and similar faculties—enter the dimension of eternity. Writing that kind of history is the most direct way of getting rid of another history that tells of arbitrariness, superstitions, privileges, and the accumulation of particularities. Freedom is a figure of meta-historicity and eternity, and the history of freedom, correspondingly, is tantamount to the history of eternity.

In the 1790s, France and England symbolized to Jefferson's eyes two contrasting visions of human potential. England was the model of the constitutional government committed to upholding the greater extent of personal liberty consonant with the flawed nature of man. In the English sense, liberty signified the *historical* rights and privileges of Englishmen. France, on the other hand, represented ideals of *abstract*, namely, metaphysical, rational, natural, and universal freedom, as the direct and necessary upshot of cutting the shackles of customs, habits, and privileges. Jefferson's optimism found inspiration in the French experience, in which humans had become citizens of another world by following the guide of reason. Jeffersonian republicans called for an informal, voluntary, political life open to all, not just sedimentary, English privileges. By choosing abstraction and eschewing the traditional linkage between past and present, Jeffersonians, as Joyce Appleby puts it, "cultivated in its place a lively connection between present and future. This substitution worked to free political discourse from the concrete imagery of historic references. Because the future is necessarily imaginary public rhetoric gravitated toward those abstract universals that Locke had introduced into politics and Adam Smith into economics."[43]

The "concrete imagery" embodied in the English ceremonies and traditions would be a hindrance to the real faculty of imagination or, better, to reason and moral sense. Following reason and moral sense was seen as the best way to increase human agency and to leap to the unconditioned realm of freedom. While ordinary history focuses on the bond between past and present and urges citizens to esteem particular institutions like family, friends, and clans above the international community, the optimistic leader puts universal and abstract institutions first. No more than a limited allegiance toward every historical government, already implicit in Locke's *Second Treatise on Government* (1690), follows necessarily from this Jeffersonian mindset. For Jefferson, as expressed in his own favorite motto, rebellion to tyrants, namely, to arbitrariness and particularisms, is obedience to God, namely, to law and universality. The idea of a universal republic must come first in the Jeffersonian context because eternity precedes time, and because universality is a whole larger than its parts, larger than family, friends, and clans.

Jefferson had unabated optimism because he believed (or at least wanted us to believe) in the real possibility of getting rid of historical "imagery." His optimism made him trust in the risk of setting reason free. This venture entailed a strong urge toward the timeless and noncircumstantial or, as I have already said, the unconditioned. That Jefferson and other American leaders introduced the problem of universal existence in secular particularity is acknowledged by historians. If time is the dimension of contingency, a rational republic should rescue itself from it. To a certain extent, it should defeat time. By emphasizing universalism, Jefferson revealed himself as more than an optimistic man of the eighteenth century, perhaps with a slight disposition to indulge in bravado. He also associated himself with the tradition of "civic humanism," which in turn affirmed the primacy of universal over particular values, and tried to build effective hindrances to the production of "imagery" and the multiplication of false values.[44]

The civic humanist ethos, which was Aristotelian, Polybian, Machiavellian, and Harringtonian, saw the course of time as moving toward the indefinite and uncontrolled multiplication of values, those I have called privileges and particularism. Historical time, in this regard, was a creative but "irrational" force, the spring from which particularity flowed. It was J. G. A. Pocock who spoke about American leaders' "attempt to escape history," and we should acknowledge that Jefferson undeniably was convinced he had found means to escape the course of time. Time qua history was a source of corruption, and according to Pocock, numerous American leaders interpreted it "as a movement away from the norms defining . . . stability, and so as essentially uncreative and entropic where it does not attain to millennium or utopia." Not that Jefferson was against novelties and modernity, as represented by industry, capitalism, or liberalism broadly defined. He was against the "uncreativity" of history—or, to put it another way, against its "irrational" and Hamiltonian form of creativity. Jefferson despised the course of history when its march blurred the distinction between particulars and universals, between idols and values, between false and true imagery, between the conditioned and the unconditioned, and between privileges and freedom. He desired to get ahead, but he also desired to do so by casting his sight on superior ends.[45]

From a Jeffersonian perspective, as I have tried to delineate it, the opposition between the ethos of republicanism or civic virtue and that of liberalism is deceptive and artificial. There is no absolute opposition between individuals who are civic and active beings, capable of perceiving things beyond their own interests and defining themselves within the framework of their duties toward the *politeia,* or political body, and liberal individuals who appear conscious chiefly of their own interests and who take part in government in order to press for the realization of their own interests, in the hope that separate interests will balance one another. Jeffersonian, rational, natural, moral-sense, good-sense individuals are universal like Adam and Eve, and their own interests overlap those of the political body, when they are well understood.[46]

This universalism was indeed the source of Jefferson's language of optimism: by using both republicanism and liberalism, Jefferson tended to rescue citizens from the specter of nonvirtuous individuals, despicable creatures of their passions and dreams. Jefferson was not hostile to the doctrine of liberalism, given that liberalism was in turn deeply unsympathetic to particularism and arbitrary dreams. Liberalism has never been a renunciation of rationality. Jefferson was willing to follow the guide of Locke's *Second Treatise,* a text that speaks about an agreement among individuals in a state of nature who formed a "social compact" anterior to any government precisely because they are rational. Following Locke, Jefferson made the individual superior, in a qualitative sense, to every government. Jefferson had always been ready to acknowledge government as a means and not as an end in itself, and individuals as free and rational creatures before entering the government. No simple contrast between "virtuous antiquity" and "corrupted modernity" can be discerned in Jefferson's philosophy.

Quite often Jefferson presented himself as an unabated optimist and a hero convinced that concrete ideals had defeated, or were going to defeat, time. Even though this type of optimism was not and could not be his unique posture, he reminded his contemporaries that human beings are universal creatures: they are free to create a social compact; they are rational in perceiving things beyond their own limited representations; they are keen on defining themselves within the framework of their duties toward the *politeia* and on taking part in government in order to press for the realization of their own *best and real* interests. When reason is left free to exert its force, Jefferson used to repeat, "I am never afraid of the issue."[47]

Because individuals would be universal, as it were, and because there would be no opposition between private/liberal and political/republican interests, there would be no resulting split between the ruler and the ruled. According to a very optimistic Jefferson, political power does not exist per se. There is no dominion of one body of society over the other bodies. Political power was for him an epiphenomenon of rational people administering themselves. Nothing could break the harmony of a universal republic. The idea of political power as a "disembodied" universality was momentous in the early American republic, and so too was the corresponding idea of power as homogeneous. Homogeneity meant that the representatives, so far as they were rational or real representatives, would not encroach upon the people because they were *the people,* and it was not probable they would abuse themselves. Representatives were widely held to be "ourselves," and political organs were denied to be foreign elements. Sure enough, disagreement arose about what level embodied true representation, whether the federal or the state level, but this is a different story. The principles were nonetheless clear. Power in America was intended to be homogenously distributed, and potentates could not thrive. John Adams's words interpreted in a magnificent way Jefferson's feelings, that the republic and only this American republic would be a universal "government of laws, and not of men."[48]

The present chapter has showed that Jefferson upheld the unconditioned, concrete ideals, abstractions, metaphysics, universals, and the timeless. He did so despite the fact that the nucleus of the Enlightenment, as explained in the previous chapter, was particularity, circumstance, the timebound, the conditioned, the limited, and the recognition of the "irrational." Although the Enlightenment was a culture of performance, it was not an easy task to perform. Some compensatory beliefs were needed, and I suspect Jefferson harnessed his unabated version of optimism to this purpose. Was this just a trick? Was Jefferson sincere in his quite precritical optimism? Why did he boast this way? These are very difficult problems to sort out. The fact remains that on a number of occasions Jefferson expressed his satisfaction about the state of things and his faith about where things were going. Whether driven by sincerity or insincerity, underscoring one's success is very comprehensible as a human attitude.

Besides satisfaction and self-satisfaction, we have to keep in mind that Jefferson was deeply and sincerely committed to the whole spectrum of the Enlightenment's discourses: he internalized an entire repertoire of lessons. Perhaps Jefferson wanted us to believe his optimism was thoroughly unabated. He may have overrated his sense of victory. He may have found in that optimism a sort of momentary relief. But, as other texts show, there is no question about his deep allegiance to Enlightenment culture, including its less consoling tenets.

Although human beings understandably like to assuage their own sense of insecurity, the Enlightenment was both a challenge to all of one's consoling beliefs and a risky venture whose outcome was far from certain. Consequently, Jefferson's worship of civilization and his optimistic devotion to the unconditioned, to a large extent, can legitimately be read as the *trembling hope* that everything would end well. Declarations of self-satisfaction were innumerable. As a man at the helm, Jefferson was not reluctant to make such declarations publicly. He often trusted the story of accomplishment that he was narrating to his fellow citizens. Moreover, he wanted to be remembered by posterity as a sort of national hero. But he enacted this role in spite of the fact that he was a genuine follower of the Enlightenment. Jefferson often detached himself from the moral and psychological burden that the Enlightenment imposed on its adepts. He had several languages and postures, and not all of them were amenable to the Enlightenment's sense of venture. "Satisfaction" is one thing, while "improvement," "mission," "attempt," and "risk" are more basic keywords to define the most important cultural trend that ran through both Europe and North America during the eighteenth century. Eighteenth-century Enlightenment was a work in progress, not the self-righteous celebration of any accomplished mission.

As a result, the most characteristic mood that the Enlightenment elicited was one of expectation and anxiety. The route proceeds from unswerving optimism to hope. For Jefferson's readers and scholars, the important thing is not to be deceived by taking declarations of unabated optimism at face value, by considering them as a conclusion, the last word on Thomas Jefferson's philosophy, rather than as the spot of blind excitement from where the real journey began.

3

From Faith to Hope

BEYOND SATISFACTION: OPTIMISM AS POSSIBILITY

Correctly understood, Jefferson's most interesting optimism was a mode of hope, not certainty. The precritical optimism discussed in the previous chapter was accompanied, in Jefferson's writing, by a critical optimism, an optimism that was at once thoughtful and problematic. The present chapter is devoted to a lengthy study of hope as opposed to assured faith. Jefferson's famous optimism is considered in a way that permits the Enlightenment's dualism, tensions, and disharmonies to emerge. To state the issue in a slightly "poetic" way, in Jefferson's critical optimism rational energy begins to face its enemy.

Jefferson's unabated version of optimism stemmed from the certainty that the unconditioned (call it nature, moral sense, reason, or natural law) had arrived on the stage of history as the true protagonist, and "uncreative" history, injustice, bigotry, and privileges had been, or were going to be, defeated. According to his critical optimism, however, this result required effort. We have reasons to be optimistic, Jefferson repeatedly averred. Nonetheless, the good outcome was more often seen as a reward to be earned than as just a blessing gratuitously lavished on the new republic. Despite his satisfaction and self-satisfaction, Jefferson put emphasis on the fact that the original night might regain its primacy. Jefferson's optimism hinged repeatedly on the doctrine that a vigilant people would act like a warning to the rulers. "The good sense of the people," he used to say, "will always be found to be the best army" against repression, violence, and tyrannical governments. Invoking this good sense did not mean, for Jefferson, that a natural wisdom was abundantly distributed among the uncultivated—despite his frequent recourse to the rhetoric of natural law. The unstated implication of such an optimistic discourse was that wisdom and right judgment among the common people were artificial tempers to be nurtured by education and information rather than a natural asset shared by the whole populace. Time and again, Jefferson made clear that the unconditioned needed nothing less than "the best army" for its defense, and that "the best army," in turn, needed to be cultivated and defended.[1]

Jefferson's critical optimism thus spoke of very precarious possibilities. This last point is exceedingly important, though generally overlooked by scholars. Despite the vast amount of literature on the subject, when we listen to someone addressing the question of Jefferson as an optimistic philosopher, or more generally addressing the nature of the Enlightenment, we are too often driven toward a facile equation of Enlightenment with some rationalistic belief that the world, or at least the American world, would be the best among all the possible ones. We are often told that the Enlightenment meant a culture of confidence and optimism, which is undeniably true, that satisfaction was absolute, which is undeniably false, and that no further analysis is required. We are frequently lured by the temptation to consider the Enlightenment as promoting the belief that reason, truth, and similar concrete ideals abounded.

Quite the reverse. Enlightenment has never been a culture of abundance. It is true that Jefferson was a steadfast devotee of the Enlightenment, but Enlightenment, to a large extent, was a form of desire, an attempt, a venture, and an effort. As such, it looked away from once-and-for-all principles, rationalism, abstract reasoning, and the satisfied sense of imminent victory, which are the spring of any precritical optimism. The language of the Enlightenment was not so much a language of optimism *malgré* the world, but rather a humanistic language of patience, fortitude, and possibility and a challenge to improve the world step by step. Jefferson's version of enlightened optimism was actually a meliorism, nurtured by those encouraging signals that had been gathered since the closing of the Revolution. His version of the Enlightenment was a conditional language of possibility speaking of a reward reserved for the intelligent, the patriotic, the virtuous, and the deserving.

Anxiety and precariousness were not defeated. Jefferson *had* optimism, but his optimism stemmed, sometimes, from a sense of satisfaction and, at other times, from the conviction that the unconditioned was possible, precious, and fragile. Jefferson made a precise use of both anxiety and precariousness in his optimistic discourses: there is a distinctive Jeffersonian way of harnessing anxiety and precariousness for practical purposes. Anxieties, fears, threats, and the sense of precariousness became modes of assertiveness and were functional to Jefferson's hope in possibility.

What Jefferson said to his friend James Madison in 1787, for example, helps clarify the point I am making: "I think our governments will remain virtuous for many centuries; *as long as* they are chiefly agricultural; and this will be *as long as* there shall be vacant lands in any part of America. When they get piled upon one another in large cities, as in Europe, they will become corrupt as in Europe." Without speculating whether or not his recipe was correct, we have to look at the structure of the statement. As is apparent, it is a conditional sentence highlighting, in turn, Jefferson's conditional way of dealing with optimism. He had satisfaction and self-satisfaction, but his dealing with conditionals was no less typical: "I think our governments will remain virtuous . . . as long as . . ." Dozens of similar sentences could be provided. There was satisfaction, it is easy to see, but the idiom of satisfaction was only one ingredient in a more articulated worldview. Jefferson knew that his beloved republic still teetered on the edge of ruin and anarchy.[2]

As a language of possible solutions, Jefferson's optimism insisted on the need of exhorting fellow citizens, talking to their sense of pride, educating them, mobilizing them, increasing the level of commitment to a common cause, and enacting rituals that would lead to the ultimate realization of the unconditioned. In his effort to gain the assent of his fellows and bring them to act by a common rule, Jefferson often played the role of a Jeremiah who foretold the most frightening scenario—"they will become corrupt as in Europe"—that would unfold if Americans did not embrace the proposed solution. In this case, anxiety and a sense of precariousness would lead people to accept the wished-for "solution." Anxiety and precariousness were companions to Jefferson's hopefulness, which was neither boastfulness nor precritical self-satisfaction, but a sense that under certain conditions the future could transcend the present and that there were grounds to promote revolutionary energies or, at least, desires for reform. This optimism took on a sense of the tragic that fueled the struggle for a better future. It held at bay both simplistic optimisms and paralyzing pessimism.[3]

To sum up, there are at least three versions of the doctrine of optimism. The first is an optimism—that Jefferson rarely took into serious consideration—stemming from a Leibnizian belief that the world had plenty of riches and that rational energy, or God's overruling providence, was the dominant presence in the universe. The second is that kind of optimism also examined in the previous chapter, stressing satisfaction for what Americans had accomplished and untrembling faith in what they were going to achieve. The third is a conditional optimism asserting that concrete ideals, to thrive in the historical world, permanently need to be succored by humans' appropriate choices. While the first two are largely precritical, only the third can be defined as critical.

As an Enlightenment devotee, Jefferson was attracted in particular by the third version. The good outcome that Jefferson hoped for would be triggered by choices that humans had not yet made and would be totally dependent on them. The unconditioned, in other words, would not be achieved by some necessity or by God's providence. Jefferson may have been confident about the success of the causes dearest to his heart, but his awareness of lurking pitfalls and human limitations was always sharp. Satisfaction apart, Jefferson's optimism was not incompatible with the worried foresight that new danger-ous phases of history lay ahead, and that the Enlightenment disciple must be alert to possible setbacks. Jefferson's version of the Enlightenment did not discount the conviction that the forces of the "counter-revolution" were rap-idly rising at home and abroad. He developed a sober awareness that ideals still had to be riskily implemented by means of a victory over obscurity and overwhelming forces.[4]

In this sense, Jefferson interpreted the Enlightenment as a desire of the heart. A heartened spirit was involved, not just reason. In order to push individu-als to action, Jefferson's optimistic meliorism needed the energy that radiates from the heart. It is true that the head provides the necessary conditions for action and that knowledge of available data is also necessary. But Jefferson's version of the Enlightenment was at once knowledge, desire, and action. It had nothing in common with a detached, "objective," and non-emotional description of the world. The Enlightenment was by definition a way to be *interested in* and *concerned about* the world, and it always tried to subordinate contemplation to action. It did not stand in awe of facts but used facts as instruments to assist hopeful ideals.

Consequently, the dialectic between "My Head and My Heart" stretched throughout Jefferson's life. The famous letter to Maria Cosway provides the best explanation of what Enlightenment meant for Jefferson. Jefferson was a man both of head and of heart because the Enlightenment was a question of both awareness of the limits—of knowledge of the pros and cons, of the possible and impossible—and hope, urging one to move on notwithstand-ing contrary evidence. "My Head and My Heart" dramatized the Enlighten-ment's basic tension, not merely the episode of Jefferson's supposed falling in love with Maria in the mid-1780s. The battle extended beyond biographical implications.

Hundreds of pages have been written on the topic of "My Head and My Heart," but Andrew Burstein seems to still have something fresh to say about it. "America's just war for independence," he writes, "could not have been conducted had not the patriots been governed by their Hearts. The Head had calculated and compared and found Britain's 'wealth and numbers' alarmingly superior; the Heart had supplied 'enthusiasm' against wealth and numbers, and in doing so, 'we saved our country.'" We could broaden the range of Burstein's comment to all Enlightenment devotees, who knew that action required the enthusiasm supplied by the heart. Generally speaking, an Enlightenment disciple knows better than any buoyant rationalist that a number of motives exist for humans to despair about any improvement. While the head compares, calculates, and often gives bad suggestions, the heart actually pushes one to be hopeful and trustful, sometimes excessively trustful, to go ahead, *to do,* to be optimistic, and to become a *philosophe.*[5]

The head is often a spur that turns sensitive human beings into "cold" philosophers, or as Jefferson said in the famous letter, it is what warns against tightening "bonds of friendship." The head warns against tightening the bonds with life and with the imperfect world. The head contrives events and often persuades people that being awake is tantamount to remaining isolated from the dangers of the half-known life. It is apparent that the Enlightenment could not have been a matter of head exclusively and of being content with an artificial and wimpy solitude. Following the head would mean to yield to pessimism. As Jefferson said, it is the heart that puts one in the condition of "justifying . . . the ways of Providence, whose precept is *to do* always what is right." It is false to assert that Jefferson, as an exponent of the Enlightenment, must have been a staunch apologist of the head. In the famous letter to Maria, he decided to give to the heart the last word. He was "attempting to convince himself that the Heart was right," Burstein correctly argues. "Only through the Heart could Jefferson achieve the optimistic state that he, as an inheritor of the Enlightenment thinking, required for sustenance." Only thanks to the heart's primacy could Jefferson voice the inauguration of the Enlightenment.[6]

The urging of the heart and the craving to transcend the present should not be interpreted as if they were a glorification of the primacy of the creative momentum. The heart does not create the world. Enlightenment was not a mystical worship of the "One" and of humans' participation in it. Vitalism, monism, the cult of the *élan originel,* or any other version of the idealistic reduction of existence to spiritual energy are perspectives that neither Jefferson nor the Enlightenment as a whole ever took into account. Present conditions, material circumstances, and all the facts that the head takes into consideration were not seen as illusions under which the "spiritual" reality would be hidden. A resolute empiricist, Jefferson took facts at face value. At the same time the heart pushed him to outstrip the limits of facts, his head consented to compromises between desires and hard reality. In a world perceived as hazardously unyielding, Enlightenment fostered a sense of urgency and cautiousness. The impression of being besieged by an unsatisfying present was altogether common, and eighteenth-century Enlightenment struggled to counteract the menace coming from hard reality with a very human attempt to introduce order.

In the context of the Enlightenment, it is apparent that words like "presence," "present," and "facts" were problematic: the desired outcome does not exist already, but must be made. Reality was not "spiritual" and humans in a mystical union with it. A realistic gaze cast on the human condition, the Enlightenment did not reduce existence to spirit and circumstances to illusions. The emphasis fell on prudence, on compromises with circumstances, on the precarious equilibrium between head and heart, and on the quest for the most suitable means to counterattack. As a form of desire, the Enlightenment began with the acknowledgment that something was missing in human life: the secret to unveil was not that humans were part of the "One." Therefore, if the heart has some predominance, it is just because the heart pushes humans forward, notwithstanding the limits of what could be attained.

The present, the facts, were problematic but extremely real, and provided the raw material on which to work. The present was acknowledged, of course, but the facts were not something with which an Enlightenment follower could have been satisfied, neither from a practical nor epistemological point of view. Real knowledge begins with the facts, but Jefferson's epistemology never leaned toward an ideal of knowledge as a pure description. Facts had to be collected, combined, and compared, and eventually a theory had to be drawn. A lot of imagination is involved, for instance, in the *Notes,* a book which is awash with theories. In general terms, that "we are to look backwards instead of forwards," exclusively to the facts instead of the ideals, was a maxim that Jefferson firmly rejected. Facts, for him, were raw material to be transformed by a restless optimistic desire to move forward.[7]

There was something tragic in this kind of optimism channeling the anxiety of one condemned to ceaseless activity and to always prefer transformation to description. A nontragic optimism would be buttressed by the delusion of a *unio mystica* and a sense of fullness, but the Enlightenment expressed the culture of a society condemned to abide by its lasting appetite. It desired to give substance to a present conceived as deficient in value and as a lack. The Enlightenment inclined emotionally toward a future as something qualitatively better than the present and thus elicited a *desperate* optimism and, accordingly, a *desperate* progressive view of history. I use the adjective "desperate" to put emphasis on the fact that, rejecting the present and the world as it is, Enlightenment devotees had no other choice than to be committed to optimism and to a better future. To the same extent, we could legitimately speak of a "desperate hope," were it not too awkward a phrase. "Desperate" also underlines the fact that the basic character of eighteenth-century culture was not that of a self-confident age and an epoch of self-satisfaction. Satisfaction was unquestionably present, but satisfaction was but one element of a broader constellation of discourses. Acknowledgment of one's ignorance, doubts, and a peculiar soul-searching character were further correlates of the Enlightenment's desire to progress.

All the symbols related to the self-righteous representation of a Ptolemaic cosmos, in which human beings were supposed to occupy the center, were rejected. The shift toward a Copernican universe, in which humans were portrayed as peripheral and dispersed beings, was complete. Humans for the first time were conscious that they inhabited a tiny, similarly peripheral and dispersed planet spinning through the void. Those who awakened from the delusion of being at the center of a "spiritual" universe described this experience through the confession of their own limits.

Elected in 1802 to the position of *associé étranger* of the Institut National de France, for instance, Jefferson unsurprisingly reacted with his typical modesty and, what is most interesting, with a clear "Copernican" spirit: "Without pretensions or qualifications which might do justice to the appointment, I accept it as an evidence of the brotherly spirit of Science, which unites into one family all its votaries of whatever grade, and however widely dispersed through the different quarters of the globe." There are of course elements of affectation, self-effacement, and mannerism in this public declaration of inadequacy. But the tone is one of sincere humility and the reference to that "brotherly spirit" reveals a lot more about a context. It tells something of Jefferson's deepest beliefs about the mission and the limits of the enlightened man of science. Jefferson was emphasizing that the "scientists," now simply researchers dispersed through this uncanny world, needed a shelter under which to find protection. We find here the admission that "Copernican" philosophy, as long as it is a human endeavor, is always tentative; that the truth is not a stable possession of a solitary thinker; that the researcher could not penetrate all the secrets of reality *via* a mystical union; that circulating hypotheses is essential; and that the acknowledgment of one's ignorance and marginality is the first step toward real wisdom. Jefferson was actually convinced that human beings should always admit they are "without pretensions or qualifications" and, in a word, peripheral.[8]

Jefferson had expressed in the *Notes* the same "Copernican" philosophy, namely, that "ignorance is preferable to error; & he is less remote from truth who believes nothing, then he who believes what is wrong." In effect, from ignorance, from a sense of inadequateness, and from the confession that we need partners, improvement can take place, while error is but the opium of the mind. The progress toward a better world began for Jefferson with a first negative step, with the rejection of deceptive idols and "Ptolemaic" self-righteousness.[9]

In its respect for both limits and possibilities, the Enlightenment implicitly highlighted the notion of choice. I am not speaking of the precritical *certitude* that Americans, through their choices, would have defeated the cycles of the past. For the Enlightenment, choice expressed nothing more certain than a hope. There was in the period a widespread hope that human societies, or at least the American one, would not remain prisoners of conditions beyond their control and hostages to false beliefs. Ignorance and limits notwithstanding, humans could set out for a new hopeful land *if they just chose it*. Jefferson and others of his age promoted the opinion according to which humans can be driven by possibilities and by their choices, and not just by needs and necessity. They cultivated the trust that human societies have a potential, which means both possibility and indeterminacy, and that humans intervene as a causal factor in influencing the course of events.

Among many other appropriate examples depicting that specific cultural climate, George Washington provided an excellent text animated by precisely this emphasis on choice-as-possibility. "It appears to me," Washington wrote in 1783, "that there is an option still left to the United States of America, that it is in their choice, and depends upon their conduct, whether they will be respectable and prosperous, or contemptible and miserable as a Nation; This is the time of their political probation, . . . it is yet to be decided, whether the Revolution must ultimately be considered as a blessing or a curse." Washington's confidence that there was an option left must not be mistaken for stubborn buoyancy. "Yet to be decided," said a very enlightened Washington. Since the Copernican universe is to some extent undetermined, historical time was humanistically considered as a never-ending probation. Choice, fallibility, responsibility, experiment, and similar human-centered notions were crucial. They discounted both the myths that reality would be essentially rational—and consequently that humans qua rational beings are from the outset the winners—or, contrariwise, that the only certain outcome of human endeavor would be defeat.[10]

What the eighteenth-century Enlightenment tried to cast off was the antihumanistic vision that the universe was closed and impervious to human decisions. Jared Sparks, the first great American historian, offers a second interesting example. Greatly impressed by another typical Enlightenment text, Ben Franklin's *Autobiography*, Sparks claimed to have drawn a precise lesson from it: "It taught me that circumstances have not a sovereign control over the mind." Circumstances definitely have a control and quite often they are unyielding and also oppressive. However, that humans could intervene as a causal factor among other causal factors was part of the Enlightenment's project of the humanization of reality. Such a humanization of reality had a limit, and it did not mean that human minds or, better, hearts were *the* causal factor. Humanization meant something less pretentious: a heuristic gaze on reality; a philosophy of history that endeavored to abandon the language of necessity; a hope in the superiority of the heart over the head; once again a desperate attempt to deal with reality *as if* the outcome was not certain. While more traditional theories held that events flowed from design provided by either God or "Spirit," the men of the Enlightenment began to look for non-necessitarian explanations of events and, accordingly, for ways of liberating the future from any teleological gaze.[11]

No simple quotation can be provided to bolster the claim that the Enlightenment's fundamental aim was an attempt at embracing choices while abandoning the language of both necessity and teleology. I have already said something on Jefferson's dialectic between heart and head. As an indirect proof, one could also reflect on the manner in which conspiratorial interpretations of events, in the second half of the eighteenth century, had spread throughout the transatlantic world. Conspiracy theories have been appropriately portrayed as a "humanization of Providence" and an attempt to exorcise any form of necessity—"An impassioned attempt to explain the ways of man to man, the crude beginnings of what has come to be called the Whig interpretation of history." According to the Whig historians, liberty, in effect, was always under the menace of the hearts of depraved individuals, such as tyrants. They interpreted the march of civilization as an ongoing and uncertain struggle between liberty and tyranny.[12]

Conspiracy theory is an interesting by-product of an enlightened *mentalité* since it focuses on human responsibility. It attributes events to the joint designs of willful individuals and deems human beings personally and morally responsible for their actions. It is part of a process of enlightenment to hold that events are determined by the human capacity to predict and control and not by "spiritual" or necessary forces.

In the eighteenth century, conspiracy was not a new tenet. From Sallust to Machiavelli, events have occasionally been considered the outcome of a calculated plot by a few powerful men in high positions. What was new, however, was the fact that similar interpretations became a common view and the banner of a new era. Conspiracy theory did not draw the attention of a small number of literati anymore but began to intimidate a significant number of American citizens. A sign of the passage from a framework of impersonal to one of personal forces, from necessity to possibility, conspiracy theory gained an unparalleled level of success. "The era of the American Revolution," Lance Banning writes, "was a period of political paranoia" in which "visions of conspiracy were endemic." Conspiracy theory was not just occasioned by particularly troublesome events, like the Revolution, but proved more enduring. "The accusations of conspiratorial designs," according to Bernard Bailyn, "did not cease with the pamphlet series touched off by the Declaration, nor even with the American successes in battle. They merely shifted their forms, and began a process of adaptation that has allowed them to survive into our time."[13]

It should be clear why the Enlightenment threw individuals into a condition of extreme emotional instability. A humanistic discourse of responsibility and maturity, the Enlightenment worked to transform the world into an arena of personal forces and impending decisions, which challenged and threatened humans' capacities at the same time. A perennial swerving between excitement and depression was the obvious consequence.

Because it is centered on responsibility, adulthood is usually burdened with anxiety. When the world began to be portrayed as Copernically open and also dependent on peoples' wills, what was elicited was at once a mature yearning to live up to better expectations—that one could be wise enough to overcome restraints by an effective resistance—and an unfathomable anxiety. Excitement aside, maturity is an emotional burden, and Enlightenment disciples were mature people who were particularly hesitant about their identity and status. They were men who were especially susceptible to conspiratorial interpretations of events. Their self was constructed out of a vision of reality that was uncertain, an arena of personal forces subjected to desires. Enlightenment was a desired coming of age, but since desire does not mean realization, the Enlightenment increased the general level of hazard and anxiety. He who awakes in the morning with the exhilarating sense of being a freshman in a world of adults, by sunset usually becomes oppressed by the burden of new responsibilities. In the same way, renouncing the dream of a *unio mystica,* the men of the Enlightenment discovered that with their spiritual independence and maturity, they had already become relatively backward, underdeveloped, limited, and weak individuals. To awake to awareness and responsibility is per se to awake to unending plights.

There was something consoling in the way premodern philosophers and mystics used to explain reality. If the world is uncontrollable and has a secret, more-than-human design, if it is ruled by the forces of the past, fate, or providence, if it is "Spirit," if it is inscrutable and necessary, there is nothing humans can do. Hope has no meaning in that world, but the level of anxiety is also lower. For those living in a premodern world, to embrace a Stoic forbearance could have probably been the only serious choice. In contrast, conspiratorial interpretations are embedded in the new tenet that historical events are amenable to humans' voluntary actions and to motives brought to bear by persons. Enlightenment gave sense to the concepts of hope and agency, but it also heralded the very ambiguous idea of an authorial control and design. It proclaimed the doctrine that, to a certain extent, history is made of events that are caused by humans, and here lies the source of ambiguity: human hearts are at times "good," other times "bad." Conspiratorial interpretations took hold in such a secularized view of history, when God's providence or "Spirit" was portrayed as merely the primary and remote cause, while for most events humans were held the immediate cause.

The empirical, causal, and descriptive line of reasoning developed, for instance, in David Hume's famous *Enquiry Concerning Human Understanding* (1748) lodged a powerful accusation against more traditional approaches. Hume's philosophy thrived on the principles that every effect has its particular cause; that particular causes are the only causes worth investigating; and that human motives, intentions, and inclinations quite often work as real and particular causes. Hume's empiricism turned into a humanism and implicitly maintained that the course of human events has purposive human agents as its cause. However, before the advent of the sciences of human processes, such as social psychology, to take account of discrepancies and conflicts among human groups meant to inevitably stand for the idea of a large-scale orchestrated deception, of corrupt doers intriguing behind the curtain. Even though at first it does not seem so, the eighteenth-century often-repeated allegation that the British were usually engaged in an endless conspiracy and that they hid their true selves to dupe the colonists is the best indirect proof of the success of "Hume's approach," as it were. Such allegations indicated the general spread of the Enlightenment and of all its by-products, such as hope and anxiety. Conspiratorial interpretations were both the cause and the effect of a high level of anxiety, but also the signal that hope, possibility, and humanism were at work.[14]

VULNERABILITY AND PRECARIOUSNESS

The Copernican and humanistic climate was propitious to the development of numberless anxieties. The peculiar situation, both geographically and politically, that the colonists found in the new continent also acted as an effective catalyst. Scholars have focused their attention on the issue that colonists "migrated in order to escape anxieties at home" and that ironically enough by coming to the new continent "they activated others and created some anew." Slavery, this "blot in our country," as Jefferson named it, is probably the most meaningful example of a typically American anxiety. Jefferson conceived slavery as both a wrong choice and a subversion of human dignity that, in the long run, would prompt God's wrath.[15]

My purpose in this section is to pursue the analysis of the dialectic between optimism and its necessary negative side, the sense of being unprotected. In particular, I would like to show that Jefferson's optimism, as an enlightened optimistic meliorism speaking directly to the colonists' hearts, found in a sense of vulnerability its fittest emotional setting. Jefferson's optimism was a reaction of heart and virtue to a context perceived as unbearably fluid. It entailed humanism, an emphasis on choices, but also realism as to the intrinsic limits and impermanence of human existence.

Actually, colonists had countless de facto reasons to be worried. Parties, factions, a defective law system, a growing North-South rivalry, wars, riots, and rebellions were real threats that worked as compelling sources of severe anxiety. Moreover, depending on the circumstance of the moment, on their personal temper, and also on their political orientation, early republicans were extremely keen on emphasizing unheard-of motives, sometimes imaginary, that added to an extant fearfulness. Size, lack of homogeneity, overpopulation, luxury, "standing" armies, corrupted representation, the lack of a bill of rights, mobs, Jacobinism, aristocracy, revivalism, awakenings, enthusiasm, Indians, the British, the Spanish, the wicked influence of a moneyed power subsidizing "artificial" monopolies that would ruin "natural" producers, to name just a few, were from time to time selected as the most obnoxious obstacles to the American cause.[16]

Jefferson, of course, was not immune from anxiety. Anxieties such as these are a well-known topic, and I need not spend too much time on it. What I want to emphasize is that the Enlightenment added to this anxiety. Enlightenment triggered a slow process of awakening. It aroused people to possibilities, to expectations, and, accordingly, to both anxiety and a very excruciating sense of precariousness. The higher the expectations, the higher the level of anxiety. The expectations of the Enlightenment were difficult to fulfill, making frustration inevitable. As stated, Enlightenment was not a culture of abundance and should not be identified with a form of self-righteousness or boastfulness. It was an effort of coming of age, which means an endeavor to uncover hard reality and unpleasant truths. Enlightenment taught Jefferson that there was a chance the unconditioned would realize itself in the world. But since possibility and not certitude was at issue, Jefferson could also see that pitfalls were everywhere.[17]

Quite frequently, the sense of precariousness was increased by the general thought that republics had never lasted for long at any time in the past. What spun off quickly into a nightmare of despair was the recognition that history did not offer any example of success. The moral premise of a republican order, as well as virtue and disinterestedness, is hazardous if not impossible to maintain. The men of the revolutionary generation, John Howe writes, "were quite aware that history offered little promise of the success of their republican experiments." The study of history disclosed republics' tendency toward internal decay. In a world ruled almost entirely by monarchies, with the exception of certain Swiss cantons and a few European principalities, the American experiment appeared to dangle over a historical void.[18]

During the most acute crises, when the sense of precariousness was at the highest peak, Americans displayed a singular mixture of fearfulness and verbal violence. The 1790s were probably the most interesting period of the national history in this respect. It is sufficient to scan the public press, speeches, sermons, and private correspondence to realize that such fearfulness and violence must have stemmed from an insupportable impression of instability. Jefferson, among other leaders, noticed that times had changed. Americans were so violently suspicious and reactive, he was convinced, that there must be something explicitly pathological underneath. Jefferson confessed to having formerly seen warm debates and high political passions, "but gentlemen of different politics would then speak to each other, and separate the business of the senate from that of society." They kept, in other words, a sense of measure and a sound realism that permitted them to separate, discriminate, and distinguish. It was not so now: "Men who have been intimate all their lives cross the streets to avoid meeting, and turn their heads another way, lest they should be obliged to touch their hat."[19]

Everybody was so convinced that the experiment was in jeopardy that over the entire decade political opponents were usually found guilty of conspiracy or of patent dishonesty and were accused of going astray, having lost the "true" American principles. The failure of nerve was so widespread that resilience and good sense seemed outmoded. It was not infrequent to come across deluded Virginians, for instance, who irresponsibly drank the toast "A speedy Death to General Washington." Under the same delusion, one anti-Federalist propagandist (probably John Beckley from Pennsylvania) composed a series of articles with the express purpose of proving Washington a common thief. One century and a half before McCarthyism, "there had developed an emotional and psychological climate," as Howe says, "in which stereotypes stood in the place of reality. . . . Over the entire decade there hung an ominous sense of crisis, of continuing emergency, of life lived at a turning point when fateful decisions were being made and enemies were poised to do the ultimate evil."[20]

As usually happens during times of crisis, people were claiming deep allegiance to stereotypes and ideology because reality was tough to bear. American citizens needed to identify external, visible enemies in order to exorcise the inner sense of uneasiness; they called for legal discriminatory devices that would allow them to put the blame on "strangers" and to cast them off. The Alien and Sedition Acts are the best demonstration that the 1790s were an age of collective delusion, and that rhetoric was more important than dialogue. The act allowed anxious leaders to fabricate proxies to simplify and hide an unbearable reality. Good sense apart, Jeffersonians thus projected on Federalists the image of staunch monarchists, while Federalists downgraded Jeffersonians to the level of dupes maneuvering to import Jacobinism.[21]

The popularity of the theme of the United States as a hazardous "experiment" reveals that precariousness was often the main category through which the political reality was interpreted. Everyone was acquainted with the prospect that the republic might succeed or fail, even ten years, a hundred years, after the Revolution. Most Americans understood their Union as an enduring experiment, and the nature of the experiment is such that the hoped-for outcome is by no means certain. The founders and, in general, American leaders were not a band of dreamers. They were brave and imperturbable realists, as Arthur Schlesinger once wrote, who nevertheless "committed themselves, in defiance of the available lessons of history and theology, to a monumental gamble." They "had an intense conviction of the improbability of their undertaking," they were "acutely aware of the chanciness of an extraordinary enterprise," and they "saw the American republic not as a consecration but as the test against history of a hypothesis."[22]

Jefferson knew, of course, that the Union was a hazardous hypothesis. When, in his writings, we come across words such as "corruption," "conspiracy," or "slavery," we should not dismiss them as mere rhetoric and propaganda intended to influence the inert minds of an otherwise passive constituency. They reveal—it is "slavery" in particular that reveals—that Jefferson was acutely aware that the Unites States was on the brink of a catastrophe. The perception of black people as consistently on the rise stirred Jefferson's deepest worries. When he published his records on the population of Virginia, his fellow Americans, and Jefferson himself, had surely flinched at the raw data that 270,762 inhabitants out of 567,614 were blacks. It was enough to feel the republic besieged. Whether or not Jefferson and his peers considered chattel slavery metaphysically and morally wrong, they definitely had to consider it a factual danger.

It was the specter of rebellion, of conspiracy and revolt, the image of legions marching against the citadel of civilization, the "storm blasting on us," that was associated with the fear of African Americans. "If I were as drunk with enthusiasm as Swedenborg or Westley," old John Adams wrote to Jefferson in 1821, "I might probably say I had seen Armies of Negroes marching and countermarching in the air, shining in Armour." Some twenty years before, commenting on the slave rebellion in St. Domingue, Jefferson had already warned about the "revolutionary storm now sweeping the globe." Sooner or later, Jefferson lamented, that storm "will be upon us, and happy if we make timely provision to give it an easy passage over our land. From the present state of things in Europe and America the day which begins our combustion must be near at hand, and only a single spark is wanting to make that day tomorrow." Whether an army or a storm, American leaders realized that they were surrounded by a black underclass and grew anxiously aware of their own vulnerability. Well-heeled citizens were terrified by what blacks could become. Far from acquiescent and fettered by their roles, slaves were perceived as a threatening source of constant insecurity.[23]

Besides the obvious menace of slave rebellions and physical confrontations, it was clear that slavery could also produce a fatal train of vices, both in the slave and in the master. The awareness of being at odds with oneself or, to use a shortened formulation, the nemesis complex haunted many Americans. There was a general perception that the United States was in contradiction with its very moral principles. Jefferson expressed the nemesis complex openly. In the sole book he really published, he took extreme care to be publicly acknowledged as outraged and even internally lacerated by the moral dilemma. His portrayal of the moral quandary of the Union is even affected by theological hues:

> I tremble for my country when I reflect that God is just: that his justice cannot sleep for ever: that considering numbers, nature and natural means only, a revolution of the wheel of fortune, an exchange of situation, is among possible events: that it may become probable by supernatural interference! . . . The spirit of the master is abating, that of the slave rising from the dust, his condition mollifying, the way I hope preparing, under the auspices of heaven, for a total emancipation, and that this is disposed, in the order of events, to be with the consent of the masters, rather than by their extirpation.[24]

Jefferson was perfectly aware of both the physical danger represented by rebellious slaves and the moral indefensibility of the institution of slavery. There were excellent reasons to tremble for the country, especially because nobody was able to envision either a peaceful or a sudden solution to the problem. The letter to John Holmes of 22 April 1820 depicted in noticeably lucid terms the extent of Jefferson's moral dilemma and its inescapability: "I can say, with conscious truth, that there is not a man on earth who would sacrifice more than I would to relieve us from this heavy reproach [slavery], in any *practicable* way. The cession of that kind of property, for so it is misnamed, is a bagatelle which would not cost me a second thought, if, in that way, a general emancipation and *expatriation* [of slaves] could be effected; and gradually, and with due sacrifices, I think it may be. But as it is, we have the wolf by the ears, and we can neither hold him, nor safely let him go. Justice is in one scale, and self-preservation in the other." The Union was a monumental gamble, indeed.[25]

Jefferson knew the meaning of humility. He knew that America was precarious, and that it was but "a child of yesterday," as he eloquently wrote in the *Notes*. He understood that the new nation was obliged to compromise, that it was burdened by moral dilemmas, and that it must enter the international scene, as he also said to the Emperor Alexander, with the credentials of an "infant nation, unoffending in its course, unambitious in its views." However, humility was not just a temporary mask that Jefferson was forced to wear: humility was not occasioned by a particular ominous circumstance that in the long run would disappear. It is true that slavery, for instance, could draw the American experiment to failure and annihilate all its possibilities. But Jefferson's humility and "un-ambition" do not seem to simply derive from this problem, although a dreadful one; it was not in one particular moment, and only in that moment, that the Union was exposed to risk. Maybe one day the problem of slavery would be solved. Jefferson set up plans for deporting slaves to "tackle" this question. But humility, for Jefferson, seems not to have depended chiefly on circumstances or on particular problems that the new nation was accidentally bound to face.[26]

My hypothesis, in other words, is that it was not slavery as such that *caused* Jefferson's anxiety and hence humility. Slavery, conspiracies, rebellions, sectionalism, and similar problems would be better understood as catalysts that precipitated Jefferson's almost "existential" anxiety. Un-ambition was not caused by Jefferson's recoiling before a problem but was an enduring stance deriving from something deeper. Problems can be solved, but the ominous implications that Jefferson discussed apropos of slavery seem, in part at least, to depend on America's being "new" and on the acknowledgment that every human venture is by definition "new." Being "new" reveals the peculiar human condition, when one intentionally abandons "the scanty field of what is known" to plunge into a boisterous ocean. Jefferson knew that every human endeavor was a risky attempt to experiment with "the boundless region of what is unknown." Jefferson's humility revealed this existential dimension of a risk that the philosopher of the Enlightenment was compelled to run.[27]

Let me develop the argument a little further. Slavery, conspiracies, and rebellions represented problems de facto. Big problems, undeniably. But to say that Jefferson acknowledged these problems and adjusted his behavior accordingly is not the whole story. There is a moment when the reader of Jefferson's writings is compelled to leave de facto considerations to enter a philosophical dimension. Jefferson's sense of the precarious is a pivotal concept in this respect. "No one was *more* conscious of the fragility of the American experiment than Jefferson himself," Peter Onuf argues. Why? For two main reasons. First, because Jefferson was aware that fragility and precariousness are essential parts of an enlightened, namely, nonconsolatory, appraisal of the human world; second, because the Enlightenment relied extensively on possibilities. The acknowledgment that humans have no better choices than to put their assets at risk, together with the recognition that they are thus precarious in an essential way, was part of Jefferson's concept of hope, of his meliorism, and of his enlightened version of optimism. The country's being "new" was for Jefferson a metaphor of an enlightened appraisal of human life, which is precarious by definition and always open to unexplored fields. To portray human life in realistic terms was to allow for precariousness, for both the unknown and the possible (considered in this chapter), and the unknowable and the impossible (considered in the next chapters).[28]

"Against us," against all those who took on a philosophical precariousness, against those who willingly pursued their enlightened plans and put their lives at risk, against the lifestyle that Jefferson revered, "are . . . all timid men who prefer the calm of despotism to the boisterous sea of liberty." Enlightened men were classified by Jefferson in opposition to all those who were "timid," namely, without heart, asleep, those who refused the risk of traveling and were addicted to self-inflicted delusions. Likewise, the "new" nation was often defined in opposition to the "old" monarchies, that kept their eyes shut, that did not understand precariousness, that did not appreciate the moral obligation to rewrite their laws every twenty years or so, and that preferred the stupor of a death-like perpetuity. The "new" nation and the "new" individual were identified by opposition to all those who did not choose to believe in their possibilities and who feared "awakening from a long stupor of many ages," as Charles Thomson stated in a famous letter to Jefferson. A crucial part of the whole Enlightenment culture, the notion of possibility, reveals the extent of America's and the "new" individual's precariousness. The structure of Jefferson's discourse, in this case also, is dualistic. Both because "new" individuals and "new" nations are opposed to old ones, and also because "the scanty field of what is known" is philosophically opposed to "the boundless region of what is unknown." "New" individuals awaken to the unknown and face their void.[29]

In Jefferson's dualistic philosophy the unknown is always opposed to what we know; timid individuals stand in opposition to the brave ones; the enlightened and the awakened nations are opposed to those that sleep; delusion is opposed to truth, and, correspondingly, the past is opposed to the future. Precariousness, in its philosophical meaning, results from all these dualisms. The enlightened life is always a challenge and encompasses opposite extremes. According to Jefferson, the enlightened man ran the risk of facing the unknown, defeating the "timid" man, awakening from the age-old slumber, letting delusions and consoling myths fade away, and heading bravely toward the future. A further opposition should be considered to complete the picture: circumstances are on one side—often in the form of the unknown, other times in the form of the unknowable—human ingenuity on the other. The metaphor of the "boisterous sea" that I have just noted in Jefferson's letter to Mazzei is probably the best means by which to clarify this last dualism.

The symbol of the boisterous sea was what helped Jefferson to grasp the essential human precariousness. He desired to convey the message that, in an essential way, humans are contingent beings, and not just because they happen to tackle problems de facto. The reverse is also true: humans have to fathom problems because their life is a continuous journey on a boisterous sea. The sea and the symbols that it elicits form the true subject, for instance, of that famous passage of the *Notes* that begins with "I tremble for my country." Slavery was the occasion de facto or the catalyst, as I have said, but Jefferson here was working on his idea that hazard, to directly borrow from his words, "is the stuff of which the web of life is woven: and he who lives longest and wisest is only able to weave out the more of it." If we continue reading the passage of the *Notes,* we discover why Jefferson was trembling for the country: "I tremble for my country when I reflect that God is just: that his justice cannot sleep for ever: that considering numbers, nature and natural means only, *a revolution of the wheel of fortune, an exchange of situation, is among possible events: that it may become probable* by supernatural interference!"[30]

Neither God's wrath nor slavery per se (perhaps slaves were the hand of God made visible, an impersonal force of justice) but the instability of circumstances and the never-ending struggle between "fortune" (hazard) and human plans (ingenuity) were the true theme that the passage addressed. It is the voice of the dualist philosopher resounding here, while the policymaker and the optimistic troubleshooter are but secondary characters.

Jefferson took into serious consideration this dualism of ingenuity and hazard, of "the scanty field of what is known," as he also said to Caspar Wistar, and "the boundless region of what is unknown." By the same token, he was almost obsessed with the correlated idea that, notwithstanding the risks, one should try oneself on a journey into that perilous element. He was attracted by hazardous plans. "I steer my bark with Hope in the Head," he declared to John Adams, "leaving Fear astern." The hope, obviously, was to resist circumstances, to make the right choice, and to convert the unknown into knowledge and an American potential. Hope and optimism apart, it is the dualistic structure of Jefferson's philosophy that is relevant for the study of the theme of precariousness. Whoever steers a bark and makes risky plans must always keep in mind that the ocean is by definition unreliable, and both error and failure are lurking. Circumstances often have an overwhelming strength, and sudden changes can always happen.[31]

A number of texts could be chosen to strengthen my argument on dualism. A good one, for instance, is the letter that the Sage of Monticello wrote to Jedediah Morse in 1822. The occasion of that letter seems far away from the theme being discussed: whether or not Jefferson should become a member of the "society for the civilization and improvement of the Indian tribes." It was a private association of "laudable views," Jefferson allowed, which could, however, "rivalise and jeopardize the march of regular government."[32]

The refusal of Morse's offer gave Jefferson the chance to philosophize a little bit and to address the general question that plans and intentions are always risky, and that human life is essentially precarious. Must we trust blindly the functionaries of an association whatsoever, as they are "men"? "Men," Jefferson said, can become a sect, a faction jeopardizing the march of regular government, combining against the rights of the people, harboring machinations "against the adored principles of our constitution." The prospect of functionaries acting not "by the laws of their station, but by those of a voluntary society" appeared to Jefferson the definitive proof that arbitrariness was a real menace, and that the sea was actually boisterous. Imaginary fears, at least at present: "The fears are indeed imaginary: but the example is *real.*" The bark of rationality, knowledge, and opportunity can easily go adrift: "The society of the Jacobins, in another country, was instituted on principles and views as virtuous as ever kindled the hearths of patriots. . . . Yet these were men; and we and our descendants will be no more. The present is a case where, if ever, *we are to guard against ourselves; not against ourselves as we are, but as we may be; for, who can now imagine what we may become under circumstances not now imaginable?*" These were humans, indeed, and humans' ingenuity is by definition exposed to both error and an overwhelming chanciness.[33]

Since the time he pondered that "a revolution of the wheel of fortune, an exchange of situation, is among possible events," Jefferson had been on familiar terms with the idea that humans are circumstantial beings. Humans are on a perilous journey in the midst of a boisterous sea. A dualist philosopher, Jefferson had always employed the binary rhetoric characteristic of the nautical metaphors—whose ingredients are the hazardous adventure in the unknown and the dualism between success and failure—even when he did not make actual nautical metaphors. The boisterous sea took different shapes, but what it symbolized remained intact: fate, fortune, circumstances, and a very romantic "spirit of the times" are different names that Jefferson gave to the boisterous sea. When in the *Notes* Jefferson spoke about religion and religious disputes, he showed his trust in the present "spirit of the times" that fortunately foils fanaticism, enthusiasm, and tyrannical laws. In that text, the "spirit of the times" looked like a calm sea waiting but for the human bark. An optimistic glance was cast on the present opportunities and on this enlightened age, but the spirit of the times was not something on which to rely. It is true that the enlightened people of this country could not suffer an execution of heresy anymore, Jefferson maintained. Nor would they accept or execute fanaticism. American citizens seemed to be rescued from tyranny. However, Jefferson was aware enough to make clear that "the spirit of the times may alter, will alter."[34]

At the end of the Query 17, Jefferson took the opportunity to give a lecture on the effects of the boisterous sea on human aspirations. The passage is worth a long quotation:

> Our rulers will become corrupt, our people careless. A single zealot may commence persecutor, and better men be his victims. It can never be too often repeated, that the time for fixing every essential right on a legal basis is while our rulers are honest, and ourselves united. From the conclusion of this war we shall be going down hill. It will not then be necessary to resort every moment to the people for support. They will be forgotten, therefore, and their rights disregarded. They will forget themselves, but in the sole faculty of making money, and will never think of uniting to effect a due respect for their rights. The shackles, therefore, which shall not be knocked off at the conclusion of this war, will remain on us long, will be made heavier and heavier, till our rights shall revive or expire in a convulsion.

Besides what the passage directly addressed, the real gist of Jefferson's argument was that human life could never be deemed "secured" in a safe harbor. It is an illusion that "we are as yet secured against them [tyrannical laws] by the spirit of the times." An apparently yielding and navigable sea, the "spirit of the times" can suddenly turn into a tempestuous and "irrational" element. Jefferson taught his readers that people will "forget themselves," the ocean "will alter," and its "tyrannical laws" will be restored. The "yielding" ocean, here under the name of a "spirit of the times," will turn into the cause of shipwreck and oblivion.

The dualism of "fortune" and human plans is evident throughout Jefferson's life, in documents and texts dating back to 1822, 1816, 1807, 1796, and to the 1780s, 1770s, and 1760s. That Jefferson's philosophy was informed by the nautical metaphor, even when he did not make actual nautical metaphors, can be argued from his enduring attention to scales, balances, measures, and their correlates. It is worth remembering here that, as secretary of state, Jefferson wrote a report to the House of Representatives, that he communicated on 13 July 1790, on the subject of uniform weights and measures. It was an exceedingly important document to him. Jefferson was looking for an internationally recognized standard, an extension of a decimal system based on plain arithmetic and common sense, that would help enlarge the province of order. The document is important also to us, since it reveals marvelously the hidden fabric of a dualistic philosophy.

Besides specific documents and texts, Jefferson's attention to viable criteria for orientation can be argued from his well-known devotion to a systematic way of living. The daily ritual of recording events in his Memorandum and Account books, for instance, gave him a satisfying sense of order in his financial world. Actually, his financial situation on a larger scale substantially escaped him, but the exactness of the entries he put on record provides the historian with the precise indication of what Jefferson's real priorities were and what his underlying operative philosophical structure was. From his lifelong interest in the theme of order and orientation, one can draw but one conclusion. Finding means, instruments, measures, and ideas to orient him in the boisterous sea was without a doubt Jefferson's main concern.[35]

Humans are not precarious de facto, only when they happen to face a particular problem. They are *essentially* precarious and vulnerable, and the enlightened ones are intensely aware of that. All who are not "timid men," all who are brave and enlightened are also essentially precarious because they have deliberately chosen to travel into and explore the boisterous element. Lives governed by the heart are even more precarious.

Jefferson traveled west of the Shenandoah Valley only once and only for a few miles. In order to take a cure, he once reached Warm Springs, Virginia, seventy-five miles from Monticello. He had never hunted the bison along the Kanawha, like Washington. In a sense, "he was neither frontiersman nor wanderer in the wilderness," as Charles Miller argued. The only gaze he cast on the West was through Lewis and Clark. However, in another sense he was an archetypal frontiersman and a philosophical wanderer. He was uncommonly comfortable with unfinished projects, with the burden of making choices, with possible solutions, with the practice of heartening himself and his friends, and with the hopeful carrying on of things more than with their completion. From time immemorial, he had internalized all the habits and the hardness of one accustomed to wander and explore.[36]

4

Nature and Time as Overwhelming Powers

HUMAN NATURE AND NECESSITY

Jefferson's hope that all will be right is not incompatible with the awareness that humans, as hoping and desiring creatures, are swept along by the boisterous sea. There is always the possibility, and perhaps the probability, that the wheel of fortune will take an odd turn. What about the necessity of a bad turn? Is the shipwreck just probable? Did Jefferson know something about necessity? Jefferson's philosophy contains discourses on faith, satisfaction, and self-satisfaction, and also on anxiety, hope, and precariousness. But that is not all. The idea that "irrational" energy might reveal itself as a fate and a commanding necessity is not irreconcilable with the Enlightenment's hopeful expectations. Quite the contrary: those expectations can be read as a sort of reaction of virtue to untamable, all-powerful, unassessable, unexhaustible, "irrational" circumstances. They derive from the acceptance of necessity.

The refusal of the Leibnizian dream—the dream that humans are spirits that dwell at the center of the best among all the possible worlds—implies two implicit assertions: (1) that human beings should be portrayed as immersed in pre-existing circumstances, and (2) that circumstances bring about human beings' multiple and conditional reactions. Human beings try to cope with circumstances, to react to them, to be hopeful and heartened notwithstanding a body of contrary evidence. The present chapter is devoted to the study of these untamable circumstances that cultures have usually put under the banner of the term "necessity."

Jefferson looked quite favorably on the environmentalist view, typical of his time, that humans like other organisms derive their characteristics from the circumstances in which they grow. The point Jefferson made in his famous Query 6 of the *Notes* to rescue the American continent from the "imputation of impotence," together with Buffon's contrary claim that in this continent nature would be "less energetic" and could produce only feeble beings, are two famous examples of eighteenth-century environmentalism. Jefferson's opinion about the aboriginal people of the North American continent was even fraught with pride. Far from being weak, such a native product of the American soil "is neither more defective in ardor, nor more impotent with his female, than the white reduced to the same diet and exercise . . . he is brave, when an enterprise depends on bravery . . . his sensibility is keen . . . his vivacity and activity of mind is equal to ours in the same situation." In the same way, the white man transplanted to this side of the Atlantic grows like a superb fruit. "Of the geniuses which adorn the present age, America contributes its full share." There is more eloquence than sound reasoning in Buffon's allegations, Jefferson thus concluded, and nature seems not to have "enlisted herself as a Cis- or Transatlantic partisan." The fact remains that "men are like plants," as Crèvecoeur used to say, and "the goodness and flavour of the fruit proceeds from the peculiar soil and exposition in which they grow."[1]

Several intellectuals of the period were sure that natural circumstances, for better and for worse, determined natural beings in a substantial sense, humans included. The classic theme of human weakness—as popularized by Swift, Mandeville, la Rochefoucauld, Malebranche, Pope, Dr. Johnson, Joseph Butler, and many others—mingled with the new theme of the dependence of human character on the environment that Montesquieu turned into a late eighteenth-century commonplace. "Circumstance" is a keyword of Enlightenment culture, because it puts emphasis on human potentialities, malleability, educability. It is no doubt empowering to know that circumstances may vary, that human characters are tied to these circumstances, and that human lives also can vary as a result. The idea that the humanity of a human being is not a substance preconstituted to its circumstances, that it is not dictated by birth, census, or race, or rooted in a metaphysical "soul," allows for a series of enticing potentialities to be realized through education. Education is the great eighteenth-century metaphor to highlight all the good things that could come from circumstances.[2]

Philosophers of the Enlightenment were convinced that the traits of human character were, to a large extent, governed by the situations, the institutions, the climate, the natural environment and the direction under which one is brought up. They knew that environment brings to the fore one set of potentialities rather than another. However, while the concept of education embodies all the positive ideals one might willingly crave, circumstances often realize unwelcome potentialities despite education and in defiance of education. As the old Jefferson asserted, "We are to guard against ourselves; not against ourselves as we are, but as we may be; for, who can now imagine what we may become under circumstances not now imaginable?"[3]

Jefferson's commitment to environmentalism is apparent from comments such as this. He was quite familiar with the fact that human beings react to circumstances not of their choice, and that the principal means through which such a reaction takes place is imitativeness. Imitativeness was, according to Jefferson, the basic psychological mechanism that best revealed that humans are environment-related creatures. In the *Notes*, Jefferson had already perspicuously commented on the commerce between master and slave as an exercise of "unremitting despotism" on the one side and "degrading submission" on the other. "Our children see this, and learn to imitate it; for man is an imitative animal. This quality is the germ of all education in him. From his cradle to his grave he is learning to do what he sees others do." The basic fact of human psyche is its imitativeness, a strategic answer to the pressures of the circumstances. This quality, as Jefferson said, is the germ of all education, but of bad education also. "The parent storms, the child looks on, catches the lineaments of wrath, puts on the same airs in the circle of smaller slaves, gives a loose to his worst of passions, and thus nursed, educated, and daily exercised in tyranny, cannot but be stamped by it with odious peculiarities. The man must be a prodigy who can retain his manners and morals undepraved by such circumstances."[4]

Jefferson accepted as normal the idea that the self is derivative; that it is a coping device employing multiple and at times incompatible sets of ideas; that the self does not create its own conditions; that it simply reacts to variable stimuli and, so to speak, that it is created with a series of mere potentialities waiting to be realized. As far as the self is concerned, Jefferson's Enlightenment amounted neither to a glorification of the creative momentum— namely, the self's creation of its own circumstances—nor to the tenet that the self is preformed when it comes into the world. By the same token, the seemingly radical call for preformism and social equality that emerges from Jefferson's famous doctrine of the Declaration that "all men are created equal" is in effect one of his first avowals of environmentalism. What he maintained is that human beings are created by "nature's God" with the same natural potentialities (or faculties), and that nurture, environment, and experience would necessarily develop them differently and unequally. This doctrine is an act of faith in the overwhelming power of circumstances.[5]

A follower of environmentalism, Jefferson trusted education. It could not have been otherwise. The ideal of education is the optimistic way of portraying humans' dependence on ever-changing circumstances and humans' naturalness. In his mid-seventies, Jefferson was still unyielding on this doctrine. Jefferson still confronted and turned down the "discouraging persuasion that man is fixed, by the law of his nature, at a given point; that his improvement is a chimera, and the hope delusive of rendering ourselves wiser, happier or better than our forefathers were." The founder of the University of Virginia envisaged himself in the role of the gardener who grafts his trees. This dependence on the environment and the implied doctrine that humans are like other organisms resulted in an extraordinary chance for improvement. "As well might it be urged that the wild and uncultivated tree, hitherto yielding sour and bitter fruit only, can never be made to yield better; yet we know that the grafting art implants a new tree on the savage stock, producing what is most estimable both in kind and degree. Education, in like manner, engrafts a new man on the native stock, and improves what in his nature was vicious and perverse into qualities of virtue and social worth."[6]

The naturalism entailed in this doctrine, as it is easy to see, has two faces. A mode of asserting that humans were not fixed at a given point and that they varied with circumstances, environmentalism made wide allowance for the influence of bad education. In other words, environmentalism recognized the accidental role of fortune and misfortune, as we have seen. But the same nature played a very ambiguous role. The "native stock," the natural moment that Jefferson alluded to in his defense of environmentalism, was a figure of necessity. Nature was a force that opposed improvement not just accidentally, but as a kind of prehistorical base that ingenuity tried fruitlessly to contrast. The question is: humans are dependent on circumstances; but to what extent can ingenuity really harness them? What if nature were an impediment that no ingenuity might ever outstrip?

In the same document that pleads for the advance of knowledge and the well-being of humankind, Jefferson acknowledged that "not *infinitely,* as some have said, but *indefinitely,* and to a term which no one can fix and foresee," improvement would have its proper march. The naturalism and the necessitarianism implied in the doctrine of environmentalism emerges unexpectedly. Despite his rhetoric of education, Jefferson admitted the supremacy of the "term" over every hope of improvement. It is true that he wanted to refuse the "discouraging persuasion that man is fixed"—as he declared on many occasions. More importantly, he acknowledged that nature acts as a necessity, and that our attempts at curbing its primordial force by painful efforts is often in vain. Improvement is not a chimera, but all we can do is carve, day by day, little pieces from nature's unconquerable territory. It is not that man is *not* fixed to a given point. It is only that we do not *know* the boundary that undeniably exists somewhere. We do not know that point, and we can (should) try to resist its tyranny.

There are some unwelcome naturalistic implications in the doctrine that "men are like plants," as Crèvecoeur said. Human beings adjust themselves to the terrain in which they grow. They float among circumstances, some not favorable, in the hope of finding an equilibrium and bettering their condition.

But they do not, cannot, exceed their natural limits. Several contemporaries of Jefferson's were much more straightforward in drawing the conclusion that stems from naturalism, namely, that necessity governs human nature. To put it plainly, naturalism as such entailed the belief in the primacy of passion over reason, as it was often labeled, of our past constitution over our future improvements.

John Adams, for one, always was extremely clear that there was no real alternative to the "federalist line," and to the endeavor to create effective barriers against passions, our natural past. No reason, no wisdom, no education, can teach humanity to become human. Only power and coercion could do that. "Lessons my dear Sir," Adams wrote to Jefferson, "are never wanting. Life and History are full. The Loss of Paradise, by eating a forbidden apple, has been many Thousand years a Lesson to Mankind; but not much regarded. Moral Reflections, wise Maxims, religious Terrors, have little Effect upon Nations when they contradict a present Passion, Prejudice, Imagination, Enthusiasm or Caprice. . . . I have long been settled in my own opinion, that neither Philosophy, nor Religion, nor Morality, nor Wisdom, nor Interest will ever govern nations or Parties against their Vanity, their Pride, their Resentment or Revenge, or their Avarice or Ambition. Nothing but Force and Power and Strength can restrain them." There is but one conclusion to draw: "A Covent Garden Rake will never be wise enough to take warning from the Claps caught by his Companions. When he comes to be poxed himself he may possibly repent and reform. Yet three out of four of them become even by their own sufferings, more shameless instead of being penitent. Pardon this freedom. It is not Melancholly: but Experience and believe me without reserve your Friend, O tempora—*oh mores.*"[7]

Adams had always been sure that the psychological principle that naturally dominates in human nature was the "Passion for Superiority." As far as psychology is concerned, Adams's stance was extremely clear: it "would seem that human Reason and human Conscience, though I believe there are such things, are not a Match, for human Passions, human Imaginations and human Enthusiasm," he wrote in 1816. Adams had no doubts that humans are natural beings and that being natural entails the fact that one is molded by nature's unbreakable laws. Adams's thought was characteristically focused not just on the necessary laws of psychology, notably, the passion for superiority, but also on other laws, on the "invisible social, economic, and demographic forces operating at different speeds and in different patterns throughout the colonies," as Joseph Ellis acknowledges. The whole sphere of nature, according to Adams, is dominated by necessity, and all scientific disciplines describe a specific form of necessity. As a consequence, history is not the outcome of some great man's rational decision. The question of the authorship of American independence is mistaken. "We might as well inquire who were the Inventors of Agriculture, Horticulture, Architecture, Musick," Adams commented in 1818. Human events were seen by Adams as evolutionary and slow transformations, not revolutionary and "ideological" upheavals. Irrational forces usually shape the behavior of the people, both aristocratic elites and the mass of populace. Adams's style here is characteristic in acknowledging the prominence of irrational forces on human motivations.[8]

Jefferson was more oblique than Adams, but to a large extent he endorsed a similar thesis. Like Adams, Jefferson did not escape the consequences of naturalism. Theirs was more a difference of style than of doctrine. The idea that rational wishes are dominated by something overwhelming and somehow "irrational" was also typically Jeffersonian, as I argue in the rest of this chapter. Not that Jefferson thought that human nature was morally bad. As historians have too often reminded us, Jefferson can be appropriately presented as the prototype of the democratic-minded leader, one who by constitution believes that governments should only remove artificial barriers to people's ingenuity. The simplest version of Jeffersonian democratic trustfulness—whether or not it corresponds to a doctrine that Jefferson ever upheld—was one that elicited easy sarcasm. "I have no doubt," Adams ironically told Jefferson, reminding him of a popular demonstration against the government in 1799, "you was fast asleep in philosophical Tranquillity, when ten thousand People, and perhaps many more, were parading the Streets of Philadelphia."[9]

It is true that Jefferson's characteristic style did not allow him to endorse the thesis that human nature is bad, but it would be too simplistic to maintain that he must have approved of the opposite thesis, as if Jefferson's only concern was removing barriers from the populace. Jefferson did not believe that humans were bad, but he "questioned the cheery view of human nature that some enlightened thinkers celebrated," as Merle Curti appropriately wrote. Despite his much-vaunted democratic trustfulness, Jefferson's discourse envisioned a clear limit to both human morality and human ingenuity. Just like Adams, although with a different style, he ruminated on the theme of necessity carefully, and he did so during his entire life. Adams's trope of human beings as potential rakes cannot be found in Jefferson's writings, but other metaphors lay emphasis on individuals as passive. The rational and moral forces of their agency appear subordinated to forces out of control.[10]

As an old man, Jefferson seemed to still chew over Adams's discourse about rakes, even though the metaphors he employed were different. The language of natural necessity, and of naturalism as a version of necessitarianism, appears familiar even to the Sage of Monticello. "This pugnacious humor of

mankind," Jefferson wrote to Adams in 1822, "seems to be the law of his nature, one of the obstacles to too great multiplication provided in the mechanism of the Universe. The cocks of henyard kill one another up. Boars, bulls,
rams do the same. And the horse, in his wild state, kills all the young males,
until worn down with age and war, some vigorous youth kills him, and takes
to himself the Haram of females. I hope we shall prove how much happier for
man the Quaker policy is, and that the life of the feeder is better than that of
the fighter." Jefferson's hope, of course, was that Americans could prove that
not all human beings must be listed among the "fighters" and among sheep,
horses, cows, and pigs. However, it would be a mistake to interpret such a
hope as if Jefferson's message, here and elsewhere, were tantamount to the
certainty that Americans were different from other animals, and that humans
were not animals. In this context, hope was trying to efface an implicit enduring fear, and perhaps the conviction, that humans were animals.[11]

Underneath his assertion of hope, we easily discover a deep-seated belief
in the power of nature to find in the natural instinct of war and self-destruc-
tion "a sufficient barrier against the too great multiplication of other animals
and of man himself," or the belief in "an equilibriating power against the
fecundity of generation," to use some of the expressions Jefferson employed
twenty-five years earlier. The old Jefferson was thus revealing his agreement
with the substance of Adams's letter of 1787, after years of rumination. For
both Adams and Jefferson, nature was a boisterous and, more to the point,
overwhelming force. Reason was at best a temper, an attitude—possibly the
only rational choice in a sea of irrational instincts, impulses, passions, and
forces that normally take over human affairs. Jefferson knew perfectly well
that human beings would not succeed in getting rid of their nature.[12]

In general terms, hope should never be mistaken for faith or for a form
of certainty. In the letter just quoted, Jefferson's hope reveals his painful en-
tanglement in an undecided dynamic between willful determination and
determinism, between individual efficacy and necessitarianism, between
humanism and naturalism. In that context, Jefferson's hope exposes a larger
tension within the Enlightenment, between the project of conceiving the individual as an agent rather than as a locus acted upon by natural forces, and
the Greek idea that the sphere of human existence is always encircled by a superior, natural necessity. The project of substituting the discourse of historical
agency and self-determination for the more traditional discourse of natural
necessity and determinism had not been completed during Jefferson's life.
Jefferson, in other words, had never been able to make a decision between
a quite modern and humanistic conception of humans as possessed of an
agency for which one is accountable, and the old-style idea of the individual

as a locus of forces. What is unquestionable is that despite a number of shallow and conventional interpretations of Jefferson's philosophy and experience, he did not live amicably in the light of nature. As Horace Fries wrote more than sixty years ago, "Jefferson, perhaps more than any other early democratic theorist, recognized that the development of social institutions and government could not be left to chance or to the 'Laws of Nature.'"[13]

NATURE AS NECESSITY

The environmentalist outlook typical of the eighteenth century, namely, that humans are like plants receiving their flavor from the nature in which they grow, was ambiguous, at once exciting and paralyzing. Americans of the future would be "vigorous" like the nature from which they come, but what happens if that nature is "irrational," destructive, and corrupting?

Before answering these questions, it is necessary to devote some attention to the term "nature." What is that entity whose power, laws, beauty, and regularity we sometimes extol, and sometimes dread? A clear-cut meaning of the term "nature" and a formal definition are extremely difficult to grasp. Arthur Lovejoy, for instance, listed sixty-six meanings. He provided a clear example of an exasperating polivocity. As far as Jefferson is concerned, the prospect does not become rosier. As Charles Miller writes, "little aware of the equivocality of 'nature,' Jefferson slipped unconsciously from one of its senses, including its antithetic senses, to another." Jefferson "seems never to have noticed the various roles that the word 'nature' played in his writings." Provided that it is impossible to arrive at a definition—and a fortiori at a consistent Jeffersonian definition of "nature"—Lovejoy's fundamental demarcation between "nature as value" and "nature as being" might be of some avail. Lovejoy's basic idea was that the various meanings of the term can be grouped into two different sets: that either the word "nature" expresses an ideal, a principle, a rule, a universal value, or it describes a reality, a force, a particular being. Either nature presides over the world or, alternatively, it is ingrained in the world.[14]

Jefferson made broad use of those concepts of nature that stand under the banner of the first set. Nature was a value for him, and quite often he lived amicably in its light. His references to nature's law, to natural rights, and, in short, to an unconditioned model upon which we should rely are numerous, from the Declaration onward. The ultimate reality to which that text appealed was nature. Jefferson's nature manifested itself, we have also seen, as the main source of our moral sense. It is this precise version of naturalism that has always urged historians to associate Jefferson with the views held by Shaftesbury, Adam Smith, Joseph Addison, Francis Hutcheson, and the Scottish philosophers, such as Thomas Reid, whose explicit mission was to emphasize the existence of the social emotion of altruism as a strong instrument to control selfish and unnatural emotions. Nature undeniably gave both Jefferson and those eighteenth-century philosophers the spur to assert that humans are imbued with a natural sociability that turns their reason into an instrument of morality and virtue.[15]

Jefferson's use of the word "nature" to designate a being, the second set, is likewise interesting. Probably more interesting. Nature, for Jefferson, was not only a collection of values, laws, and universal rules that imparted the working plan of all events. The word "nature" signified also a visible, touchable, perceivable, particular event—an array of breathtaking events. It was "this American nature," a beautiful, generous, fertile, and powerful being. Jefferson and others of his age often identified nature-as-being as a source of pride and nationalism; a weapon to counter the European haughty sense of superiority. In countless ways, both Jefferson and other leaders put emphasis on American natural supremacy.[16]

Superiority can be an agricultural advantage, for example. "The territories of the United states," Jefferson wrote in a comment to an article on the United States written by de Meusnier, "contain about a million of square miles, English. There is in them a greater proportion of fertile lands than in the British dominions in Europe." Given the rough estimate that North and South America combined contain about 12 million square miles, Jefferson concluded quite optimistically that the American continent "will nourish 1200 millions of inhabitants, a number greater than the present population of the whole globe is supposed to amount to." With this idea of a continental natural superiority firmly entrenched in his mind, Jefferson had already invited his friend James Monroe to join him in Paris and to visit Europe. The trip "will make you adore *your own country,* it's soil, it's climate, it's equality, liberty, laws, people and manners." Liberty and people, certainly, but its soil and climate first of all. Jefferson used to underline the superiority of American nature even before it was transformed by the plough. The appreciative way he described, for instance, the Ohio River, the Falling Springs, the Passage of the Potomac through the Blue Mountains, the Natural Bridge, and his "dear" Monticello, where nature has "spread so rich a mantle under the eye," requires no further comments.[17]

It does not stir particular wonder that from time to time this powerful and rich American nature also seemed to conceal a secret in its bowels and to disclose the signs of some great convulsion as in the case of the Natural Bridge, "the most sublime of Nature's work." In other words, the category of beautiful was not the only aesthetic category through which the (potential) readers of Edmund Burke valued nature and expressed their pride of treading on American soil. Since American nature held a colossal power inside itself, it was easy to disprove Buffon's thesis. Jefferson was sure that this powerful, sublime nature, which "has hidden from us her modus agendi" and exhibits the clues of its inner convulsions, could not be, as Buffon maintained, "less active, less energetic" (beaucoup moins agissante, beaucoup moins forte) than its European counterpart. In brief, both the beauty and the virtual infinitude or sublime omnipotence of American nature were undeniable facts prior to the full achievement of the market revolution. In the mid-nineteenth century, capitalism produced crushing instruments to harass nature by depleting its resources. As a consequence, its beauty, its "untamable" power, and its "infinitude" were seriously called into question.[18]

The fact remains that eighteenth-century American leaders drew heavily on American nature as the most important source of their pride and nationalism. To trust the future was for them to draw on the argument that this powerful American nature could bring about humans' regeneration. Europe was rotten, polluted, overcrowded, and corrupted, but the American nature would import a purifying strength. Human beings would be like plants and "to see this virgin terrain," as Leo Marx wrote, would be tantamount to absorbing "the rudiments of a new consciousness." If nature determined humans in a substantial sense, a virgin and powerful land called as such for splendid possibilities of betterment and hopefulness. American nature thus provided excellent circumstances. It was a plentiful sea on which to travel.[19]

The theme of the sublimity and powerfulness of American nature strikes a perilous chord. A big danger looms large when one approaches nature or selects it as a standard of judgment. Nature-as-value, we have seen, provided for laws and rights upon which responsive republicans could and should rely and that shrewd governments had to secure. Laws and rights found their ultimate origin in a nature so conceived. In a similar vein, the generous American nature-as-being seemed to abide by that same rational order; to be the physical expression of that rationality; to be wise and trustworthy accordingly. The danger lies in the fact that in the eighteenth century particularly, nature also pursued a quite different course, overwhelming, indifferent, boisterous, and sometimes cruel. Nature, as the representative of order, seemed to face its double and signify a barbarism beyond any culture.

On occasion, Jefferson regarded nature as a power that was uncaring if not openly hostile toward human plans and utility. Michael Zuckert acknowledges that Jefferson was somehow gripped with a nature that "belongs more to itself," as he powerfully says, and that reveals itself "as an awesome array of forces." "Awesome" is the best adjective to qualify a totality of primeval forces. The experience with dualism and with nature as *the* evidence that an "other" par excellence is at work was unavoidable to late eighteenth-century settlers. Facing that "real nature," as was inevitable, the American settler was almost invariably compelled to assume that overwhelming forces were in proximity, looming, and menacing. Nature the beautiful, generous, compliant, seductive "she" yielded to an indifferent and at times tyrannical and bestial "it," a forceful being whose egotism cast over human expectations a dark and deadly shadow. In this sense, nature appeared as a being upon which humans could not rely and that they could not control. Nature is wise, but as a mode of necessity, it also imposes its rhythms and its nonhuman priorities on human images of order and hierarchies.[20]

Nature imposes on us the laws of our decay and death. In an age of difficult births and too many easy deaths, Jefferson was, of course, responsive to that. One evening in early May 1782, for instance, the aurora borealis appeared in the sky of Virginia, and Jefferson duly recorded the odd sight in his *Garden Book.* In those days, that natural phenomenon was considered a sign of imminent illness or even the language nature used to speak death. It was true: two days after the bad omen appeared, Jefferson's wife gave birth to a daughter but also entered her final months. She died on 6 September. It is significant that in the months that immediately preceded and followed his wife's death Jefferson chose to lock himself in a small room that opened immediately off the head of her bed to work full-time on the *Notes,* his longest discourse on nature. The link between nature and death must have seemed evident to Jefferson, at least in those mournful days.[21]

Death "puts an end to the world as to us," Jefferson warned his daughter Martha in 1783, "and the way to be ready for it is never to do a wrong act." Sudden deaths had invaded the circle of his family and friends from the earlier stages of his life, and his juvenile *Literary Commonplace Book* is filled with that theme. No surprise that, paradoxically enough, he found a sort of Epicurean consolation in nature's immovability. "In no circumstance," Jefferson wrote to Horatio Spafford, "has nature been kinder to us, than in the soft gradations by which she prepares us to part willingly with what we are not destined always to retain. First one faculty is withdrawn and then another, sight, hearing, memory, affections, and friends, filched one by one, till we are left among strangers, the mere monument of times, facts, and specimens of antiquity for the observation of the curious." Jefferson prided himself on having been able to attain "a perfect resignation," as he said to William Duane, "to the laws of decay which she [nature] has prescribed to all the forms & combinations of matter."[22]

Nature does not only impose on us the laws of our decay and death. A nature that "belongs to itself" is something more than just indifferent toward human suffering. Occasionally, Jefferson utilized the word "nature" to express his fear of an active and almost malignant being. Nature was indifferent, for Jefferson, and elicited resignation. But it also seemed to act like a foe and actively curbed human hopes. Nature was perceived as a perennial inimical presence lurking beneath human dreams of progress; a force to be subjugated and transformed, but that threatens to reassert its primordial power. At best a precarious progress is compatible with this view of nature, a blistering, bubbling prehistorical magma over which dangle human achievements.

No more a synonym of "moral sense," or "nature's God," this feral nature contradicts itself by breaking those laws that at other times it lavishes on the human race. Nature undermines the same civilization that at other times it promotes. Cataloguing the counties, cities, and townships of his beloved Virginia, Jefferson noticed that "there are other places at which, like some of the foregoing, the *laws* have said there shall be towns; but *Nature* has said there shall not, and they remain unworthy of enumeration." We should not build a theory based on a passage such as this, of course. But we cannot overlook the fact that Jefferson was using the word "nature" in speaking of a power counteracting the ordaining power of law and civilization.[23]

Nature gives and nature takes. Nature affirms and nature denies. The problem is that the rhythms of nature, this jealous being, are cyclical, the pace of a heathen time: the time of day and night, of summer and winter, of life and death. Nature's order does not necessarily correspond to that order for which the men of the Enlightenment were looking. "The cycles of Nature compete with the linear notions of the rising mind and of human perfectibility," Irving Primer writes in his analysis of the intellectual world of a contemporary of Thomas Jefferson, Erasmus Darwin. It was not a fair competition back in the eighteenth century. Jefferson's generation had none of those technological tools that twenty-first-century societies utilize when they impose artificial days on nature, and when they transform nature's time in that linear time usually called development. No surprise that for Jefferson nature could be both the promising source of industrial and commercial enterprises and an "order" preceding civilization that still menaces human cultures.[24]

It was far from unusual for Americans to see themselves as naked individuals against wild nature, submissive preys of nature's "irrational" convulsions. Besides the most obvious ominous events that nature-the-foe generated, such as thunderstorms, blizzards, floods, droughts, famines, diseases, poisonous snakes, and bears, besides nature's vetoes cast on civilization, there was still another menace that weakened Americans' self-reliance and "virtue." Wild nature presented the opportunity of "freedom," namely, the occasion for

settlers to behave in a savage and bestial manner. Nature reasserted its primordial power in the sense that living in the proximity of the wilderness
pulled down the level of civilization. The fear of "barbarism" was widespread
throughout the country, and American nature was often blamed for this vice.
Crèvecoeur, for one, can help us clarify what it meant for Jefferson to be an
eighteenth-century settler. Crèvecoeur was well acquainted with the fact that
living on the very threshold of wild nature entailed staying beyond the power
of example and the rules of civilized society. He shivered at the thought that
a number of frontiersmen had already "degenerated altogether into the hunting state," becoming like the worst carnivorous animals. "Eating wild meat
. . . tends to alter their temper."[25]

Degeneration, temptation, and barbarism gave rise to appalling forecasts
of licentiousness. Even though Jefferson never reached the peak of Crèvecoeur's fatalistic manner, he lingered on the qualitative difference between
"Roman grandeur" and the "Gothic," which is a symbol of nature and moral
ugliness. To remain a civilized "Roman," Jefferson explained to Madame de
Tessé, one needs to turn down every seduction coming from barbarization
and exotic cultures, to refuse to become a part of nature as non-Western
people do. "I am filled with alarms," wrote the "Roman" Jefferson, "for the
event of the irruptions daily making on us by the Goths, Ostrogoths, Visig-
oths and Vandals, lest they should reconquer us to our original barbarism."
Here Jefferson was writing in a style that is half ironic, and half overblown
sentimental—he usually adopted this style when he wrote to ladies. The letter is giddily happy, it has nothing of Crèvecoeur's fatalism, and it is a typical
tourist's response to the glory of Roman ruins. Of course, the letter must
not be taken at face value. But if the fear the letter evokes is imaginary, the
example is extremely real. Hidden beneath the merry discourse, the dualistic philosopher provided a wonderful example of binary rhetoric: the tone
is ironic, but Jefferson was tremendously serious about the danger of "our"
original barbarism.[26]

Jefferson had no firsthand recollection of the American wilderness as it
was known by his father, Peter, or George Washington. As mentioned, Jefferson traveled west of the Shenandoah Valley only once and only for a few
miles. But notwithstanding his lack of direct experience, he had never ceased
"to think of himself as a man of the soil," as Noble Cunningham quite correctly remarks. Jefferson's life is the best evidence against the allegation that
Americans are disconnected, abstract, mobile, superior to place. Jefferson felt
his personal destiny as manifestly tied to the American land and to the bleak
prospect that was open in the western parts of Virginia. The distance from
European standards of civilization was geographical evidence to him. Jeffer-

son realized that America was exposed to nature in a way that Europe had not been for centuries. A man who perceived himself through the lens of the soil, he must have felt a contrast between the American republic and the two thousand years of cultural achievements accumulated by Europe. Such a disproportion must have accentuated his sense of being vulnerable. Jefferson's playing sentimentally with the idea of "our original barbarism" is not a confutation of the fact that he was compelled to see in the state of nature the real power lurking behind. In America the state of nature was incomparably stronger than in Europe: a geographical fact, not just a philosophical thought.[27]

Like every other human being, Thomas Jefferson inherited a world. He performed his mission to enlighten and moralize within a specific American context. Like other eighteenth-century settlers, Jefferson's world was a distinctive wilderness, a continent without clear borders, a nature in some sense infinite and untamable, all-powerful, and visibly nonhuman.

This frontier was the context of Jefferson's personal enlightenment. But "frontier" triggers the positive ideals of progress, emancipation, liberation, forward and onward moving. A better term would be "marchland," as Bernard Bailyn suggests. It was not just that Jefferson and his generation faced a frontier, and that they were enthused by that challenge. In a way, the frontier is an invitation, and Jefferson quite often accepted it. However, to live in a marchland means to come to terms with a ragged place dominated by hazard and violence, a daunting space where the commitment to the ideals of civilization, humanity, and rationality is always weakened by rough practicality and the "other" side of human enlightened ideals. "Marchland" is something more than "frontier." It is an outlandish place where one finds order and disorder mingled in an inseparable compound; where one bumps into limits impossible to overcome, and where the experience of hope is tempered by violence, progress by regression, and civilization by its barbarian counterpart.[28]

The reason why Jefferson saw in the American state of nature the blind force of necessity was not that he was influenced by John Bunyan's *Pilgrim's Progress* (1678), by Benjamin Keach's *Tropologia* (1682), or by John Winthrop's writings. Those seventeenth-century classics portrayed wild nature as a symbol of anarchy and evil, opposed to Christian ideals, and standardized the Puritan theme of the errand into the wilderness. American Puritans longed to carve a garden from the wilds, an idea born in Europe and transplanted to the new continent. The argument for a Puritan influence ignores an important detail: that, in several cultures across ages and places, wild nature was often construed as a barrier—quite often an enemy—to everything deemed good and desirable, call it "progress," "prosperity," or "godliness." It was the simple fact of a "constant exposure to wilderness," as Roderick Nash also acknowledges, not so much a formal acquaintance with an ideological tradition such as Puritanism, which "gave rise to fear and hatred on the part of those who had to fight it for survival and success." Why should Jefferson have made an exception to this dualism?[29]

From a dialectical perspective, the more Jefferson put emphasis on the frontier-man mentality, on possibility and optimism, and on the "sufficiency of reason for the care of human affairs," as he said in 1790, the more apparent it becomes that he voiced a fundamental opposition between civilization and nature. By repeating the maxim "reason is sufficient," Jefferson betrayed the conviction that reason was far from sufficient. Jefferson's wish that reason would be sufficient to take care of human affairs did not foreclose his secret conviction that reason was limited by a necessity that no human talent could ever harness. Our dreams and desires sometimes obscure reality, giving us the delusion that there is no gap between the two, but the gap persists. The stronger the need to express our desires, the more acute our awareness of the wide-open chasm between hopes and reality.[30]

Nature was for Jefferson a value and a being on which to rely, or, at least, he often seemed to convince himself and the large majority of his readers that his dream about nature corresponded to reality. Robert Booth Fowler acknowledges that Jefferson "constructed a nature that embodied his values and employed it as a force against much in his own society—and many other societies—that he disliked." However, the rhetoric of the laws of nature and of nature as order, beauty, and a benign power was not to be confused with the content of his deepest beliefs. It was basically Jefferson's favorite operative device.[31]

If one really believed, totally and unconditionally, that nature is order, a human (or humane) order, why would one insist on producing devices to enhance control of the conditions under which one lives? What is the significance of Jefferson's report to the House of Representatives on the subject of uniform weights and measures, for instance? Why was Jefferson so characteristically taken by classes, orders, genera, species? By calculating the precise span of time of a generation? Why was he so insistently looking for an internationally recognized standard? More in general, why was he so much concerned with universals? For the extension of a decimal system based on plain arithmetic and common sense? Why such a remarkable devotion to a systematic way of living? What should we say about his daily ritual of recording events? What about Jefferson's famous dictum that "the eye of vigilance" must "never be closed"? An appeal to mere utilitarian reasons is not the answer but just a part of the question: why in all Jeffersonian intellectual productions is it so easy to find such a characteristic, unmistakable utilitarian style? Evidently, these "utilitarian" devices gave Jefferson an artificial sense of order in his world and helped him articulate the painful dialectic between artificial and natural, civilization and barbarism.[32]

The sense of control provided by the exactness of his entries and the rationality of his projects counteracted some contrary impression of a widespread disorder. The feeling, probably, was that human projects were, in the last analysis, artificial and had to be imposed upon nature; that nature was a mere fact that needed to be superseded; that nature had to be reworked by imagination and the energy that radiates from the heart. Not that nature, for Jefferson, was chaotic and anarchic. Nature exhibited an order different from the wished-for order that he usually identified with civilization.

This was Jefferson's real situation: each time he looked at "real nature" he also confronted a basic dualism. The sense of political anxiety connected to the turmoil of revolutionary and early republican times enhanced, to use Robert Ferguson's phrasing, "the difficulty of perceiving an experimental republic on the edge of a vast and unformed new world." And vice versa: the gaze on untamed natural vastness increased political and existential anxiety. The unformed realm broke every form and every "Roman" equilibrium; its excesses represented an alluring temptation to which republicans should never yield. The problem was that republicans could not help looking at that "unformed" natural world. The reason why American intellectuals of the formative era, as Ferguson acknowledges, were "obsessed with the half formed, the partially visible," is that they had but to look through their windows to find the evidence that an awesome array of forces and a wild nature belonging to itself were at work.[33]

This is the emotional consequence of Jefferson's dualistic Enlightenment: to be at once enthused and paralyzed by the opposition between order and disorder, between society and nature, between "the scanty field of what is known," to cite once again his own words, and the "boundless region of what is unknown," between nature (as law) and nature (as a being enforcing an *original* barbarism). Human beings react to circumstances in the same way that they react to their environment. But Jefferson's vast natural environment was not just a neutral epistemological "unknown" containing the promise of its future becoming known. His "unknown" was also unknowable and the embodiment of a wild necessity. Human beings are formed by their natural environment, but what happens if that environment is itself wild and unformed?[34]

It would be an extreme simplification to say that for Jefferson two natures existed, one ordered, beautiful, and beneficial, and another chaotic, indifferent, and evil. In the present section, I argue that Jefferson used the word "nature" throughout his writings to articulate his emotions. A wide range of emotions. Following Charles Miller (who in turn follows in the footsteps of Arthur Lovejoy), I make a distinction between "nature as value" and "nature as being." Neither a systematic philosopher nor a professional logician, I show that Jefferson slipped unconsciously from set one to set two. Like probably the rest of us, he was highly "inconsistent." The hypothesis I offer is that each time Jefferson drew on the word "nature" to express a value, a law, or some idea of human order (set one), the emotions he conveyed were accordingly positive. When nature appeared as value he was full of hope. On the other hand, whenever he used the word to describe some sort of being (set two), the emotions he conveyed were sometimes negative. Quite often, through the word "nature" Jefferson described a being and communicated to his readers a sensation of beauty, pride, or even a sublime pleasure. Other times, by using the word "nature" Jefferson imparted sensations of deep disconcert: "nature" could describe a being that was, for him, indifferent, cruel, or even wild.

TIME AS NECESSITY

Dumas Malone clearly set the standard according to which Jefferson's philosophy of time is customarily evaluated. Jefferson nurtured a complete confidence in both the "laws" of nature and time. Undoubtedly Malone had an abundance of arguments to accentuate Jefferson's "congenital optimism and his unshakable confidence that time was fighting on the side of the causes he most valued."[35]

Jefferson's optimistic visions can be easily corroborated, provided the historian hypothesizes that his was *exclusively* an optimistic mind. It depends on what the historian is looking for: if one seeks unshakable optimism, then optimism will be found in abundance. The American myth, as narrated by Jefferson, would tell that time is essentially "yielding," just like nature. Understandably, historians are fond of Jefferson when he rejoices for "this march of civilization" and for the enticing fact that "where this progress will stop no one can say." Historians are captivated by Jefferson when, in turn, he eulogizes "the immense advance in science" seemingly taking hold during his lifetime.[36]

Furthermore, to add to such a "congenital" faith in the course of time, Jefferson nurtured a strong confidence in the power of human ingenuity. I have already noted that besides trusting "progress," Jefferson also endorsed the idea of the "efficacy of man": that humans can be driven by possibilities and by intelligent choices, not just by needs, by necessity, or by an inexorable law already written somewhere. In effect, in addition to what Malone pointed out, Jefferson also tried to build a humanistic language of possibility, of liberty, of responsibility. He tried to abandon the image of historical time as an ominous decree encompassing future generations. Time as such would be largely benign, but in addition human beings would have good sense and reason enough to give a desirable direction to civilization. The direct implication was that an ethical and social language would be able to account for human events.[37]

Jefferson suggested that every hypothesis of historical determinism, including more traditional ideas of "progress," must be dismissed as obsolete. The new Jeffersonian vision recommended trust in time because our fate depends on the decisions we make, and human beings have the major part in affecting the course of civilization. We should trust the future, Jefferson seems to tell us, because history is something humans make, not a river into which they are immersed, and because humans are intelligent. Thomas Paine made very clear that it is in "our power" to reshape and redesign the world "over again." The emphasis on "our power" epitomizes the true novelty of the Jeffersonian persuasion. Like Jefferson, the majority of father figures sincerely tried to give up the traditional biological metaphor, which held that historical time revolved through natural phases, by necessity, both in the body and in the social body. According to that metaphor, not only individuals but societies as well would travel through phases, youth, maturity, and senescence, to end up inexorably in death.[38]

A pragmatic and Emersonian effort to rescue America's future from the teleology of nature, from the specter of necessity, and from the biological metaphor excited Jefferson's mind, or at least some levels of his philosophy. The fact, however, is that Jefferson did not live up to this tenet in the way Malone assumed he did. He did not succeed in exalting the category of possibility over that of necessity and in freeing himself of reservations about the vision of time as yielding to human effort.

Negativity, for Jefferson, affected historical time as well as nature. Neither Jefferson nor his friend John Adams, for example, was fully successful in convincing himself that possibility and ingenuity rank higher than some form of appalling necessity. That they abundantly used the rhetoric of both possibility and unabated optimism can be easily mistaken for "evidence" that they had an unshakable confidence. But this same abundance could be seen as an evidence for a quite opposite case. What is undeniable is that the Epicurean Sage of Monticello continued to warn his friends of the awful truth that "everything has its beginning, its growth, and end." Each time the issue of the course of time was to be weighed, Jefferson's philosophy was thus caught in a fundamental dilemma. The dilemma lies in that historical time was and was not conceived as nature, alternatively as a mode of necessity and as an expression of human freedom and civilization. In accounting for social phenomena, Jefferson was fascinated by a moral language centered on notions such as possibility, hope, and choice; he was allured by the prospect of historical time as an encouraging process that would spring from humans' decisions. However, the naturalistic language of necessity never abandoned him: events must often be interpreted as the necessary outcome of hidden forces.[39]

Jefferson by no means *had* an exclusive and firm confidence that time was fighting on his side or that history was the territory of human rational decisions. Jefferson had hopes and positive discourses that pointed expectantly in that direction, needless to say, but this is quite a different story. The inclination to confound "having" with "being" is always dangerous when the historian narrates the story of a life. As a rule, one routinely has a number of colliding ideas, opinions, desires, discourses, allegiances, and emotions, and not all of these are assets. Both positive and negative discourses form the normal tools one is compelled to bear. We cannot expect that real persons should be entirely faithful to some artificial theory or a philosophical system. In other words, we cannot assume that a person is either an optimist or a pessimist and, more generally, either something or its contrary. Even though historians like to portray human beings as philosophers who act only after they have formulated a theory, and act consistently with that theory, this is not what usually happens. While it is understandable that historians define one theme as shaping a person's agenda, the reality is usually less coherent.[40]

Moreover, what makes the question of Jefferson's view of time even more complicated is that his hopes and discourses, like everybody else's, did not hover in a cultural void and a characterless milieu. Those hopes and discourses were tentatively upheld in a culture that was characterized by the unappealing view that time was unyielding. The standard discourses against which wrestled Jefferson's optimistic meliorism conveyed the message that rational human decisions had little or no determining impact on the course of events. Eighteenth-century American leaders were not accustomed to portraying themselves as winners. Jefferson's optimism collided with powerful and persuasive discourses whose tenor was very different: fatalistic, distrustful, and negative. In the same way nature was acknowledged as an untamable and somehow selfish being whose order is not a human (or humane) order, late eighteenth-century settlers saw time as crushing. I want to repeat once again: publicly avowing the idea of a yielding time and the notion of the efficacy of human ingenuity must not be taken as "proof" that Jefferson effaced the opposite conviction within himself. Time *was* commanding, and its course could turn, would turn into a curse. I cannot help thinking that hope and despair, and possibility and necessity, are interrelated concepts.

Jefferson's actual philosophy of time was at variance with Malone's suggestion that he was unshakably confident that time was fighting on the side of America's ideals. Undeniably, early Americans wished to be winners. They wanted to convince themselves that the march of civilization was linear and progressive and a non-zero-sum game. But this is the point: we are speaking of the Enlightenment's hopes and desires. It was an expression of desire, for Jefferson, the tenet of the "efficacy of man," his language of possibility, liberty, and responsibility. A desire is not its realization. A desire devours one's energies. A desire does not satisfy appetite. A desire conceals, or tries to, the awareness that facts are tough and unbearable. If one was satisfied with the present reality as it is, desiring would be pointless. To some extent, a desire is, hence, a procedure of removal and denial. Activities such as hoping, wishing, and desiring lie at the very opposite of, for instance, willing. An unshakable and overpowerful being, such as a god, might *will* something but would not desire anything. Desiring is a signal of a constitutional weakness and, as it were, of an existential failure: a desiring being is, by definition, a limited and ephemeral being.

Unshakable confidence cannot be the entire story if desire is present. Jefferson's life does not show that Americans actually "saw life and history as just beginning" and subjected to one's reason, heart, will, and efficacy, to recall Lewis's statement cited above. American leaders longed to believe the theory of the "efficacy of man." They wanted to see history as both dependent on their will and as an original narrative unlike all those that had been written before. They described themselves as hopeful, sometimes even as unshakably confident. They gravitated toward the idea of "initiative" and made a number of proclamations about time as fighting on the side of American ideals. From the early days of the Revolution, American leaders often told the story that Americans had the chance to make the world over again, that they were responsible and free. But we should not be deceived: the stronger the professed desire, the more evident the level of their discomfort.[41]

The eighteenth-century American leader may have felt he had to foster a vision of history as something fresh. He felt, occasionally at least, that the history of the American republic did not resemble any history that had been written in the past. For him, the past was wrong when compared to the present. History provided only the exempla one had to know in order to avoid earlier mistakes. American leaders read Whig historians, as has been stated, and conceived human actions in terms of an *uncertain* struggle between "liberty" and "tyranny." But the time was not ripe for those leaders to become followers of some form of romantic idealism. Romantic idealism was the tenet that "liberty," in the long run, would necessarily prevail, and civilization would necessarily defeat barbarism. As the German philosopher Georg Wilhelm Friedrich Hegel said, history was the development through which the "Spirit" became different from itself just in order to reconquer itself in a final and superior synthesis. Had they been idealists, we would have been quite right in taking literally their avowals that the United States was a success. But had they been idealists, they would not have been so anxious.

Only in the 1830s did the optimistic persuasion that Malone and Lewis described eventually take hold, at least within some restricted intellectual circles. It was in the 1830s that America became something whose glorious "Manifest Destiny" no one could seriously deny. Such a vision of America as a radical rupture in the order of time was mainly a by-product of the romantic climate in which Jefferson never lived.

George Bancroft was the intellectual whom we should take literally when he portrayed American history in unshakably confident language. Bancroft was a Hegelian idealist and a Platonic thinker. In his perspective, the American republic could hardly be understood as the product of necessary and natural conditions. As far as America was concerned, the course of time was a providential march onward. Bancroft was sure there must be a pre-ordered and intelligent design, be it due to the hand of God or, better, to the "idea" realizing itself in and as history, à la Hegel. He never consented to naturalistic patterns of explanation: that contingencies have a real causative role; that civilizations face real impossibilities and go down wrong tracks; that all events in historical time can be explained without the intercession of extra-historical characters, such as Hegel's "Spirit" or God's millennial plan. Bancroft's philosophy of harmony was monistic, which Jefferson's was not, its goal that of synchronizing our individual wills with the great "Will" governing the universe. Circumstances were part of the realm of illusions, for Bancroft, and human beings (Americans, at least) had the chance to pierce this veil to get to the spiritual reality beneath. What Bancroft revealed was the spiritual closeness—what would make us really unshakable—between the new republic and the universal "Spirit."[42]

The dissemination of this romantic, idealist, and Hegelian persuasion had first to overcome more multifaceted and less consolatory visions. Late eighteenth-century leaders did not perceive themselves as radically (and simplistically) separated from the past, circumstances, and laws of nature and connected with a spiritual dimension only. They felt they were not "emancipated from history," as Richard Lewis said, or taken by the hand by providence. Although they often asserted their optimism or paid lip service to the legend of an overruling providence, they felt they were ruled by a pre-existing necessity. If we look closely, late eighteenth-century leaders portrayed the nation's destiny according to naturalistic, not romantic, idealist, and Hegelian metaphors. We have seen, for instance, the amount of polivocity in Jefferson's ideas of nature. Late eighteenth-century leaders like Jefferson knew better than their Bancroftian inheritors that the new nation was interrelated to larger contexts; that it was new and old at once. For them, possibility was forestalled by a larger necessity, and benevolent and "rational" energy was always encompassed by nonbenevolent and "irrational" powers. The affirmation that much is in "our power" was an attempt to expunge the unpleasant truth, as old Jefferson said, that "everything has its beginning, its growth, and end."[43]

Ideas of "progress" that Jefferson inherited and with which he was acquainted were not a prelude to celebratory myths or Bancroftian self-endorsement. They emerged from the Enlightenment cultural context that was not idealist and monist but naturalist and dualist. The kind of "progress" articulated by Helvétius, the Abbé de Saint-Pierre, Turgot, Adam Ferguson, Lord Kames, John Millar, Adam Smith, and the French Encyclopedists, among other philosophers who had a role in Jefferson's formative years, centered neither on the certainty of the absolute "efficacy of man" nor on the unlikely intimacy between human beings and the universal "Spirit." The conclusion we have to draw when we read those writers is that all societies *naturally* proceeded through several phases of organization, ranging from simplicity to civilized complexity.

Through their specific and personal language, all those writers described the passage between hunting, pasturage, agriculture, and commerce—the "four stages theory"—or between the ten epochs, as in the case of Condorcet's famous treatise on the progress of the human mind. The emphasis fell on the inevitability and "naturalness" of the process, not on the human initiative or spiritual design behind it. Progress was customarily listed among those events that do not depend upon the human heart for their fulfillment. Progress was a mode of necessity and was interchangeable with the awareness that humanity is *destined* to advance in a definite direction. We can safely assume that Jefferson used precisely this naturalistic language when he declared, in 1818, that progress had its proper march, "not *infinitely*" but "*indefinitely*, and to a term which no one can fix and foresee." Evidently, Jefferson's hope was that human beings would be clever and efficacious to the largest possible extent, and that the course of time would be kind to the American republic. In fact, who would disagree with Jefferson's hope qua hope? This does not mean, however, that for Jefferson limits did not exist, that there was no difference between hoping and knowing, or that he had special reasons to be unshakably confident. An eighteenth-century natural philosopher, Jefferson knew what lay beyond his hope: that progress could not be reduced to a variable of human heart, will, and effort.[44]

Jefferson's philosophy of time did not and could not ignore this more traditional insight that the course of events was in continuity with nature's necessity, even in the new continent. Nature was often beautiful, benevolent, and caring, of course, and a generous mother upon which to rely. But "it" also belonged to itself: it imposed its amoral rhythms on societal hopes.

A number of eighteenth-century thinkers upheld this vision of a necessity-ridden course of events, well before Jefferson appeared on the scene. Some scholars have underscored this far-from-enticing detail. Interpreters who put emphasis on Jefferson's optimism should not ignore it. What Jefferson's philosophy had to resonate with, as Stow Persons clearly explained in the 1950s, was a naturalistic conception of the course of sociopolitical events as an "endless cyclical movement analogous to the life cycle of the individual organism." Inevitable decay of social bodies was a commonplace idea, even in late eighteenth-century America, and Jefferson must have been receptive to that. The cyclical theory, as the model is customarily labeled, was to become, for a brief period at least, "one of the distinctive historical conceptions of the dominant social group in America." Drew McCoy agrees that "the metaphor of a cyclical social process, with all of its pessimistic implications, retained a significant, if not dominant, place in the eighteenth-century mind." In fact, Persons explicitly warned the modern reader against over-emphasizing optimism. "Actually," he wrote, "most enlightened thinkers had a keen sense of the precariousness of the felicity which they enjoyed, of the moral and social conditions which would make its continuation possible, and of the ultimate likelihood of its dissipation." Persons' conclusion is significant: "By reading back into their thought ideas which more commonly belong to their descendants [Bancroft and Hegel, among others], we may seriously misunderstand their point of view."[45]

According to this cyclical model, societies must be coupled with natural organisms, as they both were born, mature, decay, and die. For eighteenth-century philosophers, historical time consisted, to use John Howe's phrasing, of the "gradual rise and fall of successive empires, each for a period dominating the world and then giving way to another. . . . This process was often described in terms of a biological analogy; that is, political societies were believed to pursue a natural cycle of infancy, youth, maturity, old age and death." The cyclical theory provided a way of interpreting the "signals" that the American republic was an organism that had already reached the summit and had begun its decline: moral decay, personal extravagance, and internal bickering seemed to indicate that the country had entered the downward slide. During the eighteenth century, it was commonsensical to recognize that the seasonal and necessary rhythms of nature had a determining influence even on higher-order biological entities, such as human societies, whose destinies were like those of other animals.[46]

Notable testimonies are numerous. I present a few examples to give the reader more precise clues about the culture in which Jefferson made his way. The cyclical/naturalistic view has an ancient history. Niccolò Machiavelli, to begin with, clearly set the stage of subsequent social and political thought when, in the *Discourses on the First Ten Books of Titus Livius* (1531), he wrote that "there is nothing more true than that all the things of this world have a limit to their existence." Gianbattista Vico's cycle of barbarism-heroicism-classicism-barbarism deepened Machiavelli's naturalism. Well into the eighteenth century, the famous Viscount Bolingbroke regarded those ideas as self-evident and also tried to suggest some remedies:

> The best instituted governments, like the best constituted animal bodies, carry in them the seeds of their destruction: and tho they grow and improve for a time, they will soon tend visibly to their dissolution. Every hour they live is an hour the less that they have to live. All that can be done therefore to prolong the duration of a good government, is to draw it back, on every favorable occasion, to the *first good principles* on which it was founded. When these occasions happen often, and are well improved, such governments are prosperous and durable. When they happen seldom, or are ill improved, these political bodies live in pain or in languor, and die soon.[47]

The naturalistic pattern was clearly established within the Scottish Enlightenment also. Adam Smith mulled extensively over the necessary price to be paid for progress and in particular over the fact that beyond a certain point civilization seemed always to turn to a process of corruption. Reflecting on the destinies of human societies, Adam Ferguson laid clear emphasis on that "kind of spontaneous return to obscurity and weakness," which was the rule, not the exception of progress.[48]

Less momentous figures, or not so illustrious philosophers, cherished very similar ideas. The "standard" view as expressed, for instance, in Cadwallader Colden's *History of the Five Indian Nations* (1724) was that the course of events is cyclical—societies were born, went through the stages of growth

and development, and then entered old age and death. Central to the maintenance of youth would be morality. The idea that public morality acted as a
remedy was part of the civic humanist tradition.[49]

Governor James Bowdoin of Massachusetts provided a lively portrait of
the conceptual link between biology and history that is worth a long quotation: "It is very pleasing and instructive," Bowdoin acknowledged,

> to recur back to the early ages of mankind, and trace the progressive
> state of nations and empires, from infancy to maturity, to old age and
> dissolution:—to observe their origin, their growth and improvement
> . . . to observe the progress of the arts among them . . . to observe the
> rise and gradual advancement of civilization, of science, of wealth,
> elegance, and politeness, until they had obtained the summit of their
> greatness:—to observe at this period the principle of mortality, produced
> by affluence and luxury, beginning to operate in them . . . and finally
> terminating in their dissolution. . . . In fine—to observe, after this ca-
> tastrophe, a new face of things; new kingdoms and empires rising upon
> the ruins of the old; all of them to undergo like changes, and to suffer a
> similar dissolution.[50]

That societies decline, like organisms, was a common idea in the new
continent. The anonymous author of "Thoughts on the Decline of States"
argued that all nations inevitably decline and die according to a natural necessity: "He must think little of *the order of nature* who sees not that *all of our
efforts must be defeated at last,* whether for the preservation of individuals, or
the body politick." Benjamin Smith Barton, author of the *New Views of the
Origin of the Tribes and Nations of America* (1797), mulling over the "present
savagery" of the Indian tribes, drew an interesting conclusion: their savage
status "teaches us, a mortifying truth, that nations may relapse into rude-
ness again; all their proud monuments crumbled into dust, and themselves,
now savages, subjects of contemplation among civilized nations and philosophers." Years before the painter Thomas Cole gave vividly pessimistic representations of the concept of cyclical history, Americans could have been easily
instructed also by Constantin François de Volney's *Ruines, ou Meditations
sur les revolutions des Empires* (1791). Volney's text is perhaps the best-known
example of eighteenth-century cyclical theory.[51]

Every pessimistic stance could easily turn into a jeremiad and a means
of urging fellow citizens to hasten, to become more obedient, to seize the
"unique" opportunity to secure one's liberty and future, or at least to retard
the unavoidable process of corruption by abstaining from excesses. The use
of jeremiads in America has been repeatedly surveyed by scholars. What they

have found is that insisting on the negative prospect, such as unavoidable and natural decay, could boost virtue and become a means of increasing the sense of honor and self-empowerment. However, the fact remains that Americans of the period were singularly ready to see signals of senescence everywhere. Americans were ready to react to such signals because, evidently, the vision of time as a natural and necessary cycle was widespread. Not all Americans believed that the country had already entered the downward slide; most of them were still frenzied by the revolutionary events. But Volney's idea that historical time is necessarily "revolving" was commanding.

That human civilization must be interpreted in a cyclical way and historical time as unending *revolutions,* as Volney had it, were *the* ideas late eighteenth-century Americans considered the most evident. They formed the normal pattern of explanation. Americans knew—even though their hopes may have pointed in a different direction—that each society shared the fate of individual organisms. "The highest degrees of civilizations border upon the savage life," Benjamin Rush was certain. In "The Former, Present and Future Prospects of America," 1787, a young John Quincy Adams philosophized in a very similar vein: "There is never a rising or meridian without a setting sun.—We it is true have happily passed the dangerous period of infancy;— we are rising into youth and manhood, with encouraging prospects. But let us remember we shall fall . . . into the decline and infirmities of old age." Noah Webster referred to the idea approvingly: "Every person tolerably well versed in history, knows that nations are often compared to individuals and to vegetables, in their progress from their origin to maturity and decay." A young nation might be brought to a flourishing maturity, but its death would follow inexorably. Moral vices were seen as bad habits that could hasten the process of physical decay. Given this naturalistic framework, the only realistic aim, as Webster said, was "to retard, if possible, and not accelerate the progress of corruption."[52]

Being acquainted with the cyclical theory did not imply a formal adherence to the doctrine of cycles. It was more like having an appalling thought in the back of one's mind, an obligation with which to comply or, more likely, against which to fight. Jefferson was a champion of humanism and optimistic declarations. And this is precisely the point: did Jefferson—or some among his contemporaries—actually contend that possibility was at the core of history, or did he simply *hope* that possibility could aspire to a similar role? The answer is that his philosophy was a matter of aspirations, and the discourse on hope and optimism did not efface the discourse on necessity and fate.

Jefferson has often been accused of being naive and unrealistic. Henry Adams, for instance, observing Jefferson's assertion that humans were endowed with reason and able to implement the nation's real self-interest, argued that he ignored the hidden forces that control human societies. Adams spoke of this as Jefferson's "heroic failure," namely, his endorsement of a false doctrine of freedom and ingenuity. However, the fact is that Jefferson's philosophy was far from unrealistic. His reliance upon human ability to forecast and forestall threats and upon history as the field of human rational decisions was a doctrine of hope, not a claim of knowledge and certainty. Jefferson did not "fail," as Adams maintained, because he was aware that the only freedom humans have was the freedom, through hope, to fight against forces more powerful than their reason and eventually to be wrecked by them. This is the function of Enlightenment's hopefulness: to state something in the face of the known evidence.[53]

No compelling argument prevents us from extending to societies—and to American society, at that—what Jefferson the natural philosopher clearly knew about individuals and their necessary life cycle: "Everything has its beginning, its growth, and end." The idea that time would head toward consummation, not toward an ultra-natural eternity, was firm in Jefferson's philosophy. "Man, like the fruit he eats," he wrote in 1821, "has his period of ripeness. Like that, too, if he continues longer hanging to the stem, it is but an useless and unsightly appendage." Humans cannot continue longer when their time is over. Like other eighteenth-century figures, Jefferson was convinced that real, historical time was a cycle, not a line to be prolonged ad infinitum. In this sense, time was always the *proper* time. "There is a fulness of time," Jefferson wrote to Benjamin Rush in 1811, "when men should go, & not occupy too long the ground to which others have a right to advance."[54]

The famous letter to James Madison, dated 6 September 1789, in which Jefferson stated his doctrine that "the earth belongs in usufruct to the living" may be interpreted as further evidence that he was well aware that the line of time could not be prolonged without end. It would be absurd to deny that there is a "fulness of time." Humans do not deal with infinite lines. They deal with continuous "revolutions," measured by birth, maturity, and death. That the earth belongs in usufruct to the living meant for Jefferson that nobody, neither individuals nor societies, had a right to live forever, to "eat up the usufruct of the lands for several generations to come," because in that case "the lands would belong to the dead." The living generation had no right to bind the future generation by stepping out of their "due" time, namely, their natural and biological time. Jefferson's statement is important not only for its appeal to a notion of intergenerational responsibility and its use of the term "usufruct" (expressing in turn an idea of a precarious and limited property), but for its startling use of the term "generation." "The people" of the *Declara-*

tion, by comparison, is abstract. "The people" never die. Jefferson drew on "generation" when concrete historical time was concerned, and not the realm of the unconditioned. "Generation" is specific, biologic, characterized by a precise duration (nineteen years, according to Jefferson), and conveys the image of something necessarily "revolving," a life determined by the rhythms of birth, maturity, and death.[55]

Nobody has the right to step out of the cycle of generations; neither individuals nor societies should do, or might do, that. What is true for the individual is also true for society. Since "the rights of the whole can be no more than the sum of the rights of individuals," as Jefferson said in the same letter to Madison, neither individuals nor societies have a right to make decisions, acts, choices, that would deny the cyclical nature of time and, thus, would bind the destiny of future, not-yet born generations. Ancestors have no more rights than successors. By the same token, "no society can make a perpetual constitution, or even a perpetual law." Any act, decision, choice that would bind acts, decisions, or choices of future generations (which would try to convert the cycle into a line) would impede the freedom of the living generation, and would be "an act of force, not of right." The time of nature, the circular time of biology, was the source of right. Nobody could extend his own proper time beyond its natural limit. Nobody, including the body politic, could live forever. That would be against nature, as well as against the right. Any form of perpetual existence, or perpetual property, would both be an act of abuse against the not-yet-born generations and a denial of the essential limit, precariousness, and temporality of human existence. It was that simple: no real death, no real life.

From reflections such as these we need not conclude that time qua nature, for Jefferson, was evil. Time could be indifferent to human ambitions, self-referential, and far from respectful to human hopes and human images of equilibrium. There might be something "barbarian" in the way epochs and civilizations usually attained their momentary glory by means of revolutions. But this is not tantamount to being evil.

Whether virtuous or vicious, time's condemnation of humanity to transience, compelling humans to change their lives, including their political frameworks, over and over again, might turn us to skepticism and pessimism. Time was menacing, a dangerous and consuming power, but not because it was criminal, or because its intentions were evil. Time had no intentions, no will, no purpose, for Jefferson. It was menacing simply because it was seen as a necessity operating in the world and a nonhuman force indifferent to the discourse of hope. Time compelled both humans and societies to live their lives and eventually to die. The danger came from the fact that both humans and societies were drawn through time's irresistible cycles (neither good, nor bad) as fish caught on a hook. McCoy makes this point when he realizes that Jefferson "assumed the inevitability of a particular pattern of social growth" and "perceived an intimate relationship between this pattern and the American experiment in republicanism." Jefferson turned to pessimism each time he acknowledged necessity as a real historical force.[56]

It was daunting to realize that time follows its own rules and pathways: not immoral, but simply "irrational" and far beyond the reach of humans' best hopes. Jefferson's hope, for instance, was that the people of the United States could enter the realm of the unconditioned, realize the ideal, and break the cycles of recurring despotism that had plagued the nations of the Old World from time immemorial. Nevertheless, he realized that hope does not rule the world. It was not just a remote possibility that the United States too, as he said in 1816, "shall go on, as other nations are doing, in the endless circle of oppression, rebellion, reformation; and oppression, rebellion, reformation again; and so on forever." In the new continent, too, the course of time might or, better, would become part of such an endless cycle, "and so on forever." Here lies the "irrationality" of time: that time's law is one of nonhuman necessity.[57]

In 1784, Jefferson already knew that the course of events was determined by uncontrollable forces, beyond the reach of human hope. Humans cannot forestall those forces, as if they were a fate. "All the world is becoming commercial," Jefferson had declared to Washington. "Was it practicable to keep our new empire separated from them [other nations] we might indulge ourselves in speculating whether commerce contributes to the happiness of mankind. But we cannot separate ourselves from them." Were it practicable to keep Americans separated, Jefferson would have developed a quite different kind of optimism than his typical, dualistic optimism of hope. Similarly, Jefferson's grim awareness, as expressed in the *Notes,* that "the spirit of the times may alter, *will* alter," and that "from the conclusion of this war *we shall be going down hill,*" conveys the clear message that humans must trim their expectations to necessity. This means that rational projects of civilization and ideals are on the whole restrained by overwhelming forces, and not the other way around. Given the extreme tension between hope and Jefferson's clear sense that time is stronger than hope, it is quite appropriate, as Malcolm Kelsall suggests, to portray Jefferson as the famous "angel of history" in Walter Benjamin's *Illuminations.* The angel is blown from paradise by a storm. The storm propels the angel into the future, while time keeps piling wreckage and hurling it at his feet. We call that wreckage "progress."[58]

It was alluring, to Jefferson, the image that progress would be an ascending line eternally determined by human decisions. As Paine wished, and Jefferson agreed, it is in "our power" to begin the world over again. However, alongside this hope that the course of events be interrelated to human decisions and reliant on the "efficacy of man" were other Jeffersonian discourses that put emphasis on some sort of necessity. The notion that time is a cycle is the clearest example. That humans may contribute to the process through which history grows was undoubtedly an enthralling opinion. Even so, the view that historical time is such a linear expansion with the human race at the helm was considered quite unrealistic during the eighteenth century.

Albeit Jefferson's hopes were strong, he surely could not overlook the "modernity" and perhaps the unlikelihood of his view. Jefferson's contemporaries made a number of enthusiastic statements about progress. But it would be a mistake if we severed those statements from the cyclical theory, as if they indicated a confident belief in linearity. The idea of historical time as a never-ending ascending line drawn by human beings as they march gloriously toward the unconditioned, Stow Persons wrote, "was repugnant to the characteristic convictions and temper of the class of men who in the generation prior to the Revolution had synthesized enlightened ideas in America." It was a completely new point of view that Adams and Jefferson, for instance, often wished for America. Each time they pointed out that certain innovations had a permanent character, that some discoveries and conquests seemed not to be temporary and likely to be followed by contrary movements, that "progress" did not take place within an invariable framework, they must have been conscious that they were introducing a radical novelty.[59]

Jefferson's hopeful views had to make a break with older conceptions of time that survived almost intact through eighteenth- and part of nineteenth-century America. Jefferson longed for modernity and sometimes even avowed unabated optimism. But his modernity and optimism had to cohabit with traditional visions of time that, as has been observed, fused "past and future in an instantaneous present." The new understanding of historical time as organized serially and implying forms of human control and a radical separation between past and future was basically a reaction against the Greek notion that humans would necessarily become what they were, what they had been from eternity. The wisdom of ancient philosophy was that the past returns, that the past informs the future, that it is the future's real substance. More generally, heathen philosophy knew that the real and the substantial (as opposed to the deceptive and the illusive) always have to be described as *to ti ên einai* (the essence or, literally, the "what it *was* to be"), to use Aristotle's famous expression. It was the perception of the past as the only real substance that characterized premodern philosophy.[60]

The Greek view of time dealt with the fundamental problem of rendering the world of change intelligible by considering it as "participating," as Reinhold Niebuhr once wrote, "in the changeless world through a cycle of changeless recurrence." Moreover, since Greek philosophers clung to the principle that what is true, real, and important must always have been true, real, and important, they held that the world could perhaps be understood, but that it never could be modified, let alone improved. Ancient heathen philosophy was extremely clear about the fact that the only virtues a wise person could foster were resignation, self-restraint, obedience, and forbearance. It acknowledged explicitly that the forces operating in the world were not human forces, but were far greater. "Do not forget your impotence," "do not yield to the delusion of portraying yourself as the master" were the maxims that lay at the core of the wisdom of the Greek world, and they resounded for centuries. We are not to suppose that such a heathen mindset suddenly disappeared. Quite the reverse. It was not just by accident that Seneca's work was on Jefferson's reading table when he died, despite his undeniable commitment to modernity and Enlightenment.[61]

The hope was that humans could be in control of historical processes. But Jefferson lived in an epoch in which it was extremely clear that events, most events, followed nonhuman laws. Contemporaries of Jefferson could find physical evidence of the forces of fate and necessity right beyond the west border of their backyard, from a geographical perspective, and right beyond the border of the young republic, from a historical perspective. There was something typically Stoic in Jefferson's admission that the march of time was not tantamount to a plan that humans fully understand, let alone control: irrelevant details, chance, or fate seemed to have a big part in the proceeding of events. Take, for instance, what Jefferson said in his *Autobiography:* the young American republic "is a wonderful instance of great events from small causes. So inscrutable is the arrangement of causes & consequences in this world, that a two-penny duty on tea, unjustly imposed in a sequestered part of it, changes the condition of all it's inhabitants." The arrangement of causes was actually inscrutable, for Jefferson, and the outcome thoroughly unpredictable.[62]

Likewise, something characteristically Stoic was couched also in the customary way Jefferson and his contemporaries experienced the devouring quality of time. Whether or not time was fighting on the side of the American cause, it was undeniable that it manifested itself as consumption. Time is an ally (hopefully), but it also consumes relentlessly. Not just bodies (both physical and social) are pledged to death, but memory as well—another figure of linearity and continuity—is lacunose, patchy, doomed to disappearance. Jefferson the natural historian and collector—a prop to Jefferson the man who devoted his energies to systematic enterprises, to eternal vigilance, to daily rituals of recording events—puts on view the sinister nature of time against which his optimism was fighting. Why was Jefferson so characteristically obsessed with collecting things? William Wirt, for instance, was quite right in portraying Monticello, the best window one has into Jefferson's secret life, as "a vast collection of specimens of Indian art . . . an array of the fossil productions of our country . . . and a variegated display of the branching honors of those 'monarchs of the waste,' that still people the wilds of the American continent." Generally speaking, collecting is the most reasonable response to time qua time of consumption, piling wreckage and hurling it at someone's feet.[63]

The whole story of Jefferson's historical optimism is, thus, that he both relied on and feared time and tried to build islands of resistance. He clearly realized that time passing put the law—the best symbol of national and political continuity—in serious jeopardy. Jefferson always feared that the corpus of American laws could be lost, because "many of them were already lost, and many more on the point of being lost, as existing only in single copies in the hands of careful or curious individuals, on whose deaths they would probably be used for waste paper." The problem was very simple to formulate, but much more difficult to fathom: since continuity and linearity do not exist either in nature or in historical time, they had to be built. To save the national memory "from the wreck" was Jefferson's priority. "I set myself therefore to work," he declared to George Wythe, "to collect all which were then existing." His concern for "preserving these remains from future loss," for securing them "from the worm, from the natural decay of the paper," had an enormous importance for Jefferson's equilibrium and for his role as a man of the Enlightenment. "How many of the precious works of antiquity were lost, while they existed only in manuscript?"[64]

The arrangement of events was inscrutable, chance had a role, and it was quite impossible for Jefferson to hide the unpleasant truth that time did consume. Time consumed and repeated the same old story: the feeling that America was not so "young," that Americans would soon become what they were, namely, inescapably British, did not solely stir up speculative fears; it grew into a certainty. McCoy draws attention to the general acknowledgment "that America was not the 'young,' vibrant society that Franklin and others had assumed it to be. Widespread unemployment, swelling poor relief rolls, an upsurge in crime and immorality—there was apparently no end to the signs of decay and old age. The new nation seemed to be afflicted by the very symptoms of the British political and moral economy that the Revolutionaries had risked their lives to escape." By the 1780s, especially in the coastal areas, "evidence" heralded the new republic as firmly on its way to replicate the British society. An unmistakable condition of "crowding"—which meant an increase of social stratification, growing concentration of wealth, a mobile and visible class of poor people—seemed to many citizens the clear signal that the republic had prematurely reached its elderly phase.[65]

It was a widespread opinion that in the short run America would come to resemble Europe. Even though he was excessively pessimistic, John Adams was in this sense emblematic. "Our country," he declared, "will do like all others—play their affairs into the hands of a few cunning fellows." There was no hope in Adams's thought. No education, no reason, no natural virtue, perhaps only force, could restrain Americans from replicating old patterns. Of course, what for the frankly pessimistic John Adams was a certainty, to be announced loudly, for less talkative fellows, like Jefferson, was an intolerable suspicion. But whether publicly announced or secretly mumbled, the idea that time repeats itself was firmly entrenched in American minds.[66]

Jefferson could not have denied that time casts its decrees: it consumes, it amasses the things humans long for in that repository usually called "oblivion." Time thwarts. Time repeats its circles and compels civilizations to retell the same old story. It forces humans, enlightened leaders included, to swerve from hopefulness to pessimism and from pessimism to hopefulness. Not that we have to expect from Jefferson a formal adherence to the theory of cycle, as said, or a capitulation to that kind of pessimism à la Adams. Jefferson was not the kind of philosopher who builds a pessimistic system of philosophy out of his feeling of an essential identity of past and future. The impression that the course of events is a steady state regulated by necessity does not solely trigger resignation. Nevertheless, why should we expect that Jefferson ignored these insights and that he was not touched by them as his contemporaries were? The truth is that Jefferson rose up against the dominant view of historical time with every fiber of his heart and virtue.

Jefferson hoped for irreversibility, linearity, and modernity. But such a hope is not to be confused with nineteenth-century historical optimism. George Bancroft, William Prescott, John Motley, or Francis Parkman, for instance, conceived the march of civilization as pre-ordered. Such a version of historical necessity, moreover, was nourished by the firm confidence that the outcome must be favorable to the American nation. Malone's hypothesis that time was fighting on the side of America applies to nineteenth-century historical optimism without reservation. American history, Dorothy Ross writes, was presented by those authors as "a radical break in history and a radical breakthrough of God's time into secular history. The country's progress would be the unfolding of the millennial seed, rather than a process of historical change."[67]

The idea that the course of events would be a pre-ordered "unfolding" of a seed was alien to Jefferson. Jefferson was sure that the arrangement of causes was inscrutable and that insignificant causes, like a two-penny duty on tea, could also change the condition of a whole nation. It is true that Jefferson sometimes spoke about the seed of American liberty. Douglas Wilson, for instance, calls attention to "Jefferson's own most cherished" historical notion, the so-called Saxon myth. The myth tells the story of an alleged representative democracy and an "ancient constitution" that had existed in the Anglo-Saxon period before the Norman conquest, and that the English civil wars of the seventeenth century and the American War of Independence had vindicated against the usurpations of the Crown. Jefferson considered the idea of the "seed" of such an original democracy. But Jefferson's "seed" was an *exemplum virtutis* that wise Americans *might* and maybe *should* decide to follow. His seed was not necessarily ordained to grow and blossom. Jefferson remained faithful to the Whig interpretation of history as an ongoing and uncertain struggle between success and failure.[68]

Bancroft, Prescott, Motley, and Parkman also believed that American liberty was born among the Teutonic tribes that vanquished Rome. They maintained that the seed of republican government was brought by the Saxons to England, preserved there in the Magna Carta and the Glorious Revolution, and then planted and fully grown in the American colonies. The difference was that in their picture there was no room for chanciness and insignificant events, such as a two-penny duty. The arrangement of causes was far from inscrutable. They were sure that the seed *had* to expand into the perennial tree of the American republic. God's time had entered natural history, and the cycles had been broken. Jefferson's hope was that the growing tree could be perennial. But he also knew that the tree, as a natural organism, must follow nature's cycle of life and death.[69]

I have said that Jefferson tried to build islands of resistance. That was his general attitude. And the notion of progress as a linear, irreversible, noncyclical process was alien to the temper of the individuals who voiced resistance and identified with Enlightenment values. Jefferson's unmovable conviction, let me repeat it again, was that "everything has its beginning, its growth, and end." The hope he nurtured was tantamount to resisting a necessary force, be it nature, the course of time, or the specter of barbarism.

To slow down the pace of historical change—more specifically, to restrain those leaders who wanted to accelerate social and economic development—was the only chance to forestall the ultimate destination, decline. According to Washington, Adams, or Jefferson, Stow Persons wrote, "social and political institutions were . . . but temporary bulwarks against the inexorable processes of nature and history." For many American leaders of the postrevolutionary period, the real question to fathom was how to build effective barriers against the inevitable. Jefferson was no exception. Christopher Looby correctly notices that "despite a few well-known expressions of a contrary opinion, he [Jefferson] could scarcely conceive of social process—the movement of a nation through time—except in negative terms, that is, as decay, corruption, and degeneration." As a consequence, Jefferson's obsession with the task of building barriers and finding remedies to curtail the inevitable was more than comprehensible. We are very far from the idea that the march of civilization would be the unfolding of the millennial seed. Jefferson's favorite barrier was hope. Hope was an effective instrument to propel fellow citizens and not to accelerate their fate. As Jefferson eloquently said, "we are never permitted to despair of the commonwealth." The reason they were never permitted to do so, as Adams too often did, was evident, at least to an Enlightenment devotee.[70]

Americans desired to create their own time. They wished to believe they were not characters in a story that time and nature had told again and again. They wished to believe they were at the beginning of something fresh. That America was but "a child of yesterday," to use Jefferson's famous phrase, can generate anxiety but could also foster positive reactions. Jefferson had some characteristic modes to convince himself and others that society's youth might be indefinitely prolonged. Keeping a life-long reliance on hope—this emblematic youthful sentiment—was perhaps his most celebrated mode. Jefferson hoped to prolong youth by always trying to think and behave like a young man. It is not accidental that he always liked to be surrounded by persons who were his junior.

The utopian scheme of creating an agricultural society was another. At least for a certain period, Jefferson was thoroughly convinced that the only kind of society that had any chance to forestall the process of corruption was one that could be regarded as existing outside historical time, as it were. Concealed beneath Jefferson's agricultural scheme that he devised at the time of the Revolution was the idea that given a potential for limitless geographic expansion, America would not soon reach the final corrupt stage of social development, while commerce and an advanced division of labor would precipitate America's old age. Jefferson's philosophy of time had a very practical target: to help find a way both to prolong youth and to resist the passage of seasons by means of space.

Jefferson, on the whole, was a creature of space. Space was what he always really and totally trusted. Spacious was the American continent. Space was what was doubtless promising to the new nation. Space was what the Louisiana Purchase and Lewis and Clark's westward journey bequeathed to the new republic. Spatial, more generally, was Jefferson's mode of thinking. To put it succinctly, law (scientific law) was a reduction of historical time to space, to diagram, and to a synthetic vision. One of Jefferson's primary modes of pursuing order was the elaboration of artificial synchronic and synthetic orders: Jefferson's fascination with charts, diagrams, graphics, tables, lists, and similar "two-dimensional formats," to use Christopher Looby's definition, is probably the best evidence of his dream of a synchronic world, a timeless order that could avert time's necessity. In history things are not the way they are in the field of mathematics, the synchronic science by definition, and, as Jefferson confessed to his friend Rush, "ever my favorite" study. While in mathematics, "all is demonstration & satisfaction," the kind of truth that history seemed to elicit was something appalling: decline and transience.[71]

To conclude, let me provide a summary of how this section has portrayed Jefferson's philosophy of historical time. Emphasis has been put, first, on the fact that Jefferson desired to see time as a stream taking Americans along the direction of their cheerful future. Perhaps a stream that runs forever. Call it republicanism or, more generally, modernity and civilization. Second, Jefferson deployed the idea of the "efficacy of man" (in particular, the American man) to reinforce that desire. The problem, however, was that such a desire, third, collided with more traditional ideas that Jefferson inherited and in which his mind continued to float. Tradition saw historical time as something necessary, to a large extent biological, and quite disrespectful of humans' (including Americans') hope to attain some sort of eternal life: the ultimate prospect was death and defeat. This explains why, fourth, Jefferson repeatedly sought to slow time, to remain young, and to draw on space to counteract the dreary effect of the time passing. Insofar as they centered on some form of resistance, the practices of Jefferson's dealing with time were at variance with his optimistic vision.

This way of treating Jefferson's philosophy of time is a partial revision, not a refutation, of more conventional interpretations, such as Malone's, that do not call sufficient attention to the dualism between desiring/hoping and knowing/inheriting, between the heart and the head, and between innovation and tradition. That Jefferson desired to portray the march of civilization in optimistic, linear, and ascending terms cannot gainsay the fact that he lived all his life immersed in an inherited culture. The Enlightenment was aware that "everything has its beginning, its growth, and end." As the examples I have selected show, late eighteenth-century culture did not break suddenly with the vision of time as a series of cycles of forces indifferent to the discourse of hope. Rather, it wrestled incessantly with that vision.

5

Impossibility & Despondency

Jefferson's language of satisfaction, we have seen, was a radical strategy to resist the burden that the Enlightenment imposed on its adepts. More interesting, at least for those readers who look for tension and conflict, he also made frequent use of the languages of projection and possibility, and even with that of anxiety and precariousness. Whoever relies on the heart and hope by living in the continuous anticipation of a better future likely becomes prey to anxieties, fears, tremors of reservation, confusions, forebodings, and a sense of threat. As an enlightened traveler, he confronted limits, and negativity had always been acknowledged in his realistic platform. The Enlightenment mission was itself accompanied by the awareness of specific forms of darkness and negativity.

In this chapter, negativity is still the central character of the story (as in the previous two chapters), but here the subject goes beyond anxiety, the negativity that haunts one's expectations as an ominous possibility. An enlightened realism like Jefferson's was also consistent with—and to a certain extent called for—a definitive and absolute negativity and a sense of impossibility. In the previous chapter, negativity takes the form of both natural and historical necessity. We are here concerned with the sense of impossibility, which is the psychological aspect of necessity, and with those reactions that necessity routinely triggers in people's mind. Impossibility, in other words, is necessity described *a parte subjecti*.

Jefferson was an experienced traveler who spoke several languages. There is no wonder that under certain conditions he was inclined to jettison hope. Quite often, his heart was muted. Jefferson confronted limits in a very radical way, going beyond the languages of hope, activism, and meliorism. Jefferson's philosophy of the Enlightenment did not yield to a delusive self-confidence both because it took into consideration the *possibility* of failure and, also, because it was familiar with the *certainty* that human life is limited, that as such it is open to an abyss and to a realm of impossibilities. Jefferson's philosophy was not one of naïveté in that it allowed for both a strong sense of hope (and anxiety) and, in addition, for the acceptance of an essential powerlessness.

Being limited, human hopes, endeavors, and aspirations have by definition a contour, and something—an overwhelming something—must always lie out of their reach.

Jefferson knew that the realm of impossibilities, so to speak, casts its lethal shadow on everything that is human. Not that he delved into that realm as if he were a speculative philosopher and an American Schopenhauer. If he did so in the solitude of his alcove in Monticello, he left no trace in his writings. Nevertheless, he was a very perceptive human being, and the historian can safely surmise that he acutely sensed the impossibility of all his projects. The paralyzing effects that such a realm triggered on his ideas and discourses are quite visible. These effects are evident, albeit the realm from which they spring never became the object of Jefferson's direct speculation.

The aim of this chapter is to uphold the hypothesis that the realm of impossibilities was an important presence in Jefferson's enlightened philosophy. By this expression I mean a negativity lying beyond human reach and, correspondingly, an appalling ocean that humans can neither conquer nor control. Jefferson had experience of this eerie realm, and its repeated intrusions can be inferred by the effect—despondency—it triggered. It was the realm of impossibilities, as we have seen, that prompted a dogged, almost desperate commitment to projects. Optimism qua hope was for Jefferson a virtuous response, a compensatory activism aimed at resisting precariousness and the specters of despondency. Occasionally, as we have also seen, he compensated with a form of precritical boldness of rhetoric. But the realm of impossibilities also prompted a deep-rooted hopelessness.

Jefferson responded to impossibility in quite different terms than did, for instance, his long-standing friend John Adams. Not surprisingly, indeed, given the huge difference between the two men. Often alleged to suffer from bad temper and even from mental instability, Adams nurtured very negative feelings about the character of both the American people and the human race at large. He often made very "existentialist" and anti-Jeffersonian reflections on the emptiness of human life. Let me just quote a famous example: "After all, What is human life? A Vapour, a Fog, a Dew, a Cloud a Blossom a flower, a Rose a blade of Grass, a glass Bubble, a Tale told by an Idiot, a Boule de Savon, Vanity of Vanities, an eternal succession of which would terrify me, almost as much as Annihilation." John Adams was, as Trevor Colbourn put it, "essentially pessimistic" as he lacked Enlightenment's hopefulness. He discovered in history only the record of human errors. Not believing in the possibility of any great change in human nature (which for him was fundamentally bad), he spent his entire career devising and then defending political institutions calculated to protect American society against human fundamental shortcomings. In this respect, the difference between Adams and Jefferson appears enormous.[1]

Jefferson neither succumbed to despair as Adams did, nor did he make similar frank admissions of defeat. In spite of this, Karl Lehman may have been right in his claim that "Gibbon's pessimistic characterization of history as a register of crimes seems to have exercised a powerful influence on him. The alleged utopian Jefferson nurtured, by sober contemplation of actual events, a deep-rooted pessimism and skepticism about human history." At least to some extent, Jefferson continued to believe that history was something more than the record of human crimes. Old Jefferson still believed that history gave some *exempla virtutis*. While in the past some people had been clearly wicked, others had been undeniably virtuous, and those examples should be presented to everyone. In fact, Jefferson himself wanted to be remembered by future historians as a positive figure and an "Apostle of Freedom." He kept organizing his documents and papers to this purpose. It is possible that he neither was "influenced" by Gibbon nor became a "convert" to his pessimistic philosophy of history. Moreover, Lehman did not give any clear explanation as to when and why such a "conversion" to pessimism would have taken place. But extreme though Lehman's hypothesis was, we would be completely wrong if we thought that Jefferson was untouched by pessimism. Pessimism was quite compatible with Thomas Jefferson's experience of the Enlightenment. Jefferson turned to pessimism and despondency each time he acknowledged necessity as a real historical force.[2]

Let me start with the old Jefferson. There is a story that is often told about why and when Jefferson "converted" to pessimism. According to this story, the process of Jefferson's growing old affected a radical transformation in his whole character, what might be called a failure of nerve. Gordon Wood points out that after he retired from public life in 1809, "he became more narrow-minded and localist than he had ever been in his life." In fact, when he left the presidency, he was to return to Virginia, never to leave his "country" again. A pessimist Jefferson, parochial and alarmist, seemed to make his appearance when the public man yielded to the private one. "He had a lot of gloomy and terrifying moments in these years between 1809 and 1826," Wood says. The turn of American society in the direction of Jacksonian democracy, the strengthening of the federal government, banks, "tricks upon paper," a bullying individualism, and an aggressive capitalism stirred up the demons accumulated in Jefferson's fatigued mind. His old age compelled him to react by turning against his long-standing hopefulness. Jefferson's final years were marked by disillusionment and the grim awareness that the world around him was rapidly changing in a way that he deemed bewildering and terrify-ing.[3]

At a certain moment, Jefferson seemed to completely reject his present. To Nathaniel Macon, for instance, he declared: "I feel a much greater inter-est in knowing what passed two or three thousand years ago than in what is passing now. I read nothing, therefore, but of the heroes of Troy, of the wars of Lacedaemon and Athens, of Pompey and Caesar, and of Augustus, too, the Bonaparte and parricide scoundrel of that day." In an analogous way, when Jefferson discussed with Adams the miseries of South American states and a likely recipe to get self-government there (mainly through education, free-dom of commerce, freedom of the press, trial by jury) the conclusion he drew could astonish the reader. Where had the "familiar" Jefferson disappeared? "You see, my dear Sir, how easily we prescribe for others a cure for their dif-ficulties, while we cannot cure our own. We must leave both, I believe, to heaven, and wrap ourselves up in the mantle of resignation."[4]

In the same essay, Wood acknowledges that something more than a reac-tion to traumatic external events must be at stake. "Something more is in-volved in accounting for the awkwardness of his years of retirement than these outside forces, and that something seems to lie within Jefferson himself—in his principles and outlook, in his deep and long-held faith in popular de-mocracy and the future." The reason for the mounting resignation to which Wood alludes was that Jefferson was "emotionally unprepared" for what was happening. This "pure American innocent" was "victimized by his overween-ing confidence in the people and by his naive hopefulness in the future."[5]

Is that the whole story? Did Jefferson become a pessimist because, in his old age, he *realized* that his confidence in people and ideals was stupid? That he *comprehended* he was unprepared to deal with the human capacity for evil? Did he at some point *become* a pessimist?

Wood's story is an excellent story on the whole. Only a few details should be changed and the impression of a transformation be downplayed. Simply stated, there are good reasons to question the idea of a transformation. Actu-ally, Jefferson did not become a pessimist, as he did initiate one major project in his last years that was very concrete. The founding of the University of Virginia was a proactive undertaking revealing that Jefferson did not lose his hope in a sanguine future. My argument is that Jefferson was not subject to a qualitative transformation. He did not, at a certain point, start to become progressively anti-Jeffersonian, as it were.

Despondency was not an attitude that burst out at a certain moment as a biological effect of aging. In this respect, there was complete continuity in his life, and the pessimistic discourse had always been present. It was present but best kept hidden. Jefferson's awareness of negativity, and the unavoidable resultant despondency, was like a subterraneous stream that emerged from time to time. The only difference between the young and old Jefferson was that as the time went by he had less energy to resist the realm of impossibilities. The change was only in quantity. The terrain of Jefferson's hopefulness became more and more porous, making it easier for the historian to discern both his pessimism and his awareness of an underlying negativity. There was no break with his past, as the recognition of an inescapable negativity was part of the Enlightenment canon. We might better say that the process of growing old made Jefferson less self-censoring, but the optimistic discourse was still there. Resignation became a sort of customary habit albeit, as stated, not Jefferson's unique posture.

Take the Missouri Crisis, for instance. On February 1819, Representative James Tallmadge Jr. of New York proposed an amendment to a bill about Missouri's admission to the Union that would have banned slavery in the new state. The Missouri Crisis was, in those years, the most powerful factor that hastened Jefferson's decreased assertion of will. It was a catalyst, an occasion, but no particular event could have been the cause of Jefferson's "*radical disillusionment*," as Peter Onuf names it. "Radical" here is opposed to "occasional" or momentary disillusionment. Actually, there is no clear explanation for the reason why Jefferson's disillusionment should have been so intense, so "radical," given that in 1784 he had drafted a Territorial Government Ordinance that proposed the substance of Tallmadge's amendment, to ban slavery from all the new western states.[6]

Pessimism, clearly a pre-existing theme, resounded through Jefferson's letters of the period. The one he wrote to John Holmes, on 22 April 1820, is an eloquent example of an increased receptiveness to impossibilities and a decreased capacity to react against the negative. Jefferson was upset to the point of seeing in the Missouri Crisis the ultimate confirmation of all his longstanding fears about the future of the republic. In his opinion, northern authoritarian "restrictionists" (a new word for "federalists") had eventually succeeded in throwing away the principles of self-government, gradualism, reformism, and progressivism, and, hence, the foundation of Jefferson's republicanism. We are dealing with nightmares, of course, and this is why Jefferson's heart resounded so promptly at the news that reached his mountaintop. "I regret that I am now to die in the belief," he wrote to Holmes, "that the useless sacrifice of themselves by the generation of 1776, to acquire self-government and happiness to their country, is to be thrown away by the unwise and unworthy passions of their sons, and that my only consolation is to be, that I live not to weep over it. If they would but dispassionately weigh the blessings they will throw away, against an abstract principle more likely to be effected by union than by scission, they would pause before they would perpetrate this act of suicide on themselves, and of treason against the hopes of the world." Then the letter ends.[7]

Objectively, the future of "self-government and happiness" was not impaired by the Missouri Crisis. By the same token, it was certainly excessive to grieve over the "useless sacrifice," over "blessings" that would have been "thrown away." It was likewise excessive to denounce a "treason against the hopes of the world." Jefferson could well have "sensed" the inescapability of the Civil War, as interpreters sometimes say; but the despondency of Jefferson's letter to Holmes, obviously, did not grow out of the actual experience of that war, and the growing North-South rivalry had been abundantly clear to everyone at least since Jefferson's first presidency.

There was nothing so dire, sudden, or decisive in the Missouri Crisis. Jefferson did not become a pessimist as an effect of a sensational event. The pessimism of the letter to Holmes was a question of loosening self-control. Jefferson's pessimism derived not from the discovery of new evidence, but rather from how he decided to read the events. Jefferson had become inclined to portray himself as an ineffectual being and to increasingly confess his powerlessness, at least to selected recipients and friends. With Adams, who for his part was not a champion of self-control, Jefferson felt entitled to freely pursue his philosophical meditation on negativity. To step aside from optimism became a priority for the two old philosophers who were looking for new terms in which to properly express the theme of human transience. With increased frequency, the old Jefferson merged his version of the Enlightenment into a "romantic" atmosphere both by occasionally quoting Young's *Night Thoughts* and, in particular, by devoting his precious time to meditations on the inexorability of human destiny: "When the friends of our youth are all gone, and a generation is risen around us whom we know not, is death an evil?" The question has clearly a negative answer, as death is portrayed as the dwelling to which one wishfully returns: "The rapid decline of my strength during the last winter has made me hope sometimes that *I see land*."[8]

The ambiguity of Jefferson's reflections of the 1820s—plus the bewildering portrayal of death as a home—does not allow one to determine if this Virginian Odysseus was prophesying about his personal destiny solely, about the destiny of particular human beings, or if at stake was a rumination on a generalized "triumph of death," a famous Gothic theme that would affect human creations and human aspirations, including the young republic. We cannot exclude this last option. What is certain is that Jefferson increasingly spurned the new democratic world that was emerging in America.

"Evidence" that death was already triumphing seemed to gather around this grieving prophet of the Enlightenment. From time to time he must have looked at his beloved optimism and buoyancy as if they were dead languages, still spoken by academics but ludicrously outdated. Speculation, banks, paper money, evangelical Christianity, consumerism, a growing population, and politics turned into a profession, for instance, were the incarnations of Jefferson's worst nightmares. He felt himself cast off by the new democratic forces he had helped to create and, in a sense, he must have perceived himself as an (unaware) agent of the spreading of generalized destruction. As a consequence, when in 1825 he wrote "All, all dead, and ourselves left alone midst a new gener[atio]n whom we know not, and who know not us," there was no longer any limit to Jefferson's sense of solitude and failure; to his conviction that he, John Adams, Francis Adrian van der Kemp—the addressee of the letter—and a few others were the only living men amid walking ghosts already seized by cosmic death.[9]

The reality was different, of course. From the society of the 1820s, Jefferson selected those elements that fit into the discourse of pessimism. He was not quite accurate in believing that the "younger recruits" of the American political life had "nothing in them of the feelings or principles of '76." The new men "look to a single and splendid government of an aristocracy, founded on banking institutions, and moneyed incorporations under the guise and cloak of their favored branches of manufactures, commerce and navigation, riding and ruling over the plundered ploughman and beggared yeomanry. This will be to them a next best blessing to the monarchy of their first aim, and perhaps the surest stepping-stone to it."[10]

He could not have been so upset just because of the Missouri Crisis. That crisis did not change the fate of the republic radically and all of a sudden. Objectively, the society of the 1820s had not become so dramatically different from the world President Jefferson knew during his stay in the new capital city. The Missouri Crisis had been a significant phenomenon, but we must not overstate its importance. Jefferson was not crazy, certainly, and occasions for mourning the fate of the republic were actually abundant. But those occasions had been abundant at least since the Peace of Paris.

Every human being takes up pessimism from time to time, particularly during an ailment or when growing old. The point, however, is that the expression "from time to time" can range from the minimum of two, three times in a life, to a regular habit, the timbre of one's personality. What I am arguing is precisely that Jefferson's despondency is more similar to a habit than to an occasional emotional setback occurring in an otherwise untroubled and healthy life. In other words, pessimism was among the discourses that Jefferson routinely made use of to give sense to his world. To recall Onuf once again, Jefferson's pessimism was "radical." We cannot dismiss Jefferson's pessimism, as if it were but an irrelevant mood, just because pessimism does not match with our classical image of Jefferson's life as an example of abiding Americanism.

There is no suggestion of a passing mood, for instance, in the bad light he cast on the whole of human civilization in his letter to Adams of 11 January 1816. The Missouri Crisis was not on the scene, and this time Bonaparte was the catalyst he selected. Jefferson's eulogy of the eighteenth century has a remarkable epilogue. In that letter, he refers mainly to Europe. It was Europe that could "again become an Arena of gladiators," but more than Europe was at stake.

His bitter considerations can be easily generalized: Jefferson was speaking about humanity and human civilization as such. Sciences and arts, manners and morals, not just European staples, "advanced to a higher degree than the world had ever before seen." However, the partition of Poland inflicted a wound to this century, and a dreadful reflection spontaneously arose: "How then has it happened that these nations, France especially and England, so great, so dignified, so distinguished by science and the arts, plunged at once into all the depths of human enormity, threw off suddenly and openly all the restraints of morality, all sensation to character, and unblushingly avowed and acted on the principle that power was right?" Jefferson did not know the reason why these ominous events had taken place. Note that Jefferson was talking about events that had already taken place, irreparably, not of fears about distant future occurrences. "Whatever it was, the close of the century saw the moral world thrown back again to the age of the Borgias, to the point from which it had departed 300. years before." There are no hopes or, it might be said, this time Jefferson's heart relied on an empty wish: "My wishes . . . "[11]

A number of letters show that Jefferson was on familiar terms with despondency and made habitual reference to it. The year 1816 must have been difficult for Jefferson's inner life. No visible ominous event befell him, but two days before sending the letter to Adams just quoted above, he had already written to Benjamin Austin about France and England, the "true" motives for the gloomy prospect for America. Jefferson started by observing that thirty years earlier he had been an advocate of America's dependence on England for manufacture. Thirty years later, he disclosed his disillusionment in the course taken by events, in the impossible American agricultural future he had foreseen, and in a reciprocity among nations that did not occur. "Let our work-shops remain in Europe," had said the author of the *Notes*. The general tone of the letter to Austin is clearly nostalgic. "We were then in peace." There was then "such an immensity of unimproved land," and husbandry seemed to "add most to the national wealth." The prospects seemed rosy. "But who in 1785 could foresee the rapid depravity which was to render the close of that century the disgrace of the history of man?"[12]

"Who could have imagined," Jefferson asked Austin, "that the two most distinguished in the rank of nations [France and England], for science and civilization, would have suddenly descended from that honorable eminence, and setting at defiance all those moral laws established by the Author of nature between nation and nation, as between man and man, would cover earth and sea with robberies and piracies, merely because strong enough to do it with temporal impunity." Time had not been complaisant to America, and America was compelled to awaken from a dream, a dream that Jefferson himself used to have: "We [Americans] have experienced what we did not then believe, that there exists both profligacy and power enough to exclude us from the field of interchange with other nations: that to be independent for the comforts of life we must fabricate them ourselves." Not that the prospect of fabricating those "comforts" by "ourselves" was per se a motive for the pro-technology Jefferson to become pessimistic. This was the lesser evil. National industry was compatible with Jefferson's hopes. The real evil, and hence the cause of the pessimism of the letter to Austin, was that thirty years after 1785 something compelled America to pursue "rapid depravity" and the hegemony of "power."

The evil was the "fact" that morality was over, and that a nation could believe it had the right to plunder other nations just because it had the force to do it. It is the *contrappunto* between "now" and "then," the acknowledgment of present "depravity," of events that have "irremediably" taken place, that pushed Jefferson in the direction of a clear-cut despondency. Such a *contrappunto* between "now" and "then" forced him to conjure visions of European nations treading in the footsteps of the barbarian tribes, strong enough to deluge the world, as Jefferson said, with "rivers of blood" and "scenes of havoc and horror."

That the present was unsatisfying was clear to Jefferson even at the end of 1814, when the peace treaty with England was about to be signed at Ghent. Although deliberately pursued and "entirely justifiable on our part," the war was judged by Jefferson as a debacle, a "deplorable misfortune to us." The main reason was that the war heralded an American present that Jefferson was by no means willing to accept. In mourning this "misfortune," he was not just playing the role of a Jeremiah. He was not pretending to shiver or to make others shiver at an ominous prospect in order to wake them up. Once again, it was the "irreversibility" of events that had already taken place—not a gloomy possibility—that he narrated in the letter. Those irreparable events undermined Jefferson's confidence. The War of 1812 "*has arrested* the course of the most remarkable tide of prosperity any nation ever experienced, and *has closed* such prospects of future improvements as were never before in the view of any people. *Farewell* all hopes of extinguishing public debt! *farewell* all visions of applying surpluses of revenue to the improvements of peace rather than the ravages of war. Our enemy has indeed the consolation of Satan on removing our first parents from Paradise: from a peaceable and ag-ricultural nation, he makes us a military and manufacturing one." The war "has arrested," not "could arrest," the realization of a long-awaited present, and "farewell" is crucial to Jefferson's demurring.[13]

Instead of considering despondency as a retreat from the "normality" of a naive strain of optimism, I would prefer to regard optimism and pessimism as two discourses to which Jefferson frequently recurs. Pessimism was neither an accident that occurred because some uncommon events took place, because American society had suddenly become different from what it used to be, nor because old age affected a drastic transformation in his philosophy. If there is a state of mind specific to Jefferson's later years, it is only the dwindling of the self-censorship that accompanied his recurrent pessimism. This means that his roles as a public optimistic man (an educator, a promoter, a Jeremiah, and so on) were dramatically in conflict with other roles; and discourses were in conflict with other discourses.

Jefferson's enlightened realism and perspicuity had been on alert through-out his life. Things could not have been otherwise. An enlightened realist, he had to face facts and rebuff self-edification. "When you and I look back on the country over which we have passed," Jefferson wrote to John Page in 1804, "what a field of slaughter does it exhibit! Where are all the friends who entered it with us, under all the inspiring energies of health and hope?" Jefferson was not just a creature of the heart. Regarding this enlightened life from close range, the historian may tell various stories, not just that he was hopeful, that he went ahead, that he achieved, that he had optimism, that he trusted the good outcome. It was part of the Enlightenment's mission to warn fellow travelers that slaughtering is the general rule of human civiliza-tion and that the downfall of ideals, not just of "friends," is unfortunately the norm. When one deals realistically with human affairs, there is but one conclusion: "What a field of slaughter does [our country] exhibit!"[14]

The letter he wrote to Madison, 1 January 1797, is worth a detailed analy-sis in this respect, as it expressly targeted the theme of civilization as a field of slaughter. This letter is an interesting specimen. Despondency appears in its purest form, not balanced by any opposite view.

In that letter to Madison, Jefferson made reference to a pamphlet by James Callender, *The Political Progress of Britain* (first published 1792), in which the British empire was compared with classical Rome. Commenting on Callender's pamphlet, Jefferson delved into the "ulcerated state" of the human mind and presented reflections that, by his explicit admission, "are not flattering to our species." The way Jefferson formulated his conclusion is remarkable:

> In truth I do not recollect in all the Animal kingdom a single species but man which is eternally and systematically engaged in the destruction of it's own species. What is called civilization seems to have no other effect on him than to teach him to pursue the principle of bellum omnium in omnia on a larger scale, and in place of the little contests of tribe against tribe, to engage all the quarters of the earth in the same work of destruction. When we add to this that as to the other species of animals, the lions and tigers are mere lambs compared with man as a destroyer, we must conclude that it is in man alone that Nature has been able to find a sufficient barrier against the too great multiplication of other animals and of man himself, an equilibriating power against the fecundity of generation. My situation points my views chiefly to his wars in the physical world: yours perhaps exhibit him as equally warring in the Moral one. We both, I believe, join in wishing to see him softened.[15]

The humanistic perspective that marks the closing of the letter stands in a singular contraposition to the nonhumanistic, almost fatalistic tone of Jefferson's general reasoning stressing eternal and systematic destruction. Moreover, the finale which Jefferson expressed in the form of a desire ("We both . . . join in wishing to see him softened") is a further revelation of powerlessness. Jefferson's observation that nature has put in man's brutality "an equilibriating power against the fecundity of generation" was clearly not a comfort and accentuated the grotesque conclusion of the letter.

It is probably true that "*Bellum omnium in omnia* [war of all against all], which some philosophers observ[e] to be so general in this world," as Jefferson in a completely different mood said to Samuel Kercheval in 1816, is but the "abusive state of man." Perhaps Jefferson assumed that nature was not responsible. Perhaps the general slaughtering pointed out in the letter to Madison should not be mistaken for the natural and the necessary state of human history. Nevertheless, the "nature" that appeared in the letter to Madison was unmistakably brutal, Darwinian, and clearly not the one upon which

Jefferson often relied. Such a nature was not the basis of moral sense and did not provide for the best direction in the matter of human choices. Nature seemed to be a cure more dangerous and more loathsome than the malady it was designed to cure. Like the pursuit of general destruction, nature acting in human history was something that Jefferson wished could be "softened." Be it a necessary or just an "abusive" state, the effect of the "bellum omnium in omnia on a larger scale" was not susceptible to an efficacious therapy. Humans were "eternally and systematically" engaged in a work of destruction.[16]

"Civilization and corruption," said the *Boston Independent Chronicle,* 24 November 1785, "have generally been found to advance with equal steps." An Enlightenment devotee, Jefferson understandably wanted to resist this thought. This does not mean that he disregarded the truth that the idea conveyed, or that the idea of rejecting civilization entirely was unknown to him. In some deeper levels of his psychological life, he approved of an idea he himself sometimes expressed: "What is called civilization seems to have no other effect on him than to teach him to pursue the principle of bellum omnium in omnia on a larger scale."

A gradualist and a meliorist, Jefferson did not like to take on confrontational stances, such as the refusal of civilization. Benjamin Rush, in contrast, had a confrontational way of addressing the question. Since 1769, Rush was clear that "there is no life so agreeable as that of [the] savage. It is free and independant, and in this consists [the] highest happiness of man. When he is removed from it he is perpetually striving to get back to it again." Likewise, Crèvecoeur voiced extreme criticisms of "civilized society." In comparing the state of human beings in the woods to that of humans in a more improved situation, he noted pessimistically that "evil preponderates in both; in the first they often eat each other for want of food, and in the other they often starve each other for want of room." The two states seem to be equal in this respect, but Crèvecoeur's conclusion was that "the vices and miseries to be found in the latter, exceed those of the former; in which real evil is more scarce, more supportable, and less enormous. Yet we wish to see the earth peopled; to accomplish the happiness of kingdoms, which is said to consist in numbers. Gracious God! to what end is the introduction of so many beings into a mode of existence in which they must grope amidst as many errors, commit as many crimes, and meet with as many diseases, want, and sufferings!"[17]

Jefferson did not like to formally endorse the refusal of civilization. However, in some deeper levels of his psychological life, he must have acknowledged the truth of the idea. Life lived and actual experience can easily give rise to "contradictions" that an artificial thinking mind—or a philosopher—

cannot tolerate. Life is not a question of being faithful to *one* set of ideas or to *one* discourse. There is probably nothing improper in the assertion that Jefferson, simultaneously, spoke the language of optimism, that he believed in the hopeful future, in industry, technology, and modernity, and that he avowed the equivalence between civilization and corruption. Of course, he did not reject civilization in the form of an articulated philosophical doctrine that he explicitly endorsed, but rather he nurtured this critique in the form of impressions that, quite often, he grudgingly betrayed. In this sense he was neither Benjamin Rush nor the poet Crèvecoeur. His negative words somehow escaped him, and the conscious level of his psychological life was not always censorious enough.

Let me use a metaphor. If we dig into the darkest levels of Jefferson's philosophy, we discover rich veins of dissatisfaction. These veins were what substantiated his language of pessimism and were a constant in Jefferson's life. "What a field of slaughter does [our country] exhibit," he commented in 1804. In the 1780s, beneath his optimism and outside the realm of his public roles, Jefferson's grievances about America's departure from the "good" pattern were already simmering. To Washington, as has been noted, he had already admitted that the course of events was going in unwelcome directions. Events were determined by uncontrollable forces beyond the reach of human hope, forces nobody could foil, acting as a fate: "All the world is becoming commercial." Whether his words expressed despair about human hopes in general or simply about what Jefferson the eighteenth-century Virginia planter wished for America, it is clear that he was grasping the difference between his ideals and real historical development. A follower of the Enlightenment, he was quite realistic and lucid in his appraisal of the course of history. Were it practicable to impress a different direction to American history, we would have already made that decision, Jefferson was telling Washington. But relying on the favored alternative was tantamount to speculating.[18]

The factual reasons for despondency were, of course, manifold. The Missouri Crisis, we have seen, provided one excellent reason. Similarly, Jefferson could easily draw from the anti-Federalist repertoire and linger on jeremiad-like mourning of the growth of luxury and the departure from the simple life. However, in no sense was Jefferson's pessimism entirely determined by external or occasional events. It was neither wholly motivated by facts, nor by age and biology, nor was it a tribute that from time to time he paid to the anti-Federalist line-up. The old anti-Federalist adage that speculation produced the banks, and the banks had spoiled the country, was superficiality, a motto, a slogan. I am not maintaining that Jefferson could not have been seduced by this form of un-thought. Anti-Federalist slogans had something of an aristocratic ring, a high-brow scornfulness that would have appealed to him.

In spite of this, Jefferson's despondency stemmed from the more secret and enduring suspicion that events do not proceed, have not proceeded, along "rational" and hopeful patterns. Necessity would be maneuvering behind the scene. In other words, Jefferson's pessimism echoed his negative philosophy of time that, in turn, echoed his negative philosophy of nature.

In the 1780s, Jefferson the prophet of the Enlightenment already ruminated that history was not the embodiment of reason or desires, that it was not the servant of the unconditioned. We find the same opinion even in the 1790s and well into the new century. A man of the Enlightenment, he had the insight that historical time was not an ascending line, let alone a preordered plan that would help America thrive. On the contrary, deep in his mind, Jefferson saw time as the necessary march from life to death, or from self-possession to dispossession. It was the perception of this fatal change from self-possession to dispossession, portraying the life-cycle of the American republic, that formed the real root of Jefferson's pessimistic discourse.

Several leaders feared the bank and the novelty it represented. A number of them were actually frightened by the "discovery" that fellow Americans had become dogged advocates of a "despicable" trend. In the 1820s, Jefferson mourned the prospect of the loss of "real" values, those in accord with his way of understanding wealth, and their substitution with what to him was just "nominal" gain. "At home things are not well," he wrote to Albert Gallatin. "The flood of paper money, as you well know, had produced an exaggeration of nominal prices." Andrew Jackson, as Richard Slotkin writes in this respect, "was, for Jefferson, the type of this rising class, and he regarded Jackson as a sinister figure: a border warrior without Boone's philosophic restraint, who had scrapped his way from low estate to membership in the slaveholding class, but who remained a frontier brawler, duelist, speculator, and demagogue." What was undeniable was that Jackson refused to adapt his manners and morals to the high-brow standards of Jefferson's way of envisioning republican culture. But the fact that the new class of leaders seemed to Jefferson to be motivated exclusively by the urge to exploit resources, and limited only by their self-interest, did not mean that Jefferson was right in deeming that the new generations were simply outlaws.[19]

It is extremely difficult if not impossible to demonstrate whether or not the nightmare of a nation dominated by anticitizens, namely, by border warriors and frontier brawlers devoted to the mere transfer of money, had become a reality. Jackson seemed the prototype of the person incapable of planning beyond the short term and industrious only in the wicked sense of one who is driven by the urge of financial success. Nevertheless, we are walking on an unsteady terrain, and what seems nominal to one individual—or to one epoch—is extremely real to another.

The old Jefferson could promptly recognize in the emerging class, represented by Jackson, downright advocates of localism and short-termism and a
bunch of individualist money-seekers because the language of despondency
was already operative in his psyche. A code to interpret the signals of an unwelcome America was long in use. We are not dealing with sudden discoveries and an unexpected disappointment. Since the 1780s, Jefferson had been
willing to let his friends know his private suspicions that the world around
him was slowly but inexorably becoming a barbarian world of which he had
never dreamed. His dualistic obsession with "border warriors," "frontier
brawler[s]," "rivers of blood," "scenes of havoc and horror," and "our original
barbarism," as he eloquently said to Madame de Tessé, dates back to Jefferson
in his forties, when Jackson was but a boy. "What a field of slaughter does
[our country] exhibit," he commented in 1804; "What is called civilization
seems to have no other effect on him [man] than to teach him to pursue the
principle of bellum omnium in omnia on a larger scale," he said in 1797;
"All the world is becoming commercial," Jefferson maintained as far back as
1784.

The American republic was actually becoming "commercial," and worst
of all, in his deeds as a public man, Jefferson had helped the transition to the
new social order. Like his Federalist foes, he had responded favorably to the
new economic opportunities opening before America. Scholars have demonstrated that Jefferson accepted the fundamental economic premises that
served to rationalize the nascent capitalism. From practice to beliefs the gap
can actually be huge: his active advocacy of capitalism did not thwart his
sense of being swamped by the "commercial" North.[20]

The fear of having been abused by the northern agenda was characteristic
of the multifaceted philosophy of this atypical "westerner" and self-styled
"mountain man." Although he never went beyond the Shenandoah Valley, he
always maintained close emotional ties with those peripheral areas and with
the way of life and the symbols he was sure those "young" men represented:
the very embodiment of the principle that the highest level of freedom is
the freedom to help oneself, to decide for oneself, to be the *master* of one's
own sphere of activity. Jefferson actively worked to convey to the eyes of his
contemporaries the image of himself as "an obscure youth of the American
forest," as he was labeled in the 1830s. Since he presented himself as despairing about the North's copying the "corrupt" economic models of England,
he wanted to be seen as looking to the West and the South as the future of
American republicanism.[21]

Jefferson always had clear in his mind that any Hamiltonian doctrine intended to create an "American System"—the formation of an integrated econ-

omy based on a national bank, protective tariffs for large-scale production, and federally funded programs of improvements to boost a national market (canals, turnpikes, and so on)—represented a perversion of the principle of self-government. The reason for his aversion is apparent. Hamiltonianism increased the level of mutual dependence and thus impaired the principle that freedom is the power to help oneself, to be uninhibited by subordination to external agents, to decide for oneself against external constraints, to be free of the fluctuations represented by a growing national and international market, to share in the power of the government, and to be an operative agent—the real master—in the process of making and executing decisions. Hamiltonianism, for Jefferson, was despicable, as it wanted to put a stop to the freedom to fix the conditions and the rules under which the control of the territory and of the subordinate classes took place. Jefferson must have realized that "a society in which every man is subservient to every other man, because dependent on him for any means of judging his own existence," as Pocock writes, "is corrupt within the accepted meaning of the word, in a very special way and to a very high degree."[22]

Jefferson was enlightened enough to recognize that the North represented the embodiment of what the republic was going to become once it was old. Hamiltonianism, with its allegiance to growing complexity and mutual dependence, was a truthful prophecy about America's last phases: clear signals showed that interconnectedness and "subservience"—the direct refutation of republican *vita activa* as seen from the eye of a Virginia master—were inexorably approaching. On the other hand, it was also apparent that the cultural and economic models represented by Virginia were on the verge of failure. Virginia itself was not so young. A sense of ripeness, of decay, decadence, and ennui, was widespread even in Jefferson's beloved "country." As Wood puts it aptly, "Jefferson's turning inward was matched by a relative decline in the place of Virginia in the union. Decay was everywhere in early nineteenth-century Virginia, and Jefferson felt it at Monticello."[23]

The impression that republican Virginians and in general the post-Revolutionary South were living in an old society was recounted by numerous travel reports. These reports, Thomas Clark wrote,

> far from conveying the feeling of a fluid new society taking a fresh start in a bustling, hopeful new land, seem to leave the opposite picture. Those writers who stayed any length of time portray a rather settled and elegant social life and an economy ridden by the problems of old communities. The South of the late eighteenth century was tardy in repairing the ravages of war. Its fields were invaded by imported and domestic

pests and diseases; worn out and eroded, they were being abandoned. There were already signs of the depletion of the forests. The towns, although losing trade to more aggressive rivals, had problems of housing and sanitation. Almost the only college seemed to have lost hope as well as merit. Ripeness and decay show through the traveler's pages.[24]

For decades Jefferson must have gathered evidence to confirm his suspicion that the historical course was unavoidably going from self-possession to dispossession, and from youth to old age. It was definitely not the Missouri Crisis that triggered his feeling that the citizens of the American republic had moved from the freedom to decide for themselves to the constraint of being dependent on others for values, ideas, goods, possibilities, and any means of judging their own existence. Jefferson's acknowledgment that the march of civilization was heading toward mutual dependence and, hence, dispossession cannot be understood separately from his continuous laments over the emergence of "interests."

It had been clear for decades that events were inexorably producing a new kind of human beings, ones who were slave to their own interests. The dependent citizen would be a "private" man who would be compelled to jostle for his own advantage, passions, and desires. In the short run, this decadent citizen would replace those republican and independent young masters who had no interests of their own to seek and with whom Jefferson aligned himself ever since his well-known praise for "cultivators." That praise did not express an abstract preference for agriculture and an abstract disdain for commerce and industry. The conflict between agriculture and industry is a false one, and Jefferson was never worried about industry, commerce, and capitalism per se. However, the citizens that the Hamiltonian order was producing were able to stir Jefferson's deepest sense of powerlessness.

That citizen would no longer be a master and a "cultivator," and not because agriculture would no longer be the basis of the economic structure, or because farmers and landowners would disappear from the scene. The fact is that Jefferson was convinced that an anthropological decay was poisoning the very seat upon which republicanism rested. American farmers, just like all other "private" men, would participate in the commodity market and would become dependent upon external constraints, just as the elderly are dependent on their canes. Like every other man, the "cultivator" would crave money in order to purchase manufactured goods, to fulfill contrived needs, and to satisfy artificial desires.

During his lifetime Jefferson beheld a process of dissolution of the original order and was quite an "active" spectator in the transition from the society of masters to the nineteenth-century society of common and private men. The transformation of a noncapitalist economy to a capitalist one entailed the disappearance of the independent, disinterested, self-possessed young citizen. The creation of integrated markets, the formation of a transportation system linking local, regional, national, and international markets, the hiring of substantial wage labor, price convergence, and the purchase of urban manufactured goods were clear signals of a transformation of the revolutionary agenda that had subordinated trade to consumption and, once again, dependence to independence. This process of aging identified a growing struggle, of which the protagonists usually were unaware, between "westerners" like Jefferson, who saw development and growth through limited access to regional markets, economic independence, and total control over their household, and the new "interested" men who were the byproduct of an integrated and interdependent market. It was a slow and irreversible process. The "people" who won the Revolution—those same "people" with whom Jefferson allied himself—used their newfound power to sustain their independence, which was embedded in the production of goods by members for consumption *and* trade, in this precise order. Over the decades Jefferson had gathered evidence to sustain his impression that an aged man had replaced independence with interests, and consumption with trade.[25]

It is extremely difficult to locate a precise threshold and to say when the change from consumption to trade, from youth to maturity, and from independence to "dependence" took hold in America. It may be impossible to say when Jefferson was compelled to bow to Hamilton's prophetic views. What is certain is that Jefferson beheld and to a certain extent also helped bring about this slow and inexorable transformation, and he was informed by it. At some point, however, he must have acutely felt he had no other choice but to adapt his vision of an export-centered, youthful republic—one that, as McCoy puts it, "would escape to the greatest possible extent the adverse effects of social development through time"—to the new priority of a nationwide, large-scale production. Jefferson did not bewail the alleged transition from republicanism to liberalism. He simply grasped the necessity of aging and identified signals that America had already entered the last phase. Undoubtedly, neither Jefferson nor Madison nor other Jeffersonians yielded completely to pessimism and despair. However, it was impossible for them not to realize that the society they had labored so long to secure was just a phase. They could not ignore that the independent farmers, owners of household manufactures, were clearly condemned by the process of time that leads toward the general increase of the level of "dependence."[26]

Jefferson was not shocked by the Missouri Crisis, nor did he become a

pessimist because old age affected a radical transformation in his whole character, or because at a certain moment he realized that his confidence in the
people was, to say the least, mistaken. Jefferson *progressively* lowered his self-
censorship, and with increased frequency, he discussed with his friends his
realistic insight into the course, or curse, of America's aging. At least from
the time he wrote Washington that all the world was becoming commercial,
Jefferson knew what civilization meant and what were its costs. The naturalist had collected evidence to buttress his feelings that old age was inexorably
approaching. The move toward a society dominated by Jacksonian "ordinary
people," the emergence of the mass society spreading uncontrolled in all directions, an "egalitarian" society, namely, a society dominated by a new elite
class with very pecuniary interests, precipitated eighteenth-century elites into
pessimism. "No wonder those of the Founding Fathers who lived on into the
early decades of the nineteenth century," Gordon Wood writes, "expressed
anxiety over what they had wrought. Although they usually tried to put as
good a face as they could on what was happening, they were bewildered, un-
easy, and in some cases deeply disillusioned. Indeed, a pervasive pessimism, a
fear of failure runs through the later writings of the Founding Fathers."[27]

Independence was the keyword of the youthful republic, but Jefferson
had always been caught in a drama. He simultaneously upheld the idea of a
modernization of the American economy while trying to avert its northern
aberration, heading toward old age and the increase of "dependence." At the
same time, he must have realized that "dependence" was the core of progress, not just a northerner aberration. Dreaming of a modern country meant
to *exclude* the possibility that industrious and independent citizens-masters
could remain young forever, marketing their surpluses in Europe, developing
household manufactures, and purchasing abroad the finer goods they desired.
The drama is that Jefferson at once yearned for adulthood and was frightened
by the biological cycle entailed in the process of coming of age.

Jefferson, in other words, was torn between his approval of commerce,
manufacture, and industry as subservient to his vision of republicanism, and
the acknowledgment that the hope of industry, manufacture, and commerce
as subservient to something else (agriculture, for instance, or Virginia's interests as well) was antihistorical. Jefferson's drama was that he envisioned
modernization—of which in general and "philosophically" he approved—as
at once the buttress of independence and the main cause of the increase of
"dependence." Did Jefferson really believe that modernization could protect
(southern) farmers and let them trade their surpluses abroad while forestalling
development based on the national production of superfluities and a growing
internal market? Did Jefferson ever really believe that foreign demand for the
(southern) agricultural surplus would in perpetuity be high enough to permit

the majority of American workers to be self-possessed, employed on the land, and young?

This philosopher of the Enlightenment and prophet of technology was acquainted with the unavoidable prospect of a future shaped according to a new social order, disrespectful of Virginian hierarchies and priorities. Jefferson liked technology, capitalism, industry, modernity, and progress. But he mostly liked the idea that eminent generals *should* be in control of events. Jefferson's vision of progress did not speak of shifting social currents and masses to be treated by statistics. The fact that nineteenth-century society was increasingly shaped by a chaotic multiplicity of busy private persons chasing their desires and rescued from aristocratic restraint does not prove that Jefferson planned to make an assault on old elites, causing the dispersion of authority. Jefferson's obsession with reason, control, order, and natural aristocracy and his *peculiar* passion for measuring, weighing, observing, recording, cooking, gardening, and, in general, for every form of culture, betray a deep fear of social revolution, a fear of losing control. In his vision, capitalism and industry were not to be a radical alternative to the organization of agricultural production that he was trying to devise, but rather were its most obvious enlargement. Industrialism and progress were expected to stabilize the power structure.[28]

Arthur Schlesinger Jr. recently observed that "history is the best antidote to illusions of omnipotence and omniscience. It should forever remind us of the limitations of our passing perspectives. It should strengthen us to resist the pressures to convert momentary interests into moral absolutes. It should lead us to a profound and chastening sense of our frailty as human beings—to a recognition of the fact, so often and so sadly demonstrated, that the future will outwit all our certitudes." That history will outwit, and has outwitted, all certitudes was entrenched in Jefferson's thought. He was a good historian, in a way, and a good historian is acquainted with the idea of necessity. A good historian knows impossibility also. Jefferson learned that kind of lesson from history, and when in the 1820s he realized he was cast off by the same modernization and adulthood for which he had craved and that he had helped to establish, he could promptly recognize his failure. Passivity, frailty, and transience had long since been the habitual discourses through which he portrayed his life. This modernizer and ambitious conqueror recognized that every conquest will be in turn conquered.[29]

We should not expect that Jefferson would gush in a flood of "existentialist" declarations and open assertions of discontent with the future he foresaw. Direct assertions are not the only way to give legitimacy to the claim that Jefferson, from his youth, knew the language of despondency and that his mind was familiar with the realm of impossibilities. Public assertions of hopeless-ness, Arthur Dudden wrote, "reveal an emotional frame of mind which to other persons might better be concealed as unmanly or unpatriotic if not defeatist or downright un-American." There is no doubt that Jefferson tried to conceal, not always successfully, those discourses that reveal passivity, help-lessness, wariness, or hopelessness.[30]

For years he had presented himself as a general firmly in command, an ambitious man fully confident in the success of his venture, and we like to portray him that way. Constrained by his public roles, he was convinced he had no other choice but to try to become a source of inspiration to others. Jefferson was undoubtedly successful in the promotion of his own image as a modern, optimistic man. Maybe too successful given that "success" is still the main lens through which we tend to look at him. Success tolerates temporary setbacks and mistakes, of course. Historians who often make allowances for Jefferson's mistakes are thoroughly fascinated by the idea that Jefferson was an achiever, a man convinced of his personal victory. Those who are capti-vated by his monumental achievements tend naturally to overlook Jefferson's helplessness, even when they admit his big mistakes—slavery, Sally Hemings, the embargo, his financial debt. But the well-established tendency to turn Jefferson into an achiever does not mean that he did not cultivate the im-age of himself as a weak man, defeated by all-powerful events, beaten by the course of events, and wrapped up in that famous "mantle of resignation."

Not only success, but passivity, impotence, and resignation were also tropes that Jefferson normally employed in relating the story of his life. Not infrequently he stressed his role as an inactive passenger in the ship of state or on the voyage of life. As Charles Miller acutely argues, passivity was prob-ably the mode Jefferson always favored most. "No matter which variety of the metaphor he deploys," Miller writes, "we find a good deal of passivity in Jefferson's expression. He is a mere passenger aboard the ship of state and on the voyage of life." Whether it was "the" favorite mode or just a mode among others and a discourse among other discourses, it is indisputable that since his youth Jefferson had employed an antiheroic way of portraying his person. "Antiheroic" carries an emphasis on his being a mere "passenger in our bark." Passivity, impotence, or despondency—the very opposite of stubborn opti-mism and self-satisfaction—undoubtedly had an impact on Jefferson's phi-losophy. It is not an easy task for the historian to find such negative language within the narrative of a life of successes. Negativity is usually well hidden. However, recognizing the presence of a deep-running tide of despondency is of paramount importance in giving a realistic portrait of this sanguine, enlightened, and realistic worshipper of the future.[31]

As previously stated, open declarations of pessimism are not the only evidence that Jefferson acknowledged the realm of impossibilities as a real limit to human potential, and that he regulated his behavior and his spirit accordingly. That his life was also informed by the language of despondency and that he conveyed an image of himself as a meek creature defeated by all-powerful events and outwitted by time can be argued from his constant yearning for shelter and his characteristic worship of home. Home, "the only scene where, for me, the sweeter affections of life have any exercise," had a paramount importance in Jefferson's philosophy. Such a worship seems significantly at odds with the conventional reading of Jefferson as a man of the world and a victorious general.[32]

In the previous chapter I argue that Jefferson's life is the best refutation of the myth that Americans are disconnected, abstract, mobile, and superior to place. This conqueror and man at the helm was characteristically a domestic creature always craving protection and willing to return home. Home, not the state, the world, or the country, was for Jefferson the only place secured from time in which mortals can dwell, at least momentarily. A traveler, he was trapped in a chronic search for residence and for stability to counteract an unbearable sense of impermanence. He went optimistically onward, in the large world, but his most enduring desire was always to return, to retire.

The oppositions between dwelling and traveling, as well as those between permanence and transience, or between belonging and passing, are distinctive of Jefferson and mirror the dualism between his hope in a remedy and his recognition of a mortal malady. In 1787, Jefferson wrote Dr. George Gilmer from Paris, one among his good neighbors in Albemarle County, already expressing his (home)sickness: "I am as happy no where else and in no other society," he wrote, "and all my wishes end, where I hope my days will end, at Monticello. Too many scenes of happiness mingle themselves with all the recollections of my native woods and feilds, to suffer them to be supplanted in my affection by any other. I consider myself here as a traveler only, and not a resident." Outwitted by the passing of time, deluded by progress, made dependent by the forces of the market, for Jefferson the "native woods and feilds" became the residual locus for self-possession. Whoever looks romantically back at the native dimension is implicitly drifting away from an optimistic stance. Jefferson's life-long obsession with "retiring" has something to do with a desperate search for self-possession and, hence, with a certain amount of pessimism as to the actual chances a given generation has to realize itself in history. The transformation from a passive and static domesticity to a fully forward-looking and "modern" life was never complete.[33]

Jefferson dealt repeatedly with residual values. To regain the only viable opportunity to get back his youth and the hope of self-possession, he often looked back; in doing so, there was much he had to abandon. Dreaming of home, in the way Jefferson did, meant to not fully trust the march of civilization. An exclusive community and a society of peers, Monticello reflected Jefferson's yearning to create an enclosed and protected place. Monticello was a kind of aristocratic nest or bosom, a residual space that would fit the fears of a despondent man and counteract the forces of necessity. Monticello meant a small rural scheme, a geographically limited place for the benefit of a little community that, as an island, was in the boisterous sea of events. World and events are, thus, essential to Monticello in the sense that they are its negative counterparts and form the uncanny ocean where aspirations could never thrive. In this sense, Monticello is the symbol of the true Epicurean garden: a compromise, a symbol of philosophical renunciation and an "asylum from grief."[34]

Monticello is the clearest demonstration that Jefferson spoke languages that were locked in the past and that lingered on a vague nostalgia about what was passing and missing. In effect, by means of his narratives of Monticello, Jefferson gave voice to the aristocratic Epicurean—a pessimist by definition—craving for his little and exclusive community and for the "solace of our friends." This backward-looking desire fits very well with a life lived according to a pessimistic language: life is smoother if and only if a little community succeeds in insulating itself from the troubled world. The pessimistic story holds that life should be adjusted to the idea of insulation, and that life is an unremitting quest for shelter. Optimism, modernity, confidence in humanity, and a modern sense of projection toward the future do not portray the whole of Jefferson's philosophy. Seized by a premodern selfishness, Jefferson esteemed family, friends, and property above universal and philosophical standards such as country or humanity. Time and again, Jefferson showed no philosophical love for humanity. He was often disloyal to the universalism of the *philosophes* and, somewhat tragically, to himself. His very idea of friendship was habitually highly selective and, consequently, premodern.

Friendship was not based on a moral instinct, on eighteenth-century sympathy, on humans who were supposedly friends to every other human. Jefferson's idea of friendship was rather the cavalier's club. Accordingly, a conflict existed in Jefferson's philosophy between a modern notion of public property and the idea that only propertied peers could enjoy friendship. While Jefferson was trying to convince Madison to buy land on which to settle down near Monticello, he made clear that "*agreeable* society is the first essential in constituting the happiness and of course the value of our existence." "Agreeable" is a key term for every aristocrat. Not society per se, but a selected guild enticed Jefferson's refined taste. When, in a previous letter to Madison, Jefferson remarked that "with *such a society* I could once more venture home and lay myself up for the residue of life," he once again referred clearly to his peers: not society in general, but "such a society." Small properties and little towns, where people live in aristocratic retirement and rural simplicity, from which to regard the boisterous sea beyond, were for Jefferson the best conditions to exert the "good" art of life reminiscent of a long-lost, young society.[35]

Whereas ambition and a sense of yearning are signs of modernity, in several texts speaking of Monticello Jefferson put forward a non-ambitious worldview. At home Jefferson became just a typical man of his own generation. It was not unusual for him to be centered on the prospect of an aristocratic domestic "tranquility," turning away from the idea of coming of age, despite the fact that throughout his life he had been actively engaged in promoting hope and progress. In this sense, Monticello is the best demonstration that not all the layers of Jefferson's philosophy converged in a desire to go onward and upward. Jefferson's hilltop allowed him to step back from the modern trust in endless possibilities and to maintain his allegiance to a less dynamic worldview. As should be clear, I am not alluding to an "either/or" perspective; that either Jefferson was an exponent of the Enlightenment, of optimism and modernity, or he must have been a one-sided pessimistic advocate of an older "good" society. Similarly, Jefferson's doctrine that "those who labour in the earth are the chosen people of God" did not mean that he should have refused to advocate "farms as productive units" or rejected productivity and large-scale agriculture. This well-known Jeffersonian tenet, just like his desire to dash home, was simply a vindication of the ideal of self-possession and one outcome of his struggle with "dependence" and the forces of necessity operating in the world.[36]

While Jefferson optimistically trusted the future, he also betrayed a sense of standing outside any "glorious and progressive" course of time. The fact that Jefferson unquestionably was a man of the Enlightenment did not prevent him from acknowledging that human ventures were impossible to achieve, and from seeing retirement as the only feasible chance for one generation to be content. His prospect of the future as a movement onward, upward, and forward for a society that could not be smaller than humanity as a whole existed alongside a desire for a self-contained society of peers.

Jefferson's optimism joined the sorrow of one who realistically knew that no happiness could be found outside a limited community, and for a limited span of time. Visions of the big world coexisted, paradoxically perhaps, with concurrent visions of the little world and residual values. This Enlighten-

ment devotee had always been biased toward a peculiar version of the premodern "Good Society." Moreover, Jefferson was biased toward the "Good
Society" because he was always aware of what despondency meant, and of
the role of the negative in the course of human lives. Given that modernity
and maturity headed necessarily toward "dependence" and becoming an interchangeable part of a nation-wide network, Jefferson resisted that inescapable turn and avowed his deep allegiance to self-possession and youth. While
Americans had to learn to become disconnected, abstract, mobile, universal,
and superior to place and generations, Jefferson resisted this dimension of
American identity. Components of frustration, failure, and defeat associated
with his retreat into premodern habits did not prevent Jefferson from striking
progressive tones. "Getting on" was not a standard from which Jefferson de-
viated accidentally. Likewise, he did not become a pessimist at some point in
his life. On the contrary, Jefferson's philosophy was consistently an unstable
compound of progressive and conservative, forward and backward, universal
and particular, optimistic and despondent beliefs and discourses.

6

Dream, Imagination, & Expediency

FROM HOPE TO DREAM

Thomas Jefferson dealt extensively in hope, but what is the exact boundary between hoping and dreaming? Between hope and self-deception? As a hopeful man, Jefferson knew anxiety; he knew the unyielding law of necessity; he knew, as well, impossibility and pessimism. It is likewise legitimate to expect that, to some extent at least, he recognized that his hopes might have been no more than daydreams. Jefferson was a creature of hope, but might he also have been a deluded man? This question forms the content of the present chapter.

In general terms, the difference between hope and dream or between hope and self-deception is embarrassingly slender. Hope, of course, does not stem from the certainty that an eventual success is awaiting. In fact, there cannot be real hope for those who know from the start they are going to be victorious. Nor does real hope stem from evidence readily available, like flowers ready to be gathered. Hope is rather an assault on the present and against existing evidence. Just like despair, it is a refusal of the present, but one animated by the heart. Those who hope see the existing world, in its present state, as a kind of failure and a minus, unacceptable, intolerable, excruciating. Hope stems from the knowledge, not of eventual success, but of the appalling fact that the world-as-it-is is fallen. The only knowledge that is implicit in the act of hoping is, thus, that the present does not offer reliable clues that "everything will be all right." The garden from where the flowers are plucked is an imagined garden. Hope does not stem from present evidence or from the certainty of success. Hoping is setting out for an exotic land. In a word, hope stems from imagination or, better, from a *desperate* reaction of imagination.

If so, once again, what is the difference between hoping and dreaming? Between Jefferson-as-a-creature-of-hope and Jefferson-as-a-creature-of-dream? In both cases, visions and imagination abound and conspire to dethrone the present.

Imagination had an enormously important role in the style Jefferson usually adopted to approach reality. Jefferson's reality was usually filtered through images. To outline the argument that is discussed throughout this chapter, let me start with an example drawn from politics.

Jefferson was a life-long foe of Federalist policies severely thwarting citizens' *vita activa*. The desirability of *vita activa* and, hence, ingenuity on the part of the people was one of Jefferson's central visions. Another, one of his most famous, was that people "are" trustworthy, and, therefore, "democracy" to a great extent is a good word. Jefferson trusted self-government because all his life he had been convinced that in the last analysis "republic"—this term "of very vague application in every language," to borrow his words—meant democracy. "It means a government by its citizens in mass, acting directly and personally, according to rules established by the majority." Jefferson had always seen something good in the possibility of a majority rule. Every government is more or less republican, as Jefferson explained, "in proportion as it has in its composition more or less of this ingredient of the direct action of the citizens." Jefferson could not help allowing that a pure democracy is severely restrained, for instance, "to very narrow limits of space and population." Nonetheless, that special ingredient that alone is able to turn a government into a real government *by* the people should always be looked after. The "direct and constant control by the citizens" was always something highly desirable, and Jefferson was never wary of appealing to that democratic principle.[1]

Of course, the excesses of democracy must be feared, as Jacobinism demonstrated, but they must be feared less than the prospect of losing that "ingredient" completely. This is the typical Jeffersonian conception: that people were to be trusted and entrusted. Like every vision, this one could not be drawn *from* evidence. Instead, evidence comes second. One has necessarily to follow the guide of imagination to find a direction among colliding masses of inconsequential details. Imagination tells what one has to look for, what one should keep track of, what should be placed in the forefront and what relegated to the background. It is imagination alone that turns a heap of insignificant cases, irrelevant details, and unimportant exceptions into full evidence for a convincing case. Evidence of people's trustworthiness can be gathered—as Jefferson inescapably did—only when, from the outset, one is enthused by a definite vision that "the mass of the citizens is the safest depository of their own rights."[2]

It was Jefferson's imagination that taught him that people as such are trustworthy and that the democratic seed must be sown. Jefferson's visions allowed him, for instance, to confess to Jeremiah Moore his "great confidence in the common sense of mankind in general." Given all this, we should not forget that eighteenth-century imagination, by and large, desired to differentiate republicanism from democracy. The prevalent view contradicted the Jeffersonian vision of a mass of people who in general are "endowed by nature with rights, and with an innate sense of justice," as Jefferson wrote in 1823. Eighteenth-century imagination preferred to advocate some kind of paternalism. The norm was that imagination prompted late eighteenth-century American leaders to create a government *with* the people, not *by* the people acting directly and personally, because the people, as such, was usually presented as a ghastly foundation.[3]

Baron Montesquieu, an inspirational figure for eighteenth-century American political beliefs, made clear that "republic" was the main category of government portraying authority as resting *with* the multitude. But he did not venture into open eulogy of a government by the people, like Jefferson's. Montesquieu maintained that "the common people, tho' capable of calling others to an account for their administration, are incapable of the administration themselves. . . . The action of the common people is always either too remiss or too violent." That some form of aristocracy should be preferred seemed an apparent truth to the majority of intellectuals. As a consequence, a pure democracy, namely, a direct rule *by* the citizens (the one Jefferson often upheld), seemed highly unrepublican, the populace being exclusively interested in pursuing their own parochial interests. As a rule, their imaginative vision taught Americans, and Europeans as well, that democracy would be an ineffective and unlikely means to govern the nation. If the purpose is to govern with the people and not to be dictated to by the people, a nation should take care to erect a number of shelters to protect itself from democratic frenzies. To reduce, for instance, the democratic potential of the Articles of Confederation by producing the Constitution and enhancing the filters on the powers of the ordinary citizenry appeared to many leaders as urgent as erecting a solid barrier against a dangerous lurking anarchy.[4]

At the same time as Jefferson imparted to John Taylor the democratic lesson that the House of Representatives was the "purest republican feature in the government" because it was chosen by the people directly and frequently, other leaders were guided by the vision that universal suffrage and direct election of officials would be a hallmark of anarchy, as John Adams contended in his "Thoughts on Government" (1776). Not that, in absolute terms, Adams's vision was correct while Jefferson's was wrong, or vice versa. The point I am trying to make is that eighteenth-century imagination inspired Americans with a number of contrasting guiding images, at times "democratic" and more often "aristocratic." Furthermore, it was from the viewpoint provided by imagination that, as a norm, evidence pro and con the people was assembled.[5]

The imagination of the time generated both the Jeffersonian vision that the government by the people is highly promising and the paternalistic vision that sought to check daydreamers by preventing unicameralism and extolling separation of powers along with checks and balances. Several Americans were persuaded by their imagination that if the purpose was to safeguard the public interest, there was no alternative except to secure the national government against the more "democratic" state legislatures. Anti-Jeffersonian visions were abundant in the period. After the unsuccessful attempt to convince the Constitutional Convention of the dangers of allowing the state legislatures to elect the senate, James Madison set out from Philadelphia with the apprehension that not even this Constitution would efficiently *"answer* its *national object* nor prevent the local *mischiefs* which every where *excite disgusts* against the *state governments."*[6]

Anti-Jeffersonian visions endowed some leaders with the fittest instrument for highlighting those "facts" that were customarily ignored or undermined by other leaders who complied with the Jeffersonian visions.

Shays' Rebellion, to provide a further example, seemed to some leaders the best illustration that people must not be trusted; that they were irrational, extravagant, passionate, degenerate, foolish, and unbearably "feminine." While some leaders considered Shays' Rebellion as the ultimate proof that popular demands must be curbed and the frightening swell of democracy must be curtailed, others imagined things in a very different way. "Yet where does this anarchy exist?" Jefferson asked. "Where did it ever exist, except in the single instance of Massachusets? And can history produce an instance of a rebellion so honourably conducted?" Jefferson was clearly conveying the idea that Shays' Rebellion was an imagined rebellion and that no importance should be credited to that episode. Anti-Jeffersonians were sure there was plenty of evidence to question Jefferson's "prejudice" in favor of the populace. Jefferson was analogously persuaded that it was just because delusion and hysteria had taken hold that some leaders could grieve over the "imminent" conflict between a besieged minority in power and the majority of an unrestrained and "womanly" populace. It was the way things were envisioned that allowed Jeffersonians and anti-Jeffersonians to decide whether Shays' Rebellion had only been an exceptional and irrelevant episode, a "single instance" as Jefferson termed it, or whether it was representative and of general consequence.[7]

Events were necessarily ambiguous because the United States, by its very nature, was (and still is) emotional and normative. It was born of visions. It was an invitation made in the hope that future generations would understand it and pursue the "hopeful" direction. As such the United States had an intrinsic normative feature. Everything in this country was emotionally charged and fictionalized, and nothing was a mere fact. There could not be an easy-to-see boundary between fact and fiction.

Writing to Jefferson at the time the rebellion in Massachusetts broke out, David Humphreys could not help grumbling about a baffling inconsistency, that "to judge by the face of the country; by the appearance of ease and plenty which are to be seen every where, one would believe a great portion of the poverty and evils complained of, must be imaginary." This is the real point, and Humphreys' comment should be taken as a guiding principle. Besides Shays' Rebellion, one can discover high degrees of fiction beneath, for instance, the "Revolution of 1800," the embargo and the "quasi-war" with England, beneath the Missouri Crisis, beneath the Essex Junto and several other "critical" moments that the new republic had to face over the decades.[8]

The role played by expectation and imagination was altogether enormous. Starting from the Revolution, American leaders brought to bear a utopian effort to reform nothing less than the whole *character* of American society. They did not expect to just tackle administrative, practical, and ordinary problems. They were involved with a greater narrative, the narrative of American salvation. Well before the Revolution, in the hope of "fabricating" their identity, Americans had fueled their imagination by delving into the literary texts that were easily available, first and foremost the Bible. Since colonial times, English men and women fostered images of America as hell on earth, but they also did not miss the chance to point out the way to transform the country into Eden. They at once provoked ominous images and compensatory counter-images. It was because Americans intended, as it were, to bring down to earth literary visions of peace, justice, and equilibrium, that they could repeatedly and seriously maintain that actual reality was unyielding and that everything was on the verge of failure. Expectations excite the imagination, and vice versa: an excited imagination produces motivations, ambitions, forward-moving stances but also countless grievances and an ominous fear of consequences.[9]

Americans, from the outset, relied on visions. As has been stated, they were involved in a utopian and literary effort to reform the whole character of American society. Literature was and still is endemic throughout American culture, not just a discipline within it. In this country, everything is and was literature. Americans were not just trying to fathom practical problems. They invented the literary narrative of American enduring practicality, which is a slightly different affair. By committing themselves to myth and utopia,

Americans set out for a risky venture. Perhaps, in so doing, they were complying with the style of the Enlightenment, which urged people to uproot
themselves, to set out on the appalling ocean surrounding the verdant land,
to develop a dualistic perspective, to imagine, and to see life as if it were
a novel. Much imagination is implied in this way of living. To recall once
again Robert Pogue Harrison, the Enlightenment "detaches the present from
tradition and projects it forward into an ideal secular future." If "the future
remains Enlightenment's true heritage," as Harrison correctly argued, imagination must play a crucial role.[10]

Whether Jeffersonian or anti-Jeffersonian, the whole late eighteenth-century American society chose to be committed to visions of betterment; no
matter what "betterment" meant, no matter whether the goal was envisioned
in the future or located in the past. Undoubtedly, American colonies fought
to preserve past liberties at least as much as to realize the vision of future
freedoms. To some extent at least, they seemed to draw inspiration from their
past. Almost all the colonies preserved into statehood the structure of gov-
ernance they had had before, and one could ask how much imagination entered into that work of "preservation."[11]

Imagination, the faculty that produces visions, is quite often a source of
empowerment and the very spring of human agency. This empowerment is
what the term "enlightenment" usually indicates. When triggered by hope
and buttressed by the energy of youth, imagination reveals cheerful prospects
and elicits a commitment to a desired goal.

Nevertheless, imagination can also play a contrary role by revealing one's
powerlessness. Each time imagination forsakes the comfort of hope, it becomes an evil instrument that reveals an unbearable void. Enlightenment, in
turn, implicitly unveiled a real void: the negative, as we have seen. Dreams
and visions stem from this basic ambiguity and, depending on the presence
or absence of rational energy, provoke very opposite effects. Visions empower,
but they can simultaneously be a synonym for unrealization, the sign of a
present failure. Still to be imagined? Still possible? Still to be enlightened?
Imagination is at once the art of making blueprints and the art of dreaming,
of preferring universal literary problems to practical ones. Blueprints apart,
imagination is also a strategy of denial of the world as it is. When successful,
imagination reveals and makes a new reality. When unsuccessful, it tells the
story of the looming void, or to put it another way, it reveals the naked fact
that the dreamer is a dreamer.

In everyday life, quite often, a moment comes when visions reveal their
hazy nature. When Jefferson grew old, he began to admit publicly that "mine,
after all, may be an Utopian dream, but being innocent, I have thought I

might indulge in it till I go to the land of dreams, and sleep there with the dreamers of all past and future times." Perhaps something similar happens to everyone. Perhaps at a certain point everyone endorses John Adams's famous motto, that life is "a Vapour, a Fog, a Dew." However, such an ordinary story becomes particularly intriguing when the main character is a man who, like Jefferson, always prided himself on having put his whole life under the banner of the Enlightenment. In old age, there is no doubt that Jefferson regarded his imagination as mere dreaming, but a more intriguing question is: are we beholding the ending phase of the very process of enlightenment? Its logical conclusion? Perhaps every Enlightenment devotee, if sincere, must develop this way.[12]

There is something of special value in Jefferson's sweeping acknowledgment that "the natural course of the human mind is certainly from credulity to skepticism," as he once said to Caspar Wistar. The last phase of one's enlightenment is probably a demythologization of the very faculty of imagination and the unpleasant revelation that imagination means fantasy and dream. Perhaps the Enlightenment had to turn into some form of Romanticism and reverse itself completely. It is because one has sincerely and ardently trusted his mission to enlighten that, when energies dissolve or circumstances become adverse, one must regard his dearest images as mere dreams, the ocean as ultimately unconquerable, and the void as the basic fact of human life. The Enlightenment devotee grows old but still uses his fading energy to announce a truth.[13]

On the demythologization of imagination that took place in Jefferson's later years, the scholar can write hundreds of pages. It is not uncommon to come across the Sage of Monticello equating imagination and wishful thinking. The two old philosophers, John Adams and Thomas Jefferson, produced striking examples of "existentialist" reflection. When Jefferson and Adams, in the spring of 1816, asked each other whether they would agree to live their life over again forever, their quasi-existentialist vein came freely to the surface, Adams's earlier, Jefferson's a little later. The letter Adams sent to Jefferson on 3 May 1816, to begin with, is a well-known masterpiece of the genre. It is an answer to the very different one Jefferson sent to Adams on 8 April where, instead, in a *too* typical Jeffersonian style, the discourse on hope was doggedly upheld. This typical Jeffersonian letter is a masterwork of conventionality and self-censorship, and it may have sounded irritating to Adams. "I think with you that it is a good world on the whole," Jefferson declared. "My temperament is sanguine. I steer my bark with Hope in the head, leaving Fear astern."[14]

Adams's famous letter to Jefferson of 3 May is a mocking response to Jefferson's conventionality. It is here that Adams tried, perhaps unintentionally, to shock Jefferson by affirming that human life is a "Vapour" and a "Boule de Savon." It is here that, with a very cunning irony, Adams poked fun at Jefferson. Let me cite a passage definitely worth a long quotation: "I admire your Navigation and should like to sail with you, either in your Bark or in my own, along side of yours; Hope with her gay Ensigns displayed at the Prow; fear with her Hobgoblins behind the Stern. Hope springs eternal; and Hope is all that endures. Take away hope and What remains? What pleasure? I mean. Take away Fear, and what Pain remains? 99/100ths of the Pleasures and Pains of Life are nothing but Hopes and Fears." Adams's conclusion is a real pearl: "All Nations, known in History or in travel have hoped, believed, an[d] expected a future and a better State. The Maker of the Universe, the Cause of all Things, whether We call it, *Fate* or *Chance* or God has inspired this Hope. If it is a *Fraud*, We shall never know it. We shall never resen[t] the Imposition, be grateful for the Illusion, not grieve for the disappointment. We shall be no more. Credat Grim, Diderot, Buffon, La Lande, Condorcet, D'Holbach, Frederick Catherine; Non Ego."[15]

Adams had no particular problems in demythologizing imagination. It was in line with the person everyone had known for decades. In contrast, Jefferson needed to be provoked to drop his self-censorship, but the Sage of Monticello seemed to readily accept the game. On 1 August, Jefferson sent Adams a letter that cannot clearly be defined as surreptitiously optimistic or openly pessimistic. It is probably a combination of the two. The ending is eloquent and marks an important step in Jefferson's painful march toward the acknowledgment of himself as a dreamer asleep in the land of dreamers. "I like the dreams of the future better than the history of the past," Jefferson said to Adams. However, the way the letter ends reveals Jefferson's acquaintance with the existential void and with imagination as essentially deceptive. One might expect that Jefferson would issue a typically Jeffersonian invitation, such as to build a greater and stronger nation. He seemed to retreat instead: "I like the dreams of the future better than the history of the past. So good night. I will dream on, always fancying that Mrs Adams and yourself are by my side marking the progress and the obliquities of ages and countries."[16]

As mentioned in the previous chapter, no real transformation occurred in Jefferson's character due to old age; more likely, old age simply allowed Jefferson an alibi to drop a self-censorship that he had tried to maintain all his life. Probably, in his old age, Jefferson felt entitled to declare a truth he had always known. For the historian, it is quite easy to detect that dreaming became a disquieting presence for Jefferson, while hope revealed its flatteries.

To Marbois, in 1817, Jefferson betrayed something more than a sense of presage. He no longer felt shame in announcing the futility of his worship of the future. Jefferson began in a typical Jeffersonian mood: "I have much confidence that we shall proceed successfully for ages to come, and that, contrary to the principles of Montesquieu, it will be seen that the larger the extent of country, the more firm its republican structure, if founded, not on conquest, but in principles of compact and equality. My hope of its duration is built much on the enlargement of the resources of life going hand in hand with the enlargement of territory, and the belief that men are disposed to live honestly, if the means of doing so are open to them." Indeed, nothing is more typical—until a complete but almost undetectable reversal of the tone occurs: "With the consolation of this belief in the future result of our labors, I have that of other prophets who foretell distant events, that I shall not live to see it falsified. My theory has always been, that if we are to dream, the flatteries of hope are as cheap, and pleasanter than the gloom of despair."[17]

This is the point: is it actually true that his theory has *always* been that the flatteries of hope are as cheap and more pleasant than the gloom of despair? Is that conditional sentence beginning with "if we are to dream" typically Jeffersonian? What about the reduction of hope to flattery? Did Jefferson always know that the future was just a consoling dream, and Americans had no special reasons to be optimistic? Is it actually Jeffersonian to allow that he preferred to be optimistic because optimism was as cheap and more pleasant than the gloom of despair? Maybe yes, maybe no. It depends on whether we believe or not Jefferson's "my theory has always been" statement. More interesting is the fact that we are here watching the reversal of a jeremiad. Such a reversal is the way imagination is demythologized. Jefferson started with vaunted optimism ("I have much confidence") and ended in the equation of hoping and dreaming, or wishful thinking. According to the jeremiad-like argument, one should exhibit pessimism first in order eventually to foster optimism and hope. Jefferson, instead, unequivocally asserted that he was in the same position as those prophets who foretold something that could not be disproved, and that he was expecting the worst to happen while dreaming for the best.

Jefferson-the-dreamer became his most characteristic stance in the early 1820s. This is understandable, as has been said, but the change is meaningful nonetheless. Let me provide a couple of further examples. With William Short, on 4 August 1820, Jefferson shared his most secret helplessness. While fancying "a cordial fraternization among all the American nations," he openly yielded to a biblical dream: "The lion and the lamb, within our regions, shall lie down together in peace." Jefferson's capacity for real hope or self-censorship did not fade entirely; neither did he completely abide by his tenet that the human mind goes from credulity to skepticism. He continued to use the discourse on hope and trusted his imagination until the end of his life, up to his very last letters. However, it is easy to see that he became embarrassingly plaintive: Jefferson must have known that nowhere do the lion and the lamb lie together.[18]

Replying to one of Adams's letters that raised the momentous questions whether we should "surrender all our pleasing hopes of the progress of Society? Of improvement of the intellectual and moral condition of the World? Of the reformation of mankind," Jefferson expressed his loyalty, once again, to dream. In a subtler form, though. "The events of Naples and Piedmont cast a gloomy cloud over that hope," he said to Adams, even though no one could know whether the hope of improvement must be forsaken. "These, my dear friend, are speculations for the new generation, as, before they will be re-solved, you and I must join our deceased brother Floyd. Yet I will not believe our labors are lost. I shall not die without a hope that light and liberty are on steady advance. . . . And even should the cloud of barbarism and despotism again obscure the science and liberties of Europe, this country remains to preserve and restore light and liberty to them. In short, the flames kindled on the 4th. of July 1776. have spread over too much of the globe to be extin-guished by the feeble engines of despotism."[19]

Are we seeing an example of hope? Or is this but a dream? Momentous questions, once again. But Jefferson's reference to a rational decision, as it seems, more than to his heart and his deepest and spontaneous beliefs ("I will not believe our labors are lost . . . I shall not die without a hope . . . And even should the cloud of barbarism . . .") reveals that he probably intended to ward off very opposite feelings. It is really hard to believe Jefferson's avowal that "this country remains to preserve and restore light and liberty." Mine is perhaps mere conjecture, but I cannot help thinking that by appealing to a decision, he was trying to give Adams and himself courage. He probably did not desire to believe what he actually believed and preferred to find some comfort in the latest version of the old story of the lion and the lamb. No one can penetrate Jefferson's mind, of course, and disclose his real intentions. However, the declaration that his hope "after all, may be an Utopian dream" must be taken seriously.[20]

There comes a time when people must be excused if they admit that hope and dream are siblings: an imagination that no longer empowers but that simply reveals one's inner void. There comes a time when one must bid adieu to the most cherished visions of an entire life and say to everyone good night, asking not to be disturbed in dreaming. Jefferson's poem directed to his daughter Martha from his deathbed brings this tendency to an extreme:

A Death-bed Adieu from Th. J. to M. R.
Life's visions are vanished, its dreams are no more;
Dear friends of my bosom, why bathed in tears?
I go to my fathers, I welcome the shore
Which crowns all my hopes or which buries my cares.
Then farewell, my dear, my lov'd daughter, adieu!
The last pang of life is in parting from you!
Two seraphs await me long shrouded in death;
I will bear them your love on my last parting breath.[21]

Of course, when one grows old and approaches death, one has to pre-
pare to regard images as dreams: "I welcome the shore / Which crowns all
my hopes." In the later phases of life, images are no longer embellished by
the hope of realization and buttressed by the energy of a young heart. But
further questions arise: Did Jefferson really and consistently trust imagination throughout his life? Was Jefferson actually and completely a creature of
hope? What I argue in the following pages is that the demythologization of
imagination began earlier. It was not an obsession of Jefferson's later years or a
transformation that occurred in his character. Jefferson accepted that human
beings, including himself, are creatures of the present and are committed to
the brutal fact of their animal survival. In a word, he admitted the brutality
of expediency.

JEFFERSON AND EXPEDIENCY

Interpreters have repeatedly emphasized Jefferson's toughness and realpolitik, for instance, during his exercise of the presidential power. Despite the
standard image of him as an impractical idealist, Jefferson showed he was
able to be a ruthless operator. As Malone wrote, "His actions against the
Barbary pirates, and those authorized in connection with the acquisition of
Louisiana, showed that he was by no means averse to the use of force when
in his judgment circumstances required it." Similarly, an antilibertarian,
"Hamiltonian," and "restrictionist" Jefferson emerged, for instance, during
the embargo he imposed on American shipping, and each time he suggested
launching surgical strikes against "gangrenous" states such as Connecticut or
Massachusetts.[22]

There is an undeniable pragmatic style of which Jefferson made large
use. At times, Jefferson's pragmatism blended with his typical republicanism,
characterized by the praise of the *vita activa*, and the outcome was a variety
of Spartan militarism. A few years after his second term was over, during
the War of 1812, Jefferson wrote to Monroe: "We must train and classify the

whole of our male citizens, and make military instruction a regular part of collegiate education. We can never be safe till this is done." Jefferson's version of republicanism called for the enhancement of citizens' participation, not surprisingly in the form of a military involvement.[23]

Likewise, the ruthless operator emerges in Jefferson's willingness to occasionally waive the principle, quite often advocated during George Washington's administration, of a strict construction of the Constitution. Condoning General Wilkinson's actions in New Orleans during Burr's conspiracy, Jefferson wrote Governor Claiborne an amazing letter: "On great occasions every good officer must be ready to risk himself in going beyond the strict line of law, when the public preservation requires it."[24]

An almost Hamiltonian use of the law seems to have been deeply entrenched in his mind, given that a few years later Jefferson restated the same idea. "The question you propose," Jefferson wrote to Colvin in 1810,

> whether circumstances do not sometimes occur which make it a duty
> in officers of high trust to assume authorities beyond the law, is easy of
> solution in principle, but sometimes embarrassing in practice. A strict
> observance of the written laws is doubtless *one* of the high duties of a
> good citizen: but it is not *the highest*. The laws of necessity, of self-
> preservation, of saving our country when in danger, are of higher obli-
> gation. To lose our country by a scrupulous adherence to written law,
> would be to lose the law itself, with life, liberty, property & all those
> who are enjoying them with us; thus absurdly sacrificing the end to
> the means.

In the same letter, Jefferson appealed to "a law of necessity & self-preservation" that renders "the salus populi supreme over the written law."[25]

It is true that Jefferson regarded these principles as not applicable to petty cases, but exclusively to great occasions, when the nation's safety or interests were in actual jeopardy. Nonetheless, he openly admitted a practice of which Colonel Hamilton would surely have approved.

Historians sympathetic to Jefferson have to guard themselves against a dangerous tendency: the tendency to underplay or even ignore those discourses and practices that are not considered "good" enough to be listed under the historian's benchmark of what the Jeffersonian worldview should be. I do not believe that Jefferson's "untypical" declaration, for instance, made after the British entered the Federal City in 1814, has to be dismissed as *merely* circumstantial. That "no government can be maintained without the principle of fear as well as of duty" is a tenet to which only fools or idealistic philosophers could not consent. The principle of expediency was no less characteristically Jeffersonian than, for instance, his trust in populace, his universalism, and his hope in common sense. He had several languages. Jefferson was a creature of hope and imagination no less than he was a detractor of imagination.[26]

Addressing the question of expediancy, I do not provide a full list of cases in which Jefferson behaved or spoke in an "unbearable" rough way. I try to look beneath those cases. The point I do make is that Jefferson's enlightened philosophy allowed considerable room for what might be called (somewhat improperly) "realism" or (better) "presentism" and for an anti-imaginative worldview. Stated otherwise, this disciple of the Enlightenment certainly tried his best to uphold and even implement his much-loved principles. Stirred by the Enlightenment, however, he also knew he did not have to live up to any idealized abstraction of Jeffersonianism. It is not a matter of inconsistency: propelled by ideals but not blinded by them, this enlightened philosopher gave flexible responses to unforeseen events and contingencies.[27]

Every scholar would easily agree about the typicality of Jefferson's tenet that "a government of reason is better than one of force," as he still wrote in 1820. Of course, a doctrine such as this fits admirably well the vision of himself that Jefferson undeniably tried to bequeath to posterity, and of which scholars are eager to approve. However, are we sure that Jefferson's ideas concerning the relation between reason and force is adequately assessed? Did Jefferson think that human reason is essentially and entirely antithetic to force? Is reason unconditioned? Perhaps reason is the historical development of our (or someone's) rules of prudence, and "rational" or "moral," thus, are labels we apply to behaviors that have proven successful. Perhaps reason is just the way someone has categorized the legitimate use of force. For twenty-first-century historians and philosophers it is somewhat commonsensical to treat every tradition and every hierarchy of values in terms of crafted and invented habits, notably, in terms of someone's traditions and someone's hierarchies. We are clear that a purely rational tradition would be a non-existent one. We know that the unconditioned could never realize itself in history, but was this fact somehow clear to Jefferson? Did Jefferson recognize that reason and values must be assessed historically?[28]

As noted above, the Enlightenment reacted against seventeenth-century rationalism and quietism. The Enlightenment was a refusal to admit that reason was a supernatural and superhistorical mark. Quietism was the stance typical of those seventeenth-century European thinkers who believed humans were affiliated with something greater than their finitude and were incomparably superior to their mere circumstantial role in the history of human events. I suspect that to Jefferson, too, reason and universality sometimes revealed themselves as historically conditioned, as a practice of prudence, the effect of particular social causes, and something effectual and successful from a mere evolutionary point of view. Of course, Jefferson would never have expressed these ideas in the language we would use today. But from Jefferson's juvenile doctrine, that we have to "*fortify* our minds against the attacks of these calamities and misfortunes," a number of Darwinian consequences come. Jefferson's emphasis on reason, ideals, and values should be demythologized and treated dialectically. To some extent, the emphasis Jefferson placed on those qualities was a strategy of denial of the world as it is. He wanted to see worth all around, not mere brutal facts. He often used his imagination to disguise the basic fact that humans respond to the circumstances of life not too differently from the way other animals do.[29]

I have said that the new republic was envisioned as the embodiment of a universal principle, a value, a concrete ideal, and the expression on earth of the unconditioned. The United States was supposed to be something more than a nation among other nations. By the same token, leaders put forward the image of the American people as if they were not merely a tribe among others that existed or had existed in a contingent history. The language of reason, freedom, law, and right was widely employed, and not just by Jefferson. The problem of the "universal existence in secular particularity," to use Pocock's phrase, was deeply felt, and the expectation was rather high. "This I hope," Jefferson wrote to Adams in 1796, "will be the age of experiments in government, and *that their basis will be founded on principles of honesty, not of mere force.*" Instances of governments based on honesty, reason, and law are very rare in history, Jefferson allowed. "Either force or corruption has been the principle of every modern government." The idea that the United States was different seems, nevertheless, to have never been called into question, at least if one is satisfied by certain declarations and by certain interpretations of those declarations.[30]

In 1788, Benjamin Rush was proclaiming that "Justice has descended from heaven to dwell in our land," but it is not clear what that avowal meant. There is no doubt that the urge to differentiate the new republic from other nations was intensely experienced, but this is not the proof that the United States *was* different. The United States *should be* different, and everybody looked forward to finding some evidence for that hopeful and decisive event. While the goal was clear, the way to achieve it remained obscure. What was actually perceived at the end of the eighteenth century was the desirability of severing the new republic from previous social and political experiments, because those experiments had obviously failed. The problem was that universalism, justice, and law are on one scale and real-world effectiveness, par-

ticularism, and self-preservation on the other. The enthusiastic declarations
à la Rush stood for the dream that the exigency to subordinate expediency
to justice be clear to every citizen, starting from those who were at the helm.
What Rush's declaration actually communicated was that there are precise
criteria according to which a government must be held a success or a failure.
The Romans, for instance, were effectively ruled by emperors for nearly half
a millennium, but everyone, both Federalists and anti-Federalists, agreed that
this was not enough to term the empire a success.[31]

Every leader would have refused to define the republic solely through
the language of real-world effectiveness. A keen discomfort arose from those
interpretations of human history, including the American cause, that reduced the conquests and the crusades to mere battles among different, but
fully equivalent, wills. In particular, admitting that law "represents nothing
but the codified will of powerful interests," as William Nelson writes, "may
give satisfaction to those who have power and may also teach them how to
maximize their well-being. But such a conception of law gives neither solace
nor protection to the powerless." Nor would it give solace, or protection, or
satisfaction, I would add, to those who desired to interpret human events
through the lens of universalism and justice.[32]

Jefferson's uneasiness with an expedient or realistic interpretation of the
American Revolution—and of revolutions as such—is apparent, for instance,
in his rejection of Hume's *History of England*. In a skeptical way, Hume held
that the English civil wars of the seventeenth century were not triggered by an
act of arbitrariness of the Crown, to which the Commons replied in compli-
ance to universal justice, but by the encroachments upon royal prerogatives
by the Commons. According to Hume, the wars of the seventeenth century
were not waged by the people at large to restore reason. Not surprisingly, as
Douglas Wilson correctly acknowledges, "it was clearly Hume's basic thesis
that the Commons encroached on the crown and not the other way around
that most offended Jefferson." Hume's reading, in effect, cast a dim view on
the supposed rationality and rightness of the American Revolution held by
Jefferson to be in full continuity with the rightness of the precedent English
civil wars. In his *Summary View,* Jefferson referred back to Tacitus's *Germania*
to demonstrate that the Anglo-Saxon "constitution" had been republican and
hence founded upon reason and justice. The Anglo-Saxon "constitution," so he
explained, assumed the validity of the universal principle of self-government
because it allowed for an elected king and parliament. Self-government was
supposedly maintained until the Normans came to overturn it and to replace
the principles of justice and reason with arbitrary prerogatives and privileges.[33]

Although Hume did not condemn the American Revolution (he published his *History* between 1754 and 1762), he clearly gave little credence to both the vision upon which Jefferson thought that the Revolution was grounded and the principle of American republicanism. The issue was whether the American experiment had been undertaken "on principles of honesty, not of mere force." Hume implicitly questioned the two basic "truths" that Jefferson firmly held: the Americans' appeal to a historical precedent for a true democracy, and people's universal sense of justice as the sole origin of all just power.

A tyrant could establish prerogatives and privileges that served his own interests while also, to some extent, taking care of his many subjects. Under these conditions, as the Roman case demonstrates, an empire might last for centuries. Nonetheless, reason would condemn the success of such a venture as well as that of any of its leaders. It is clear why Caesar was normally referred to as the most eloquent symbol of what the American rulers should never become. Caesar was a Roman emperor who never succeeded in getting rid of his original barbarism. Every social system, based on inherited hierarchies that reduce right and law to force, is likewise to be condemned. "This I believe is the case with every barbarous people," Jefferson said in the *Notes*. "With such, force is law." In a barbarous society, those who do not have force enough to sustain their prerogatives, such as women, for example, would have no hope at all. In theory at least, it is clear what right and law should amount to and what civilization should support. "It is civilization alone which replaces women in the enjoyment of their natural equality. That first teaches us to subdue the selfish passions, and to respect those rights in others which we value in ourselves. Were we in equal barbarism, our females would be equal drudges."[34]

The phrase "were we in equal barbarism" triggers momentous questions. Was the American republic emancipated from barbarism? Did Jefferson truly believe that? What America *should* become was altogether evident, in Jefferson's imagination at least. But was America founded on universal principles of right, law, and honesty, or was the American republic one group and someone's will taking over other groups and others' will? Some negative answers should be quickly taken into account, before moving to consider Jefferson's embarrassment.

Abigail Adams, for one, was sure the American republic was not founded on any kind of universalism. On 31 March 1776, Abigail made an immortal declaration—rich in irony but tremendously serious as to its content—repeatedly quoted ever since. "In the new Code of Laws which I suppose it will be necessary for you to make," she wrote to her husband, "I desire you would Remember the Ladies, and be more generous and favourable to them than your ancestors. Do not put such unlimited power into the hands of the Husbands. Remember all Men would be tyrants if they could. If particular care and attention is not paid to the Ladies we are determined to foment a Rebellion, and will not hold ourselves bound by any Laws in which we have no voice, or Representation." Seen from the perspective of this numerous "tribe"—as John had derogatorily labeled all those who were not allowed to enter the ruling group—the principles upon which the American republic was founded appear no less an arbitrary statement of privileges, prerogatives, and established traditions than any other previous example in history. By means of her irony, Abigail demythologized American imagination by giving an unvarnished representation of the American cause as a skirmish of band against band. The new republic was, for her, the brutal affirmation of some-one's will. She must have considered no less than insulting Jefferson's claim that civilization, in America, had restored women in the enjoyment of their natural equality.[35]

Thirty years after Abigail made her startling and still-valid declaration, another of the dispossessed was compelled to retell an analogous story of arbitrariness, encroachment, and total lack of moral deference.[36]

In 1806, Tenskwatawa ("the Open Door"), a Shawnee prophet, delivered a speech before the Tuscarora branch of the Iroquois Confederacy. The prophet expressed not just the serious plight of Indian people; he also revealed some-thing important about the self-deception of the American imagination. All Indian tribes "will vanish like a vapor from the face of the earth; their very history will be lost in forgetfulness, and the places that now know them will know them no more. We are driven back until we can retreat no farther; our hatchets are broken; our bows are snapped; our fires are extinguished; a little longer and the white man will cease to prosecute us, for we shall cease to exist." The prophet looked from outside the American civilization and portrayed the circumstantial event of a (white) tribe beating a different (red) tribe. He gazed at the original flaw, namely, the arbitrary violence of those barbarians who vindicated themselves appealing exclusively to their own effectiveness. Like Abigail, Tenskwatawa conveyed a relativistic perspective and discovered that reason, law, and justice did not cling to a truly universal language. The prophet did not just yield to fatalism and mourning. He had enough of a following to rally the tribes to action and, thanks to his war-rior brother Tecumseh ("Shooting Star"), to seek to create a separate Native American nation that whites were compelled to respect. His idea was that expediency must face expediency.[37]

Critical judgments made from external perspectives could easily be collected, although this is not what concerns us here. The topic of the chapter is not the "embarrassment" expressed by those who were dispossessed. Our concern is insiders. But before moving to considering whether Jefferson believed that the new republic was actually emancipated from barbarism, from "our original barbarism," let me take note of a third voice.

Besides women and Native Americans, African Americans also were the living and more often the dying demonstration that universalism was a rhetorical ploy. Like other dispossessed, black slaves gave visibility to what today we would call "cultural relativism": the acknowledgment that so-called universalism (like every other cultural phenomenon) must be depicted as a conditioned practice, and that "universal" ideals about "progress" or "government by laws" are justified by the power and arbitrariness wielded by definite human groups. Consider this episode: a slave speaking after the Gabriel Prosser slave revolt of 1800. Quite unintentionally, the slave pinpointed the dreamlike nature of American universalism. Wearing iron handcuffs, he resolutely said: "I have nothing more to offer than what General Washington would have had to offer, had he been taken by the British and put to trial by them." To the slave's eyes, the endeavor to obtain freedom for his countrymen was indistinguishable from the endeavor of Washington and other patriots.[38]

Jefferson was aware that a government of reason would be better than one of force. Likewise, together with the majority of American leaders, he was conscious that the British and French abominations were eloquent counter-examples. Britain and Napoleonic France *should* not be imitated. Bitter reflections ensued from the "enormities" of Bonaparte and "the piratical principles and practices" of the English government. To Caesar Rodney, Jefferson gave a vivid portrait of what the American republic, together with any rational republic, should never become. "The hurricane which is now blasting the world, physical & moral, has prostrated all the mounds of reason as well as right. All those calculations which, at any other period, would have been deemed honorable, of the existence of a moral sense in man, individually or associated, of the connection which the laws of nature had established between his duties & his interests, of a regard for honest fame & the esteem of our fellow men, have been a matter of reproach on us, as evidences of imbecility."[39]

It is telling that Jefferson chose to emphasize the "reproach" to those gullible philosophers, like himself, who believed in some universal law, right, reason, morality, or justice. Jefferson, of course, did not (entirely) believe the reproach. He considered reason, right, and law something very serious, and something no one should reproach. However, what Jefferson was implicitly revealing was his awareness that, as a rule, societies and nations follow a very contrary principle, the principle that force is law. Jefferson knew that men usually appeal to the use of force, and it is far from clear whether he (entirely) condemned that practice or, to some extent at least, whether he considered it as a sort of natural and unavoidable habit.[40]

In fact, Jefferson himself admitted to John Colvin, as just mentioned, that the "laws of necessity, of self-preservation, of saving our country when in danger, were of higher obligation" than any other law. It is a Darwinian statement, and it is not clear what for Jefferson should be the limit of applicability of that evolutionary principle. "The salus populi" is "supreme over the written law," he said in that same letter, but what about the *salus* of individuals? Is it actually in our power to bargain it away for some abstract universal principle of law and morality? In 1822, as discussed, Jefferson performed a dissection on the "law of his [man's] nature" and explained its mechanism by a not too honorific comparison between human behaviors and the "cocks of henyard" that "kill one another up." Reason, right, law, and morality seem to form second-order criteria, while the first and most archaic order would be the animal instinct of self-preservation. Jefferson must have been aware of the amoral basis of existence, on which both nations and individuals have to rely, albeit they should not. A natural philosopher, Jefferson had always been clear that the chance of being reconquered to an original barbarism was tremendously real.[41]

As the years passed, Jefferson became less and less intimidated by compromises when survival was at stake. In the 1820s, that tendency reached its apex. I have recalled the letter to John Holmes of 22 April 1820: in chapter 3, apropos of his anxieties, and in chapter 5, as an example of Jefferson's pessimistic discourse and increased receptiveness to impossibilities. That letter contains a further point that is worth consideration now.

"I can say, with conscious truth," Jefferson wrote, "that there is not a man on earth who would sacrifice more than I would to relieve us from this heavy reproach [slavery], in any *practicable* way." This was Jefferson speaking in the moral language. "But as it is, we have the wolf by the ears, and we can neither hold him, nor safely let him go. Justice is in one scale, and self-preservation in the other." Jefferson was not saying that self-preservation should be preferred on moral grounds. On the contrary, Jefferson was clearly implying that we have no choice, and that self-preservation is the only basis from which finite creatures are compelled to start. Seen from the Darwinian perspective of the struggle for survival, one must deplore the decision of those who in the name of an "abstract principle," as Jefferson himself allowed, are going to sacrifice their whole happiness and existence. Jefferson's view was that universal criteria of equality, justice, or morality appear as entirely secondary and abstract when compared to the preservation instinct. There is a limit beyond which criteria of morality make no sense at all.[42]

This is how Jefferson concluded: "I regret that I am now to die in the belief, that the useless sacrifice of themselves by the generation of 1776, to acquire self-government and happiness to their country, is to be thrown away by the unwise and unworthy passions of their sons, and that my only consolation is to be, that I live not to weep over it. If they would but dispassionately weigh the blessings they will throw away, against an abstract principle more likely to be effected by union than by scission, they would pause before they would perpetrate this act of suicide on themselves, and of treason against the hopes of the world." What matters here is not whether Jefferson's judgment on northeastern policies was sound and whether the weight he attached to self-government was actually a wise move. Jefferson was probably wrong in both cases. That Congress might put forth its right to regulate the conditions of the inhabitants of the states was not such an act of suicide as Jefferson believed, either theoretically or practically. Even so, the position he was defending is relevant to his view of the relative claims of morality and self-preservation: Jefferson was clearly saying that universal and abstract principles could not be pushed beyond a certain limit.

Virtue, law, and morality end somewhere. Beyond a certain point or, better, beneath a certain level, reason becomes "our reason," to be interpreted in exclusive terms, and the original barbarism emerges. Visions of universal harmony and ideals of a moral society have no sense when the survival of "our" group is at stake. Neither societies nor individuals could ever entirely emancipate themselves from barbarism. It would be wonderful if the American republic could be different from Europe and its "system of disunited sovereignties," as Onuf said, or from a system of colliding wills, as I would say. Unfortunately it is not. Despite his dreams of lions and lambs, Jefferson had always known the brutality of expediency, at least since the *Summary View*.[43]

In 1774, Jefferson made explicit what was couched beneath the inclusive rhetoric of right, reason, and morality. The British conquered America, he wrote; this is the source of their right of possession. "America was conquered, and her settlements made and firmly established, at the expence of individuals, and not of the British public. Their own blood was spilt in acquiring lands for their settlement, their own fortunes expended in making that settlement effectual. For themselves they fought, for themselves they conquered, and for themselves alone they have right to hold." Malcolm Kelsall calls attention to the radical difference between Jefferson's universal claims made, for instance, in the Declaration and the harsh effectiveness—a badly disguised form of barbarism—expressed in this document. "Nor is there any reason to suppose," Kelsall adds, "that Jefferson ever abandoned this interpretation of the Saxon myth which paradoxically links conquest with law." It is not paradoxical. When survival is threatened, when our group and our reason(s) are in jeopardy, it is almost unavoidable to embrace some form of realpolitik. From the point of view of "our" chances of survival, the whole history of the settlements in America "might be interpreted as a series of exercises in duplicity, intended to conceal in the language of law and liberty, civilization and philanthropy, the simple, material, bloody fact: 'for themselves they fought, for themselves they conquered.'" Imagination, in peace, and harsh "presentism," in the struggle for survival.[44]

It would be unwarranted to consider the Darwinism couched in the *Summary View* as the original and unique inspiration of another famous Jeffersonian doctrine, namely, that the earth belongs to the living. An element of harsh expediency, nonetheless, was clearly conveyed also by the principle that Jefferson communicated to his friend James Madison in 1789, and that has been restated several times since. Besides the reference to an intergenerational responsibility within the white family, the doctrine that the earth belongs to the living generation also articulated the exclusion of those, such as Native Americans, who were tragically caught in the past and were already seized by the seed of extinction. Properly speaking, Native Americans were not the living. The "melancholy sequel of their history," as Jefferson said in the Query 11 of the *Notes,* demonstrated that the majority of that unfortunate generation was already dead or would be dead soon. Native Americans, hence, had no real title to partake in the temporal dimension of the present and should be evicted from the ongoing debates about rights.[45]

It was an obvious consequence. Those who lived vapor-like lives, as Tenskwatawa appropriately maintained, and were embarrassingly "old," as Jefferson himself admitted in his letter to the "brothers" of the Choctaw Nation, had neither powers to exert nor rights to defend. Only the living generation, that history said to be composed of successful white settlers, had rights and powers. "Compared with you, we are but as of yesterday in this land," Jefferson said to his dying "Brothers." The tacit allegation was that youth, which also means physical strength and effective presence, would be the only spring from whence flowed all the "rights" over the land. It has been correctly argued that through his earth-belongs-to-the-living doctrine Jefferson was able to play a significant part in the intellectual groundwork for the Darwinian nineteenth-century conquest of the continent without any explicit reliance on the racist argument. It was deep sympathy for the *dying* brothers as such that pushed Jefferson toward a pronouncement of their political irrelevance, despite publicly acknowledging an abstract intellectual equality. As far as

Native Americans were concerned, conquest, once again, was tantamount to law.[46]

The duality of Jefferson's thought has clearly been noticed by historians. Malone, for instance, had been forced to write that "on the one hand he was devoted to principles which he regarded as timeless and universal; on the other he was an experienced statesman, with a keen sense of practicality, who was aware of the danger of pressing abstract principles too far in particular situations when circumstances were unfavorable, and who not unnaturally perceived difficulties the more when he was himself in the midst of them." There is nothing paradoxical in that. Principles, reason, and morality have no application when the animal, which is in us all, perceives that the real priority is to increase one's chance of survival. Both individuals and society are subject to this form of natural necessity. It is quite a different story to live in serenity with such a double standard.[47]

A huge number of human beings, in particular those at the helm, are capable of asserting principles inconsistent with their practices. Jefferson, Charles Miller acknowledges, "was indeed capable of doing that, and it was the torment of his life." There is no existential paradox in linking conquest with law; on the contrary, it is very "natural," even though it might become excruciating. Jefferson's philosophy seemed to teach that all humans are equals, persons connected through a moral tie. The social and economic system in which he was reared, and that he internalized, organized human beings according to the well-known hierarchy of master and servant, of propertied and unpropertied, of hunters and prey, of "us" and "they."[48]

It was excruciating, but Jefferson dealt with the issue of expediency throughout his life, without ever being able to unravel it. He could not have untangled the "paradox" between expediency and the universal language of reason and morality. He had always known that history is a matter of survival and reflects the point of view of the winner. Winning and losing are the only available options. The natural philosopher must have known that for themselves white Americans fought, for themselves they conquered, and for themselves alone they had the right of possession. Because survival is at stake, the march of civilization, far from being the march of reason, is a simple matter of power. "What is called civilization," Jefferson wrote to Madison in 1797, "seems to have no other effect on him [man] than to teach him to pursue the principle of bellum omnium in omnia on a larger scale, and in place of the little contests of tribe against tribe, to engage all the quarters of the earth in the same work of destruction. . . . We both, I believe, join in wishing to see him softened."

The fact that moral imagination wishes to see humanity awakened by standards of justice and equality does not prove that, in nature, things do not follow a Darwinian pattern and its law of necessity. As a work of imagination, the Enlightenment had to search harmony. As a work of honesty, on the other hand, the Enlightenment had also to resist the dream, to demythologize imagination, and to acknowledge the human condition.

An enlightened man, Jefferson knew that the right of the white settlers in America was a right by gunpowder. The founders refused British imperialism in theory and in practice, but they could not refuse imperialism and conquest *tout court*. The *practice* of imperialism in western land was admitted, and as a leader, Jefferson tried his best to promote it. Carroll Smith-Rosenberg makes an interesting comment in this regard. Republicans, Jefferson included, were "simultaneously postcolonial and colonizing subjects. American patriots faced in two directions. Looking east, they called themselves Sons of Liberty, true heirs of Augustan republicanism and the Scottish Enlightenment. Facing west, they became lords and proprietors of a vast continent." In order to become a winner, one must become a proprietor. One must simultaneously exclude other groups and one's own moral imagination.[49]

It was excruciating for Jefferson to be an enlightened man, to speak many languages, to be at once inspired and made weaker by his imagination, and to accept living in the muddy marchland between civilization and barbarism. An original barbarism was always lurking beneath Jefferson's moral conscience. His only book, the *Notes on the State of Virginia,* just like the *Summary View,* articulated all these "paradoxes." In the last analysis, they are the paradoxes of the human condition. In writing his book, Jefferson tried to convey an image of order and harmony, of universality and morality. It was his duty as an Enlightenment thinker. He spoke the language of so-called objectivity, of reason, of tables, diagrams, and philosophy in the proclaimed intent to represent his beautiful country to Europeans, to his fellow citizens, and also to himself. But speaking about order was per se speaking about several forms of disorder and negativity. Western wilderness, brutality, conquest, eviction, effectiveness, barbarism, and lack of moral deference are the unwelcome co-protagonists of that singular treatise on the tragic that characterizes human history.

As Peter Onuf says, because the phantom of negativity was always present, "An undercurrent of malaise pervades the *Notes,* and is by no means confined to the discussions of race and slavery. Jefferson's inventories and descriptions are offered in a hopeful, progressive spirit, as he anticipates a glorious future for Virginia and for America. Yet despair shadows this hope—despair that is not simply an expression of his chronic anxieties about popular slothfulness and ignorance but was more deeply grounded in a devastating judgment on himself and his slaveowning countrymen." Despair shadowed Jefferson's hope because, in the very process of enlightenment, disorder and barbarism cast their dark shadow on every venture humans undertake. It was not just because of slavery that Jefferson trembled for both his country and himself. It was because by accepting the challenge central to the Enlightenment, Jefferson got snared by the negative, this time in the form of expediency.

Let me further quote Onuf as a conclusion: "It was a problem that writing the *Notes*—the great effort to represent his country to Europeans, to his countrymen, above all to himself—had brought to the fore. This was the tragic counterpoint, the lengthening shadow of Jefferson's great project to smash the despotism of the old regime and spread universal enlightenment through words—the liberating words that articulated natural rights principles, the words by which free men signified and constituted the affectionate, durable bonds of republican government."[50]

A government of reason is definitely better than one of force. However, we have to keep in mind that Jefferson did not live in a universal and classless society. Far from being a universal man existing in a social void, that optimistic meliorist was a member of a leading group that was reluctant to bargain away its prerogatives and privileges in order to broaden the spectrum of those allowed to make decisions.

Historical human beings always live in stratified and hierarchical societies. Understandably, they normally do not want to relinquish privileges, at least as long as they perceive that they have some privileges to defend. In Jefferson's case, egalitarian visions and practices collided with de facto status privileges and a very aristocratic sense of honor, prestige, and accomplishment, as well as a penchant for "agreeable society" and *private* property. We cannot tackle the general questions whether property is compatible with democracy, egalitarianism, and morality, or whether property is, at least to some extent, synonymous with theft. Nor can we ascertain whether Jefferson's meliorism, reformism, progressivism, and gradualism were the tools he selected to get rid of the extant hierarchies, or whether they were merely his great alibis for preserving his world. Suffice it to say that Jefferson remained to a large extent a late eighteenth-century member of a propertied, slaveholding elite that thrived on the theft of both slave labor and Indian land.

This status characterization did not make it easier for Jefferson to build an inclusive, dynamic, cosmopolitan, and universalistic society in which the unconditioned would realize itself. He often dreamed of that kind of society, certainly, and allowance should be made for a sincere intent to take advantage of his social status to change his society for the better. His elite affiliations and his upper-class biases, however, do call attention to Jefferson's life-long involvement in the practice of violence and expediency. That he could not have realistically relinquished his social status—the famous wolf he held by the ears—does not make the conflict less dramatic. The brutal fact remains that Jefferson benefited *personally* from his property and from a society in which potent bulwarks existed against both lower-class interests and any possibility of making the unconditioned a reality. In other words, since he always tried to be successful, Jefferson benefited from a number of effectual barriers against American hope and imagination. He wanted to change his society at the same time as he identified with it.

Philip Burch has put emphasis on those "elite family relations" (concentration of wealth and intermarriage), both in the North and in the South, that had dramatically shaped the history of the early republic. More generally, the top officials after the Confederation period (1789–97), as Burch writes, were "essentially a reflection of the distribution of wealth and power in America as this politically pivotal regime embarked on the momentous task of providing for a sound and stable government." Virtually all national leaders of the period came from the upper class either through birth or marriage. In short, "the top officials of the Washington administration represented primarily commercial and entrepreneurial interests." The policies adopted by the Washington/Jefferson/Hamilton cabinet, as a result, boosted speculative actions based on inside information and aimed fundamentally at "stability," namely, at the protection of the status quo that came out of the Revolution. The late eighteenth-century leaders who explicitly subscribed to citizens' *vita activa* could not help favoring those economic clans that from the beginning of the nation's history had wielded power and acted largely on behalf of themselves. Though a more independent figure, the "whimsical" John Adams also had significant socioeconomic "clan" ties. Between Washington's, Adams's, and Jefferson's administrations several discontinuities existed. We should not presume the unity or cohesion of all upper-class interests. But discontinuities, factions, and discordances did not undermine, as Burch wrote, "the predominantly upper-class character of national politics in these early years."[51]

On the state level, in Virginia particularly, Republican leaders were similarly the expression of a clan, reportedly composed of no more than twenty persons, known as the Richmond Junto. It was that form of aristocracy (definitely not just of "virtue and talents") that took over Virginia's state politics from the early 1800s to the late 1820s. The consequence is that besides Jefferson the universalist, pro-democracy moral philosopher, another Jefferson existed who was a leader and an insider tied to his own class, a member of an informal oligarchic body who identified to a great extent with its *exclusive* goals. Both Adams and Jefferson had always been aware of the unbridgeable gap between universalism and particularism. "Now, my Friend, who are the *aristoi*?" Adams asked Jefferson rhetorically. "Philosophy may Answer 'The Wise and Good.' But the World, Mankind, have by their practice always answered, 'the rich the beautiful and well born.'" Unfortunately, the problem is that Jefferson *was* propertied, beautiful, and well born.[52]

That he cherished the democratic dream to turn American society into a universal society of *persons* while preventing the ascendancy of an artificial aristocracy founded on wealth and birth does not prove that Jefferson must have overlooked the brutal fact that in the historical world successful individuals like himself are by no means the most virtuous and talented in a truly universal sense. The propertied cavalier—with his shining armor, his imposing manor, and the cohort of his submissive servants—has more opportunity to succeed. The cavalier's individual relation to nature is mediated through his property, a construct from which unpropertied persons would not profit. In its most Darwinian moment, Jefferson's philosophy regarded property as an evolutionary tool to increase one's chances to defeat the forces of both nature and time. Since true democracy should privilege persons over property, we are forced to admit Jefferson's embarrassing dedication to an old-style, quasi-aristocratic idea of property and, accordingly, his unpreparedness to *fully* grasp a modern idea of the person. The propertied few cannot help shivering—just like Jefferson during the years of the Missouri Crisis—when actual democratizing forces were unleashed, and the right to property and historical privilege was seriously challenged.[53]

For all his professions of universalism, reason, and equality, Jefferson lived as a mightily privileged member of a mightily privileged elite that secured its position by the theft of both slave labor and Indian land. All his life, Jefferson was enmeshed in a regime of violence and expediency, whatever his idealistic aspirations. His success (which he also always desired) was conditioned in considerable measure *against* the realization of American hope and imagination in slaves, Indians, women, and the lower classes on which the society he supported insisted.

A philosopher devoted to travel on the ocean of negativity—which is what the Enlightenment asked that Virginia leader to do—Jefferson was suspended between his spiritual destiny, his dearest moral visions, his universal dreams, his optimism—which he could not fulfill—and his animal and historical nature, his sheer expediency and his particular privileges—which he could not retain. The conditions that made Jefferson a winner would eventually make him a loser.

Notes

INTRODUCTION

1. See Vyverberg, *Historical Pessimism,* 1.

2. Ibid., 2.

3. On an American "sense of dispersion and alienation," see also Goodman, *American Philosophy,* 16.

4. An interesting essay on Jefferson's self and personality is J. Lewis and Onuf, "American Synecdoche."

5. Silver, "Emerson and the Idea," 3, 4. An eighteenth-century man, Jefferson wanted to dismiss the "authorial" character of private texts by warning his readers that in those texts "we are careless, incorrect, in haste, perhaps under some transient excitement, and we hazard things without reflection, because without consequence in the bosom of a friend." TJ to George Logan, 19 May 1816, *Works of Thomas Jefferson* (hereafter cited as *Works of TJ*), 11:526. But that Jefferson wanted to resist the idea that private texts are often more telling than formal ones is, in turn, a telling and meaningful fact. The opinion that haste and lack of self-censorship are tantamount to irrelevance is not one modern readers are likely to share.

6. For an interesting overview of studies on whiteness, see Roediger, "Pursuit of Whiteness." My research must not be confused, for instance, with Fresia, *Toward an American Revolution.* That book portrays the framers of the Constitution, and in general white leaders, as profoundly undemocratic. The premise of Fresia's book is an act of faith in the *essential* dishonesty of the leaders. The book does not tell the story of the tensions and conflicts among the several layers of the founders' discourse. The only tension the book traces out is that between these greedy, demonic, sinful, quite unaware leaders and the (essentially good and innocent?) multitudes.

7. See Burch, *Elites in American History,* 16, 21.

1. ENLIGHTENMENT AND DUALISM

1. See Tuveson, *Redeemer Nation;* Hatch, "Origins of Civil Millennialism"; and Marshall and Manuel, *Light and the Glory.* Sacvan Bercovitch provides an excellent description of Americans' unshakable optimism. See Bercovitch, *American Jeremiad.* Bercovitch's analysis ends up in the acknowledgment of "an unswerving faith in the errand" (6). Puritans who made their settlements in the Massachusetts Bay did not minimize the threat of divine retribution, of course, "but they qualified it in a way that turned threat into celebration. In their case, they believed, God's punishments were *corrective,* not destructive," a prop to their "unshakable optimism" (8).

2. Kammen, *People of Paradox,* 12–13. Boorstin agrees: lacking the Puritan background, "the Jeffersonian boasted the unhampered prosperity of his enterprises." Boorstin, *Lost World of Jefferson,* 227.

3. Bercovitch, *American Jeremiad,* 161. See also Blum, *Promise of America.*

4. Williams, *Contours of American History,* 229.

5. D. W. Howe, *Making the American Self,* 10; Smith-Rosenberg, "Dis-Covering the Subject," 842. Louis Hartz contends that Locke was *the* source for the American Revolution, that Revolutionaries were natural-born Lockean liberals, and that their revolution was a legalistic, moderate, reasonable, nonconflictual, emotion-free enterprise, permeated from the outset by an all-pervasive consensus. See Hartz, *Liberal Tradition in America.* For the opposite view that republicanism was "the distinctive political consciousness of the entire Revolutionary generation," see Kelley, "Ideology and Political Culture," 536. See also, of course, countless well-known essays from Bailyn, Wood, and Pocock. Richard Beeman, more persuasively, tells the story of the political *behaviors* that led to the democratic result. His basic ideas raise a criticism of every synthetic view, including the republican, because it would be "impossible to talk about a single *American* political culture; . . . there existed numerous, diverse political cultures, diffuse and fragmented, often speaking altogether different political languages." Beeman, *Varieties of Political Experience,* 2. For another superb example of social history, see Waldstreicher, *Midst of Perpetual Fetes.* Waldstreicher portrays American nationalism not as an ideological consensus but as something highly unstable, something "imagined and practiced locally in distinct, changing ways by different groups for a variety of purposes" (10).

6. Onuf, "Scholars' Jefferson," 683. On late eighteenth-century American leaders' yearning for virtue and their suspicion that virtue is missing and vanishing, see, for instance, Vetterli and Bryner, *In Search of the Republic,* and Yarbrough, "Constitution and Character." The republican, backward-looking leader is discussed, for instance, in Banning, *Jeffersonian Persuasion,* and McCoy, *Elusive Republic.* On leaders looking back at the Saxon myth of the Ancient Constitution, see Pocock, *Ancient Constitution.* On leaders looking back at the Roman republic, see Pocock, *Machiavellian Moment,* and Shalev, *Rome Reborn.* On the discourses expressing enthusiasm for modernity and liberalism, see Appleby, *Capitalism and a New Social Order.* For the contention that Jefferson, like other leaders, was a forward-looking modernist enthused by Lockean liberalism and by the new individualistic forces that were liberating citizens from traditional hierarchies, see Becker, *Declaration of Independence;* Diggins, *Lost Soul of American Politics;* Pangle, *Spirit of Modern Republicanism;* and Dworetz, *Unvarnished Doctrine.* On Jefferson's attention to the Scottish moral sense theory and his interest in communitarianism and a social definition of the human being, see Wills, *Inventing America;* Matthews, *Radical Politics of Jefferson;* and McDonald, *Novus Ordo Seclorum.* On the simultaneous presence of republicanism and liberalism in America, see Appleby, *Liberalism and Republicanism.* Richard Sinopoli goes beyond a simplistic dichotomy of liberalism versus republicanism and implicitly beyond a Federalists–anti-Federalists schematic opposition: "I reject a definition of liberalism that forces the *a priori* conclusion that where virtue exists, liberalism is absent. On the other hand, it would be equally invalid to claim that where rights and interests are mentioned, liberalism is present or predominant" (Sinopoli, *Foundations of American Citizenship,* 13). Nowadays historians refuse to draw on a synthetic view of Jefferson (namely, Jefferson-as-a-republican or Jefferson-as-a-liberal) and offer more dynamic accounts of the changes and conflicts within his philosophy. In fact, a

third option is also traceable. A democratic and radical discourse exists that enhances the tension between the first two discourses. To the historian's discomfort, Jefferson upheld a number of discourses: a republican vision, a liberal one, and a third with deep roots sunk into a new world of popular political speech in a democratizing republican society. The elitist philosopher living in a "republic of letters" (it does not matter whether republican or liberal) was at odds with another philosopher experimenting with an American society increasingly democratic. The best study on the democratization of the early American republic is Wood, *Radicalism of the American Revolution*. On Jefferson as a radical democrat, see Matthews, *Radical Politics of Jefferson*. On Jefferson's thinking as being indebted to a number of different sources and several groups of writers, see Ellis, *American Sphinx*, in particular 63–70.

7. TJ to John Adams, 22 January 1821, Adams, *Adams-Jefferson Letters* (hereafter cited as *A-JL*), 2:569; Richard, *Founders and the Classics*, 180–81. On Jefferson on the march of civilization, see TJ to William Ludlow, 6 September 1824, Jefferson, *Writings of Thomas Jefferson* (hereafter cited as *Writings of TJ*), 16:74–76. Also future oriented is TJ to Roger Weightman, 24 June 1826, *Works of TJ*, 12:476–77.

8. For the notion that eighteenth-century Americans did not perceive commerce and modernity as natural and manifest assets, see Henretta, "Families and Farms."

9. Wood, "Significance of the Early Republic," 11.

10. Onuf, "Scholars' Jefferson," 674; Peterson, *Jefferson Image*, 13.

11. Zuckerman, introduction to *Almost Chosen People*, 16. On polarities, tensions, contradictory qualities, inconsistencies within the U.S. "national style," see Kammen, *People of Paradox*. In the early 1970s, years before the advent of "postmodern" culture and its emphasis on differences, Kammen complained about American historians' being "less sensitive to contradictory tendencies in the national style than foreign observers, philosophers, theologians, high-level journalists, and scholars of the interdisciplinary 'American studies' movement" (100). "American historians on the whole have been uninterested in this more European way of perceiving culture and character" (99). In other words, following Kammen, the questions to raise are not "were American leaders Jeffersonian *or* Hamiltonian," "were they trying to comply with innovation *or* tradition," "were they advocates of optimism *or* pessimism," "of civic virtue *or* liberalism," and so on. More interesting is to start with the hypothesis that they were at once Jeffersonians *and* Hamiltonians, complying with both innovation *and* tradition, at once optimistic *and* pessimistic. On Jefferson as a "grieving optimist," see Burstein, *Inner Jefferson*. On Jefferson as a "sphinx," see Ellis, *American Sphinx*. On Jefferson as a "restless mind," see Beran, *Jefferson's Demons*. See also Dumas Malone's thesis that "being a half dozen men rolled into one, he presented no unvarying image to artists or anybody else." Malone, *Jefferson and His Time* (hereafter cited as *J and His Time*), 3:452.

12. *J and His Time*, 1:389, 2:xxii.

13. TJ to John Melish, 10 December 1814, *Writings of TJ*, 14:220–21. On Jefferson's anti-systematic approach, see also TJ to John Adams, 14 October 1816, *A-JL*, 2:491. On Jefferson's looking for "ad hoc" responses, see *J and His Time*, 1:377.

14. TJ, "Eight Annual Message," *Works of TJ*, 11:72. Locke as well put emphasis on error and limits. "Locke constantly emphasized the limitations of the human instrument and the need to get along without certainty." May, *Enlightenment in America*, 5. On the earth as belonging to the living, see chapter 4. The precise measure of Jefferson's realism as to his full

acceptance of the temporality of existence is given by passages such as this: "There is a ripeness of time for death, regarding others as well as ourselves, when it is reasonable we should drop off, and make room for another growth. When we have lived our generation out, we should not wish to encroach on another." TJ to John Adams, 1 August 1816, *A-JL*, 2:484.

15. On the discovery of Enlightenments (plural), see Porter and Teich, *Enlightenment in National Context*. See also R. A. Ferguson, "American Enlightenment"; Withers, *Placing the Enlightenment;* and Manning and Cogliano, *Atlantic Enlightenment*. Without quoting Hazard, Cassirer, or Gay, a challenging and controversial recent book on the Enlightenment is Himmelfarb, *Roads to Modernity.*

16. Michel Foucault was quite right in his warning against a too facile confusion between humanism and Enlightenment. See Foucault, "What Is Enlightenment?"

17. TJ to Thomas Cooper, 7 October 1814, *Writings of TJ*, 14:200. On the Enlightenment emphasis on experience and experiment, see, for instance, Lienesh, *New Order of the Ages*, 119–37.

18. "Travelling. This makes men wiser, but less happy. When men of sober age travel, they gather knowlege which they may apply usefully for their country, but they are subject ever after to recollections mixed with regret, their affections are weakened by being extended over more objects, and they learn new habits which cannot be gratified when they return home." TJ to Peter Carr, 10 August 1787, *Papers of Thomas Jefferson* (hereafter cited as *PTJ*), 12:17. I believe this is an excellent portrait of the Enlightenment culture.

19. Wood, "Trials and Tribulations of Jefferson," 413. Harold Hellenbrand explicitly recognizes Jefferson's life-long commitment to dualism. Jefferson did not just presuppose dualism or make use of it as a heuristic device. "Jefferson's thought about nature and human nature . . . was profoundly dualistic, perceiving (and fearing) phenomenal turbulence, intuiting (and longing for) inner composure and harmony." Hellenbrand, "Roads to Happiness," 7.

20. I took the reference to Nietzsche from Slotkin, *Regeneration through Violence*, 12. To symbolize the tension between "rational" and "irrational," Slotkin also mentions the figures of Moira and Themis. The goddess Moira is a source of disorder, inciter of female violence, while Themis, Zeus's first wife, is the goddess of justice. A fundamental dualism crossing all human cultures was also analyzed by Jung, *Psyche and Symbol;* Lévi-Strauss, *Savage Mind;* and Lévy-Bruhl, *How Natives Think.*

21. On Jefferson's "binary rhetoric," see Kelsall, *Jefferson and the Iconography*, 23–24. Hannah Spahn provides another excellent analysis of Jefferson's binary rhetoric. She examines in particular the dualistic structure typical of Jefferson's temporal and historical thinking. See Spahn, *Thomas Jefferson, Time, and History.*

22. TJ to John Page, 15 July 1763, *PTJ*, 1:10.

23. In a previous letter to John Page of 25 December 1762, Jefferson asked and answered a pivotal question at once: "Is there any such thing as happiness in this world? No" (*PTJ*, 1:5). A poem that Jefferson clipped in one of his scrapbooks several years later answered the question the same way—"Answer to the Question, What Is Happiness?" by Joseph Brown Ladd:

'TIS an empty fleeting shade,
By imagination made;

'Tis a bubble, straw or worse;
'Tis a baby's hobby horse;
'Tis a little living clear;
'Tis ten thousand pounds a year!
'Tis a title, 'tis a name;
'Tis a puff of empty fame,
Fickle as the breezes blow:
'Tis a lady's YES or NO!
And, where the description's crown'd,
'Tis just *no where* to be found. (Gross, *Jefferson's Scrapbooks*, 263)

24. See Jefferson, *Jefferson's Literary Commonplace Book* (entries 172 and 141), 83, 75. See also Koch, *Philosophy of Jefferson*, 2–3.

25. TJ to Hugh Williamson, 10 January 1801, *PTJ*, 32:444.

26. Gross, *Jefferson's Scrapbooks*, 8 (illustrations following p. 270). I fully agree with the editor that "the newspaper clippings book of 1801–1808 formed a second chapter in the history of Jefferson's literary tastes" (330). The first chapter is, of course, his *Literary Commonplace Book*.

27. All these examples are also analyzed in the following chapters where further references are given. On Whig and Tory dualism as founded in nature, see TJ to Joel Barlow, 3 May 1802, *Works of TJ*, 9:371, and TJ to Marquis de Lafayette, 24 November 1823, *Works of TJ*, 12:323.

28. Beard, "Jefferson: A Civilized Man," 162–63.

29. Harrison, *Forests*, 114. See also Cunningham, *In Pursuit of Reason*.

30. Wood, "Trials and Tribulations of Jefferson," 401; Leibniz, *Theodicy*, 67.

31. On "the Enlightenment family" as "composed of rationalists," see Spurlin, *French Enlightenment in America*, 7. On the dangerous claim that rationalism was the source of the Enlightenment, see Staloff, *Hamilton, Adams, Jefferson*, 6–7. The merit of Staloff's books, however, lies in the attempt at blurring the boundaries between outdated partitions, such as that between Enlightenment and Romanticism. The third chapter is entitled "Thomas Jefferson: Romantic America." In that chapter Staloff points out that starting from the 1780s politics became for Jefferson a matter of the heart, and to his fellow countrymen Jefferson communicated a vision of the American future that was at once romantically alluring and compelling. Like other Enlightenment devotees, Jefferson worked with the imagination. See 248. On the allegation that Enlightenment would be the ideological spur of Western imperialism, see Racevskis, *Postmodernism and the Search*, and Gray, *Enlightenment's Wake*. On Jefferson's belonging to "the epoch of romantic nationalism, sharing a Koine of discourse . . . which . . . would have been immediately intelligible and generally acceptable, for example, to Byron and Shelley, de Staël and Sismondi," see Kelsall, *Jefferson and the Iconography*, 12. On Jefferson's fascination for the literature that "incorporated themes and motifs exemplifying neoclassical thought yet anticipating Romantic ideals," see Hayes, *Road to Monticello*, 103.

32. Pope, *Dunciad*, book 4, lines 653–56.

33. Helvétius, *Lettre à Montesquieu*, 285. See also Milton, *Paradise Lost*, book 3, lines 13–21.

34. Porter, *Creation of the Modern World,* 140. For matter as "spiritualized," see 141. See also Schofield, *Mechanism and Materialism;* Brown, "From Mechanism to Vitalism"; and Valsania, "'Another and the Same.'"

35. Mettrie, *Man a Machine,* 145; Darwin, *Temple of Nature* (canto 4, lines 427–28), 55; Buffon, *Histoire naturelle* ("Ier discours"), 1:15, 16–17: "La première vérité qui sort de cet examen sérieux de la Nature, est une vérité peut-être humiliante pour l'homme; c'est qu'il doit se ranger lui-même dans la classe des animaux, auxquels il ressemble par tout ce qu'il a de matériel, & même leur instinct lui paroîtra peut-être plus sûr que sa raison, & leur industrie plus admirable que ses arts." (All translations of Buffon into English are mine.) Jefferson fully agreed with Buffon's statement: "The 'modus operandi' of nature, in this, as in most other cases, can never be developed and demonstrated to beings limited as we are." TJ to George Cabanis, 12 July 1803, *Writings of TJ,* 10:404. On Jefferson's philosophy as emerging from the context of eighteenth-century materialism, see Boorstin, *Lost World of Jefferson.*

36. Porter, *Creation of the Modern World,* 55.

37. Diderot, in Raynal, *History of the Settlements* (vol. 4, book 11, chapter 10, "Colour of the Inhabitants"), 35; my translation from Dumarsais's "Philosophe"; Tracy, *Project d'éléments d'idéologie* (Préface), 3, my translation (C'est là l'objet de la métaphysique. Nous la rangerons au nombre des arts d'imagination destinés à nous satisfaire, et non à nous instruire). On Jefferson's positive appraisal of Destutt de Tracy, see TJ to John Adams, 14 March 1820, *A-JL,* 2:562. See also Chinard, *Jefferson et les idéologues.* The story of Jefferson as translator and promoter of Tracy's works and thought has been told several times. But see Koch, *Philosophy of Jefferson,* 54–64. On Jefferson's prejudice against metaphysics, see, for instance, TJ to John Adams, 21 February 1820, *A-JL,* 2:560–61, and TJ to John Adams, 14 March 1820, *A-JL,* 2:561–63.

38. On the eighteenth-century discovery of relativism, see Wolff, "Discovering Cultural Perspective."

39. Jefferson, *Jefferson's Literary Commonplace Book* (entry no. 16, from Bolingbroke, *Philosophical Works,* 2:154–55), 29; Staloff, *Hamilton, Adams, Jefferson,* 261. See also Jefferson, *Jefferson's Literary Commonplace Book* (entry no. 46, from Bolingbroke, *Philosophical Works,* Fragment 42, 4:316–20), 43–44. On Jefferson as "a friend to neology," see TJ to John Adams, 15 August 1820, *A-JL,* 2:565–69. See also TJ to John Waldo, 16 August 1813, *Writings of TJ,* 13:338–47, and TJ to Joseph Milligan, 6 April 1816, *Writings of TJ,* 14:456–66, in particular 463–64. After he had been named an honorary member of the American Academy of Language and Belles Lettres, Jefferson wrote to William Cardell, 27 January 1821: "Judicious neology can alone give strength & copiousness to language and enable it to be the vehicle of new ideas." Quoted in Burstein, *Jefferson's Secrets,* 102.

40. With John Adams, for instance, Jefferson freely conversed about Locke's materialistic hypothesis that "the mode of action called thought" might "have been given to a material organ of peculiar structure . . . as that of magnetism is to the Needle, or of elasticity to the spring." He also looked askance at the metaphysical opinion that thought, magnetism, or elasticity could "retire to hold a substantive and distinct existence." As always, Jefferson's attitude toward "speculations and subtleties" such as these was extremely cautious. Nevertheless, he declared that "I should, with Mr. Locke, prefer swallowing one incomprehensibility rather than two. It requires one effort only to admit the single incomprehensibility of matter endowed with thought: and two to believe, 1st. that of an existence called Spirit . . . and then 2dly. how that spirit which has neither extension nor solidity, can put materials organs

into motion." TJ to John Adams, 14 March 1820, *A-JL*, 2:562. On "my creed of material-ism" and the dictum that "to talk of *immaterial* existences is to talk of nothings," see TJ to John Adams, 15 August 1820, *A-JL*, 2:568. On Voltaire, who was for Jefferson "a repertory of facts, a dictionary of inventions rather than a thinker," and on Rousseau, whose ideas were "expressed in a much more logical and plausible way in Lord Kames," see Gilbert Chinard's introduction to Jefferson, *Commonplace Book of Jefferson*, 63. On Jefferson's "debt" toward Destutt de Tracy and other Ideolgists, see Koch, *Philosophy of Jefferson*, 54–82. Still an excel-lent introduction to Jefferson's thought and his several debts is Boorstin, *Lost World of Jef-ferson*. A more recent introduction to Jefferson's philosophy is Sheldon, *Political Philosophy of Jefferson*. On Jefferson's libraries, see Gilreath and Wilson, *Jefferson's Library*, and Wilson, *Jefferson's Books*. On Jefferson's readings, see Sanford, *Jefferson and His Library;* Wilson, "Jef-ferson's Early Notebooks"; and Reinhold, "Classical World." The best treatment to date of both Jefferson's early intellectual development and his reading habits is Hayes, *Road to Mon-ticello.* Hayes's study also deals extensively with Jefferson as a lover and a collector of books.

41. On the sweeping assertion that many thinkers contributed to Jefferson's worldview, see Jayne, *Jefferson's Declaration of Independence*, 168.

42. On Jefferson's positive appraisal of Ossian/Macpherson, see TJ to Charles Macpher-son, 25 February 1773, *PTJ*, 1:96–97. See also Hayes, *Road to Monticello*, 133–46. In the *Liter-ary Commonplace Books* there is an interesting passage from Young's *Night Thoughts* entered by Jefferson when still a teenager. See Jefferson, *Jefferson's Literary Commonplace Book* (entry no. 258), 103. On entries from Ossian/Macherson, see 141–45, 150–51. On Jefferson's roman-tic temper, see McLaughlin, "Jefferson, Poe, and Ossian."

43. On Jefferson's appreciation of Sterne, whose writings were "the best course of moral-ity that ever was written," see TJ to Peter Carr, 10 August 1787, *PTJ*, 12:15, and TJ to George W. Summers, 27 February 1822, *Writings of TJ*, 15:352–54.

44. Koch, *Philosophy of Jefferson*, 89.

2. OPTIMISM AS CERTAINTY

1. May, *Enlightenment in America*, 279; Wood, "Trials and Tribulations of Jefferson," 413.

2. On "compensatory consecration" in America, see Zuckerman, "Fabrication of Iden-tity," in particular 37–39. On presidential optimism as an American "counter tradition" trying to offset a widespread sense that America was an experiment, undertaken in defiance of history and fraught with risk, see Schlesinger, "America," 514.

3. Wood, *Radicalism of the American Revolution*, 6.

4. Colbourn, "Jefferson's Use of the Past," 57. Albeit history, as Jefferson said, "only informs us what bad government is," he was fully persuaded that a knowledge of history "becomes useful to the American politician." TJ to John Norvell, 14 June 1807, *Works of TJ*, 10:416. On Jefferson's conception and use of history, see also Cogliano, *Thomas Jefferson*, in particular 19–73. Cogliano's book analyzes how Jefferson sought to shape the way he would be treated by posterity. According to Cogliano, Jefferson wanted to be remembered as a successful "Apostle of Freedom" in the face of the assaults of the forces of tyranny and barbarism. See 262.

5. TJ to Elbridge Gerry, 26 January 1799, *PTJ*, 30:647; TJ to Joseph Priestley, 27 January 1800, *PTJ*, 31:341. Similar is TJ to William Green Munford, 18 June 1799, *PTJ*, 31:126–28. On Jefferson's interest for the "ocean ahead," see Boorstin, *Lost World of Jefferson*, 233.

6. TJ to Martha Jefferson, 28 March 1787, *PTJ*, 11:251.

7. TJ to William Green Munford, 18 June 1799, *PTJ*, 31:127. Condorcet's central idea, articulated in his *Outlines of an Historical View of the Progress of the Human Mind* (1795), was that humanity has passed through nine epochs, and it is entering the tenth and final one.

8. TJ to James Monroe, 24 November 1801, *PTJ*, 35:719; TJ to Benjamin Waterhouse, 3 March 1818, *Works of TJ*, 12:89–90; TJ to William Ludlow, 6 September 1824, *Writings of TJ*, 16:75.

9. TJ to Roger C. Weightman, 24 June 1826, *Works of TJ*, 12:477, italics added. On Jefferson's unremitting trust in humanity, see Burstein, *Inner Jefferson*, 238.

10. TJ to John Adams, 15 June 1813, *A-JL*, 2:332.

11. On the confidence of Adams and other leaders in God's approval of the Revolution, see Cherry, introduction to part 2, in Cherry, *God's New Israel*, 63–65. On America's millennial role, see also chapter 1, note 1. The journalist John L. O'Sullivan devised the idea of "Manifest Destiny." Arguing in 1845 against potentially aggressive deeds by Mexicans and the British, O'Sullivan wrote that it is "our manifest destiny to overspread and to possess the whole of the continent which Providence has given us for the development of the great experiment of liberty and federated self-government entrusted to us." See John L. O'Sullivan, "The True Title," *New York Morning News*, 27 December 1845.

12. TJ to William Ludlow, 6 September 1824, *Writings of TJ*, 16:75; TJ to Benjamin Rush, 23 September 1800, *PTJ*, 32:167.

13. TJ, "First Inaugural Address," 4 March 1801, *PTJ*, 33:150, 148. It is worth remembering that Jefferson ended his "Eighth Annual Message" with an overconfident appeal to his "firm persuasion that Heaven has in store for our beloved country long ages to come of prosperity and happiness." *Works of TJ*, 11:72. On Jefferson's appreciative attitude toward providence, see Boorstin, *Lost World of Jefferson*, 227, 229.

14. TJ to Benjamin Waterhouse, 3 March 1818, *Works of TJ*, 12:89–90; TJ to John Page, 4 May 1786, *PTJ*, 9:445. On Jefferson's interest in Matthew Boulton, the major figure of the Industrial Revolution in England, see TJ to Charles Thomson, 17 December 1786, *PTJ*, 10:609–10. See also TJ to Charles Thomson, 20 September 1787, *PTJ*, 12:160. On Jefferson's famous dictum "I am not afraid of new inventions or improvements," see TJ to Robert Fulton, 17 March 1810, *PTJ, Retirement Series*, 2:301. A good survey on Jefferson and science, applied science, and technology is Bedini, *Jefferson and Science*.

15. J. Clark, "American Image of Technology," 432; Marx, *Machine in the Garden*, 197. On importation as subjugation, see J. Clark, "American Image of Technology," 436.

16. TJ, *Notes*, Query 19, *Works of TJ*, 4:85–86; Benjamin Rush to TJ, 6 October 1800, in Rush, *Letters of Rush*, 2:824.

17. TJ to John Page, 4 May 1786, *PTJ*, 9:445. On cities as "quasi-feudal institutions," see Marx, *Machine in the Garden*, 238. On the qualitative difference between American and European cities, see White and White, *Intellectual versus the City*, 6–7, 9, 12. On the substantial approval of urbanity, see also Bender, *Toward an Urban Vision*, 3–51.

18. Onuf, "Scholars' Jefferson," 685.

19. On mountain men, voyageurs, and their unconditioned refusal of both city and technology, see R. F. Nash, *Wilderness and the American Mind*, 43.

20. On industry-agriculture continuity, see Benet, "Sociology Uncertain."

21. Marmor, "Anti-Industrialism and the Old South," 397. I find compelling Marmor's thesis of the southerner as a modern entrepreneur.

22. TJ, *Notes*, Query 19, *Works of TJ*, 4:85–86; Marx, *Machine in the Garden*, 126–27. On Jefferson and the environmentalism, see Browers, "Jefferson's Land Ethic."

23. Slotkin, *Fatal Environment*, 69; TJ to Horatio Gates, 21 February 1798, *Works of TJ*, 8:372; Hofstadter, "Parrington and the Jeffersonian Tradition," 400. On Jefferson's de facto approval of Hamilton's bank, see Wilentz, *Rise of American Democracy*, 104. On Jefferson and the Hamiltonian order, see C. A. Miller, *Jefferson and Nature*, 214–16. On Jefferson's favorable attitude toward surplus production and the "exploitative cast of mind," see McCoy, *Elusive Republic*, 252. On Jefferson's participation in the expanding international commerce, see Appleby, "Commercial Farming." On Jefferson's approval of labor-saving devices and the practice of interchangeable parts, see TJ to William Sampson, 26 January 1817, *Works of TJ*, 12:49–51. See also Hodin, "Mechanisms of Monticello." For the classic formulation of the "agrarian myth," see Hofstadter, *Age of Reform*.

24. TJ to Lafayette, 13 March 1801, *PTJ*, 33:270.

25. TJ to John Adams, 8 April 1816, *A-JL*, 2:467. For some examples of Jefferson's more long-lasting pessimistic stances, see TJ to John Adams, 11 January 1816, *A-JL*, 2:458–61; TJ to William Short, 28 November 1814, *Writings of TJ*, 14:211–18; TJ to Caesar A. Rodney, 10 February 1810, *PTJ, Retirement Series*, 2:209–10; and TJ to James Madison, 1 January 1797, *PTJ*, 29:247–48. On the belief that human condition will advance to such a level that there shall no longer be pain or vice, see TJ to P. S. Du pont de Nemours, 24 April 1816, *Works of TJ*, 11:519–25.

26. See TJ to William Ludlow, 6 September 1824, *Writings of TJ*, 16:75.

27. TJ to the "Brothers of the Choctaw nation," 17 December 1803, *Writings of TJ*, 16:403.

28. R. W. B. Lewis, *American Adam*, 5. See also Richard, *Founders and the Classics*, 87.

29. On Jefferson emphasizing the importance of the subject of history in his academic advice, see Cogliano, *Thomas Jefferson*, 19. Had he not been convinced that the knowledge of the past can prevent its repetition, Jefferson would not have made statements such as this: "Instead, therefore, of putting the Bible and Testament into the hands of the children at an age when their judgments are not sufficiently matured for religious inquiries, their memories may here be stored with the most useful facts from Grecian, Roman, European, and American history." TJ, *Notes*, Query 6, *Works of TJ*, 4:62. Knowledge of history, for Jefferson, was the best way to counter the fatalism and submission that religion may produce. It was the best way to protect the liberty Americans had just gained. On the "knowledge of those facts, which history exhibiteth" as "the most effectual means" of preventing the perversion of power into tyranny, see TJ, "A Bill for the More General Diffusion of Knowledge," 1778, *PTJ*, 2:526–27. On the rejection of the past as the unique repository of wisdom, see Appleby, *Capitalism and a New Social Order*, 79.

30. On "this march of civilization," see TJ to William Ludlow, 6 September 1824, *Writings of TJ*, 16:75. On good sense and reason, see TJ to Diodati, 3 August 1789, *PTJ*, 15:325–27. On "the immense advance in science," see TJ to Waterhouse, 3 March 1818, *Works of TJ*, 12:89. See also Wood, *Creation of the American Republic*, 120, and R. A. Ferguson, "Commonalities of Common Sense," in particular 491.

31. Samuel Stanhope Smith's hope, as confided to James Madison, November 1777–August 1778, in Madison, *Papers of Madison*, 1:208–9; Paine, *Common Sense*, 82, 120.

32. Price cited in Clarke, *British Opinion*, 170. On the vision of America's "stellar role," see Loewenberg, *American History*, 141.

33. Loewenberg, *American History,* 133. For examples of interpretations of the Revolutionary War as a fight for the rights of all humanity, see Van Tassel, *Recording America's Past,* 34, 38.

34. TJ to Richard Rush, 20 October 1820, *Writings of TJ,* 15:284; TJ to John Holmes, 22 April 1820, *Works of TJ,* 12:160.

35. Benjamin Rush to Elias Boudinot, 9 July 1788, Rush, *Letters of Rush,* 1:475. On the founders' acquaintance with universalistic discourses on natural law, moral sense, laws of nature, and natural rights, see Commager, *Jefferson, Nationalism, and the Enlightenment;* Commager, *Empire of Reason;* L. H. Cohen, "American Revolution"; White, *Philosophy of the American Revolution;* White, *Philosophy,* The Federalist*, and the Constitution;* and Richard, *Founders and the Classics,* 169–95. As Sheldon points out, Locke's principle of natural rights (that he elaborated in his *Second Treatise*) was actually at odds with the idea of moral sense. Locke's psychology portrayed humans as separate, isolated, and independent beings aiming at a pure contractual idea of justice. In contrast, the moral sense theory described humans in an Aristotelian way, as creatures naturally social and political, as beings who have their telos in society and who were designed to serve the good of society rather than their personal interests. Sheldon contends that Jefferson adhered to the Lockian idea of natural rights in particular when he wrote the Declaration and during the period of the Revolution (in the "destructive" moments, when the real priority was cutting the ties with England and attaining independence), and that he shifted to a moral sense position later on, and in general each time he was attempting to construct a republic. See Sheldon, *Political Philosophy of Jefferson,* 2, 9, 17, 51, 93–94. On the "nonliberal" doctrine of the moral sense, see 53–60. Notwithstanding the difference, the natural rights theory and the moral sense philosophy shared the same conviction that humans were more than historical and circumstantial beings, that they were open to meta-historical, abstract, ideal laws and standards.

36. See TJ to Thomas Law, 13 June 1814, *Writings of TJ,* 14:138–44, in particular 141. On Jefferson's use of moral sense, see also TJ to Peter Carr, 10 August 1787, *PTJ,* 12:14–19. See also Fiering, "Irresistible Compassion." Garry Wills argues that Jefferson was familiar with the basic lines of division among the theorists of moral sense because he was able to distinguish Hutcheson's moral sense from Reid's common sense. See Wills, *Inventing America,* 200–206.

37. On revolutionaries' choice to be in a state of nature, see C. A. Miller, *Jefferson and Nature,* 258–59.

38. Ibid., 278–79. On history as a chain of errors, ignorance, and superstition, see, for instance, TJ to Alexander von Humboldt, 6 December 1813, *Works of TJ,* 11:350–55, in particular 351.

39. TJ to Thomas Pinckney, 30 December 1792, *PTJ,* 24:803, italics added.

40. TJ to Thomas Mann Randolph, 7 January 1793, *PTJ,* 25:30.

41. TJ to William Short, 3 January 1793, *PTJ,* 25:14. See also TJ to Gouverneur Morris, 30 December 1792, *PTJ,* 24:800–801. In his "First Inaugural Address" Jefferson proclaimed the same "sacred" principle, "that though the will of the majority is in all cases to prevail, that will, to be rightful, must be reasonable; that the minority possess their equal rights, which equal laws must protect, and to violate would be oppression" (*PTJ,* 33:149). Not to be confused with an expression of particularism and with a "tyranny of the majority," according to Tocqueville's classical formulation, the will of which Jefferson spoke must be put under the

banner of the law and turned into an expression of universality. For an interpretation of the "Adam and Eve" letter as an explicit vindication of the holocaust, see O'Brien, *Long Affair,* 148–50.

42. TJ to Diodati, 3 August 1789, *PTJ,* 15:326.

43. Appleby, *Capitalism and a New Social Order,* 83. For the "informal, voluntary, political life open to all," see 67.

44. On the problem of universal existence in secular particularity, see Pocock, *Machiavellian Moment,* 9. See also Pocock, "Civic Humanism."

45. Pocock, *Machiavellian Moment,* 545, 551.

46. For the standard characterization of the opposition between the republican and the liberal models, see Wood, *Creation of the American Republic,* 606–15.

47. See TJ to Diodati, 3 August 1789, *PTJ,* 15:326.

48. Jefferson's optimistic belief that the American government would not encroach upon the people is well expressed in passages such as this: "A government, if organized in all it's part on the Representative principle unadulterated by the infusion of spurious elements, if founded, not in the fears & follies of man, but on his reason . . . may be so free as to restrain him in no moral right, and so firm as to protect him from every moral wrong. To observe our fellow citizens gathering daily under the banners of this faith . . . cannot but give new animation to the zeal of those who, steadfast in the same belief, have seen no other object worthy the labours & losses we have all encountered." TJ to Amos Marsh, 20 November 1801, *PTJ,* 35:708–9. On power in America as "disembodied" and "homogeneous," see Wood, *Creation of the American Republic,* 604. On John Adams's dictum, see J. Adams, *Works of John Adams,* 4:230.

3. FROM FAITH TO HOPE

1. TJ to Edward Carrington, 16 January 1787, *PTJ,* 11:49. See also TJ to Abigail Adams, 22 February 1787, *PTJ,* 11:174–75; and TJ to William Stephens Smith, 13 November 1787, *PTJ,* 12:355–57. See also *J and His Time,* 2:158–59.

2. TJ to James Madison, 20 December 1787, *PTJ,* 12:442, Italics added.

3. On the Jeremiad in America, see Bercovitch, *American Jeremiad.*

4. On Jefferson's aversion to "artificial reason" and buoyancy, see C. A. Miller, *Jefferson and Nature,* 5. On Jefferson playing in defense, see *J and His Time,* 2:487.

5. Burstein, *Inner Jefferson,* 93.

6. TJ to Maria Cosway, 12 October 1786, *PTJ,* 10:451, italics added; Burstein, *Inner Jefferson,* 95. On the heart's superiority to the head, see also Wills, *Inventing America,* 279–83.

7. That for Jefferson knowledge had to *start,* not to end, with facts can be demonstrated by passages like this: "A patient pursuit of facts, and cautious combination and comparison of them, is the drudgery to which man is subjected by his Maker, if he wishes to attain sure knowledge." TJ, *Notes,* Query 6, *Works of TJ,* 3:462. If one puts emphasis on words such as "combination" and "comparison," the passage comes to uphold an inferential vision of knowledge, not a descriptive vision. By the same token, the system of classes, orders, genera, and species—through which our mind imposes order on the infinitude of units that nature produces—is a creation of human imagination. See TJ to John Manners, 22 February 1814, *Writings of TJ,* 14:97–98. Knowledge, for Jefferson, always looks optimistically forward, beyond facts and individuals. On the importance of looking forward, from a practical point

of view as well, see TJ to Joseph Priestley, 27 January 1800, *PTJ*, 31:339–41. Similar is TJ to William Green Munford, 18 June 1799, *PTJ*, 31:126–28.

8. TJ to the president and secretaries of the Institut National de France, 14 November 1802, printed in Chinard, *Jefferson et les idéologues*, 21.

9. TJ, *Notes*, Query 6, *Works of TJ*, 3:393. Also Copernican in style was Jefferson's passage that I have just cited, that "a patient pursuit of facts, and cautious combination and comparison of them, is the drudgery to which man is subjected by his Maker, if he wishes to attain sure knowledge." Query 6, *Works of TJ*, 3:462. Certainly Copernican was Jefferson's appreciation of living in a universe that was becoming larger and larger, and in which no fixed stars (literally) were left. Commenting on the discovery of the periodical variation of light in some stars, Jefferson offered this consideration: "What are we to conclude from this? That there are suns which have their orbits of revolution too? But this would suppose a wonderful harmony in their planets, and present a new scene where the attracting powers should be without and not within the orbit. The motion of our sun would be a miniature of this." TJ to Rev. James Madison, 2 October 1785, *PTJ*, 8:576. On Jefferson's Copernican and antidogmatic dictum that "doubt is wisdom," see TJ to Chastellux, 7 June 1785, *PTJ*, 8:184–86. On Jefferson's idea that "truth advances, and error recedes, step by step only," see TJ to Thomas Cooper, 7 October 1814, *Writings of TJ*, 14:200. See also Cassara, *Enlightenment in America*, 20, 32.

10. George Washington, "Circular to State Governments," June 8, 1783, in Washington, *Writings*, 517–18.

11. Jared Sparks in Herbert B. Adams, *Life and Writings of Sparks*, 1:6. On the "invention" of historical responsibility and agency and the eighteenth-century fear of determinism and instrumentality, see Fliegelman, *Declaring Independence*, 140–50.

12. Wood, *Creation of the American Republic*, 41. See also Wood, "Conspiracy and the Paranoid Style." On the Whig historiography, see Colbourn, *Lamp of Experience*. On Jefferson's historical thinking as derived from the Whig interpretation of history, see Cogliano, *Thomas Jefferson*, 21–22. Cogliano writes that "the chief lesson that history taught, according to the whig historians, was that *liberty was always in danger* and that it could only be protected by a virtuous, informed and vigilant citizenry" (22, italics added). For interesting works on conspiracy and the psychology of anxiety, see Hofstadter, *Paranoid Style;* Burrows and Wallace, "American Revolution"; Jordan, "Familial Politics"; Waters, "James Otis"; Brodie, *Thomas Jefferson;* Mazlish, "Leadership in the American Revolution"; Shaw, *Character of John Adams;* Greven, *Protestant Temperament;* Lynn, *Divided People;* and Shaw, *American Patriots.*

13. Banning, "Republican Ideology," 171; Bailyn, *Ideological Origins*, 156.

14. On the frequent allegation that the British would be champions of conspiratorial designs, see Trees, "John Adams," in particular 399.

15. Kammen, *People of Paradox*, 113. On slavery as a "blot in our country," see TJ, *Notes*, Query 8, *Works of TJ*, 3:491.

16. The *Federalist Papers* (1787–88) probably represent the best catalogue of plain motives for colonists' shivering with precariousness. The *Federalist Papers* portray a country rich in possibility but in desperate need of a bulwark. On "artificial" monopolies that would ruin "natural" producers, see McCoy, *Elusive Republic*, 154–55. Hundreds of scholars have drawn attention to the question of American anxieties. The best large-scale examination of anxieties during the revolutionary years and the early phases of the republic is Wood, *Creation of the American Republic.*

17. Jefferson's anxieties are magisterially recounted in Malone's biography (*J and His Time*). On expectations generating anxiety and frustration, see Kammen, *People of Paradox*, 114.

18. Howe, "Republican Thought," 154. See also Rodgers, "Republicanism."

19. TJ to Edward Rutledge, 24 June 1797, *PTJ*, 29:456–57.

20. Howe, "Republican Thought," 150. On Virginians wishing a speedy death to Washington, see 149.

21. On the paranoid way—maybe a better adjective than "ideological"—Federalists perceived Jefferson and his supporters as a serious threat to the state that they worked to create, see Gannon, "Escaping 'Mr. Jefferson's Plan.'"

22. Schlesinger, "America," 509, 511, 512. On the United States as an "experiment," see also Nagel, *One Nation Indivisible;* Stampp, "Concept of a Perpetual Union"; Murrin, "Roof without Walls"; and Buel, *America on the Brink.*

23. John Adams to TJ, 3 February 1821, *A-JL*, 2:571; TJ to St. George Tucker, 28 August 1797, *PTJ*, 29:519. See also TJ, *Notes,* Query 8, *Works of TJ*, 3:491. On the specter of rebellion, see Zuckerman, "Power of Blackness."

24. TJ, *Notes,* Query 18, *Works of TJ*, 4:83–84.

25. TJ to John Holmes, 22 April 1820, *Works of TJ*, 12:158–59.

26. TJ, *Notes,* Query 6, *Works of TJ*, 3:460; TJ to the Emperor Alexander, 19 April 1806, *Works of TJ*, 10:249. On Jefferson's plans to expatriate and emancipate slaves, see Onuf, *Jefferson's Empire*, 147–188.

27. On the opposition between "the scanty field of what is known" and the "boundless region of what is unknown," see TJ to Caspar Wistar, 21 June 1807, *Works of TJ*, 10:427.

28. Onuf, "Scholars' Jefferson," 698, italics added.

29. TJ to Philip Mazzei, 24 April 1796, *PTJ*, 29:82; Charles Thomson to TJ, 9 March 1782, *PTJ*, 6:163; TJ to Caspar Wistar, 21 June 1807, *Works of TJ*, 10:427. On Jefferson's aversion to perpetual laws, see the *locus classicus* TJ to James Madison, 6 September 1789, *PTJ*, 15:392–97. I return to this famous letter, and to the idea of precariousness that it conveys, in chapter 4.

30. TJ, *Notes,* Query 18, *Works of TJ*, 4:83–84, italics added. Jefferson actually said that "error," not hazard, "is the stuff of which the web of life is woven." See TJ to Chastellux, October 1786, *PTJ*, 10:498. But in that letter Jefferson also put emphasis on the fact that "human calculations" are often "set aside by events." Events drive human calculations toward error and failure. As a consequence, to live "longest and wisest" means to accept the risk of incurring error. On the centrality of nautical metaphors to Jefferson's thought, see C. A. Miller, *Ship of State.*

31. TJ to Caspar Wistar, 21 June 1807, *Works of TJ*, 10:427; TJ to John Adams, 8 April 1816, *A-JL*, 2:467.

32. TJ to Jedediah Morse, 6 March 1822, *Works of TJ*, 12:222.

33. Ibid., 12:224–25, italics added. The theme of the strength of circumstances and of sudden changes appears also in TJ to John Adams, 11 January 1816, *A-JL*, 2:458–61.

34. TJ, *Notes,* Query 17, *Works of TJ*, 4:81–82.

35. On Jefferson's plea for order and his ritual of recording entries, see James A. Bear Jr. and Lucia C. Stanton, introduction to Jefferson, *Memorandum Books*, 1:xviii–xix.

36. C. A. Miller, *Jefferson and Nature*, 15. On the way Ladyard and other travelers "affected Jefferson's thinking profoundly," see Jackson, *Jefferson and the Stony Mountains*, 56.

On Jefferson's preference for the carrying on of things over their completion, see *J and His Time*, 4:38.

4. NATURE AND TIME AS OVERWHELMING POWERS

1. TJ, *Notes,* Query 6, *Works of TJ,* 3:438–60, passim; Crèvecoeur, *Letters from an American Farmer,* 56. Good examples of Jefferson's speaking the language of environmentalism are also TJ to Chastellux, 7 June 1785, *PTJ,* 8:184–86, and TJ to Chastellux, 2 September 1785, *PTJ,* 8:467–70. On the eighteenth-century environmentalist outlook, see Marx, *Machine in the Garden,* 109–10. See also Sheehan, *Seeds of Extinction,* 15–44, and Shaffer, *Politics of History.*

2. On Jefferson's penchant toward the conventional theme of the weakness of human nature, see, for instance, TJ, "Second Inaugural Address," 4 March 1805, *Works of TJ,* 10:136. On Jefferson's reliance in education, see Wagoner, *Jefferson and Education.*

3. TJ to Jedediah Morse, 6 March 1822, *Works of TJ,* 12:225.

4. TJ, *Notes,* Query 18, *Works of TJ,* 4:82–83. An interesting chapter of the Enlightenment use of the idea of dependence on environment was the notion of psycho-physical parallelism. David Hartley, La Mettrie, Joseph Priestley, and William Cullen articulated the thesis that mental operations reflected cerebral localization; that memory, imagination, and the moral faculties were influenced by the physical condition of the brain. Interesting arguments for upholding the correlation between mental and physiological states can be found, for instance, in Rush, *Inquiry into the Influence,* and Franklin, "Art of Procuring Pleasant Dreams," 10:131–37.

5. I draw my interpretation of Jefferson's doctrine that "all men are created equal" from Fliegelman, *Declaring Independence,* 197.

6. TJ, "Report of the Commissioners for the University of Virginia" (Rockfish Report), 4 August 1818, in Jefferson, *Writings,* 461.

7. John Adams to TJ, 9 October 1787, *A-JL,* 1:202–3. Robert Ferguson comments on Adams's passage in this way: "Ironically, the triumph of the Revolution is accompanied by a grim awareness of human limitation and continuing acrimony among those who struggle to fulfill its continuing promise." R. A. Ferguson, "American Enlightenment," 352.

8. John Adams to TJ, 2 February 1816, *A-JL,* 2:461; Ellis, *Passionate Sage,* 105; John Adams to James Madison, 25 July 1818, quoted in Ellis, *Passionate Sage,* 105. On the "passion for superiority," see John Adams to Abigail Adams, 22 May 1777, in Butterfield, *Adams Family Correspondence,* 2:245–46. See also Ellis, *Passionate Sage,* 97, 123, 237–38.

9. John Adams to TJ, 30 June 1814, *A-JL,* 2:346–47.

10. Curti, *Human Nature in American Thought,* 106.

11. TJ to John Adams, 1 June 1822, *A-JL,* 2:578–79.

12. TJ to James Madison, 1 January 1797, *PTJ,* 29:248.

13. Fries, "Varieties of Freedom," 21. On the Enlightenment attempt at the "invention" of historical responsibility and agency together with the fear of determinism, see Fliegelman, *Declaring Independence,* 140–50.

14. C. A. Miller, *Jefferson and Nature,* 6, 7. See also Lovejoy and Boas, "Appendix: Some Meanings of 'Nature,'" *Primitivism and Related Ideas,* 447–56.

15. On Jefferson and moral sense, see, for instance, TJ to Thomas Law, 13 June 1814, *Writings of TJ,* 14:138–44.

16. On nature as a source of pride and nationalism, see R. N. Miller, "American Nationalism."

17. TJ, "Observations on Démeunier's Manuscript," 22 June 1786, *PTJ*, 10:56–57; TJ to James Monroe, 17 June 1785, *PTJ*, 8:233, italics added; TJ to Maria Cosway, 12 October 1786, *PTJ*, 10:447. In the Query 6 of the *Notes* (*Works of TJ*, 3:400–408), Jefferson offered a detailed catalogue of the trees, plants, fruits, flowers, and vegetables, both native and produced in the American farms. Although the tone is generally detached and scientific, by compiling that list he put no fetters to his nationalistic pride. Philip Freneau, for one, used to do the same. He declared the Nile "but a small rivulet and the Danube a ditch" when compared to the beautiful Mississippi river. Freneau, "Philosopher of the Forest," *Prose of Philip Freneau*, 228. Like several other settlers, Freneau liked to portray his new country as "naturally invincible."

18. TJ, *Notes*, Query 5, *Works of TJ*, 3:380; Query 6, *Works of TJ*, 3:417, 415. On Jefferson and the "virtual infinitude" of American nature, see C. A. Miller, *Jefferson and Nature*, 266. See also R. F. Nash, *Wilderness and the American Mind*, 67–83.

19. Marx, *Machine in the Garden*, 110.

20. Zuckert, *Natural Rights Republic*, 61, 62. On nature-as-order and nature-as-disorder, see Kelsall, *Jefferson and the Iconography*, 166. On nature as a source of law, see Zuckert, *Natural Rights Republic*, 129. On the expression "real nature," see C. A. Miller, *Jefferson and Nature*, 10. On the American nature as the "beast," see Kelsall, *Jefferson and the Iconography*, 76. See also Scheick, "Chaos and Imaginative Order."

21. On Jefferson's *Garden Book,* the episode of the aurora borealis, and other interesting details, see Hayes, *Road to Monticello,* 253–54. For the idea of a connection between nature, death, and the *Notes,* I am indebted to Frank Cogliano.

22. TJ to Martha Jefferson, 11 December 1783, *PTJ*, 6:380–81; TJ to Horatio G. Spafford, 11 May 1819, *Writings of TJ*, 15:189; TJ to William Duane, 1 October 1812, *PTJ*, Retirement Series, 5:366. On Jefferson's preference for Epicurus, see Richard, "Dialogue with the Ancients." Douglas Wilson writes that "perhaps the most persistent motif in the Literary Commonplace Book is death. It appears early and late, in poetry and in prose, in English, Latin, and Greek." Wilson in Jefferson, *Jefferson's Literary Commonplace Book,* 16. Death is also a prevalent theme of Jefferson's *Scrapbooks.*

23. TJ, *Notes*, Query 12, *Works of TJ*, 4:4.

24. Primer, "Erasmus Darwin's *Temple of Nature*," 61.

25. Crèvecoeur, *Letters from an American Farmer,* 69, 68. On the "wilderness-temptation," see R. F. Nash, *Wilderness and the American Mind,* 20, 29. On Crèvecoeur's fatalistic attitude, his "underlying conviction of the universal presence of evil," and his certitude that "the dream must turn to horror," see Grabo, "Crevecoeur's American," 168. Like Crèvecoeur, Jefferson was aware of the danger coming from the practice of eating excessive animal food: "I fancy it must be the quantity of animal food eaten by the English which renders their character insusceptible of civilization. I suspect it is in their kitchens and not in their churches that their reformation must be worked." TJ to Abigail Adams, 25 September 1785, *PTJ*, 8:548–49. The letter is suffused with irony, but Jefferson took the argument very seriously. His alimentary diet is a demonstration of that.

26. TJ to Madame de Tessé, 20 March 1787, *PTJ*, 11:228. On barbarism, see also TJ to Giovanni Fabbroni, 8 June 1778, *PTJ*, 2:195–97. In that letter Jefferson was styling himself as

the teacher who would rescue his countrymen from their "deplorable barbarism" by introducing them to the school of European music and culture generally. According to Jefferson, not just Roman but also Greek thinkers (with the exception of Plato) presented "the lights which originally led ourselves out of Gothic darkness." TJ to A. Coray, 31 October 1823, *Writings of TJ*, 15:481. On Jefferson's distrust of Plato, see, for instance, TJ to John Adams, 5 July 1814, *A-JL*, 2:432–33. Jefferson was serious about the danger of barbarism. Writing to New York's governor DeWitt Clinton, 19 March 1822, he compared the Erie Canal with the University of Virginia. "While you get millions to employ so usefully," he wrote, "I am laboring for a few thousands to save my fellow-citizens from the Gothic barbarism into which they are sinking for want of the means of education." Quoted in Burstein, *Jefferson's Secrets*, 82.

27. Cunningham, *In Pursuit of Reason*, 2. On Jefferson's lacking firsthand knowledge of the wilderness, see Jackson, *Jefferson and the Stony Mountains*, 81. On the cultural distance between America and Europe, see Strout, *American Image*.

28. On "marchlands," see Bailyn, *Peopling of the British North America*, 112–13.

29. R. F. Nash, *Wilderness and the American Mind*, 43.

30. TJ's response to the "Address of Welcome by the Citizens of Albemarle," 12 February 1790, *PTJ*, 16:179.

31. Fowler, "Mythologies of a Founder," 131.

32. On Jefferson's interest in classes, orders, genera, and species, see TJ to John Manners, 22 February 1814, *Writings of TJ*, 14:97–98. On "let the eye of vigilance never be closed," see TJ to Spencer Roane, 9 March 1821, *Works of TJ*, 12:202. Kevin Hayes maintains that Jefferson's decision to make the issue of boundaries the first subject of the *Notes* revealed fully his personality and his real priorities: he always tried to exert control. "His desire to establish boundaries before proceeding any further reflects his personal need to exert control over his subject." Hayes, *Road to Monticello*, 237.

33. R. A. Ferguson, "American Enlightenment," 374.

34. TJ to Caspar Wistar, 21 June 1807, *Works of TJ*, 10:427.

35. *J and His Time*, 5:9. The present section has largely benefited from Spahn, *Thomas Jefferson, Time, and History*. Jefferson used the word "time" (and its equivalents) to articulate several emotions. Just like "nature." Besides, he gave the word several meanings. While here I am exclusively concerned with Jefferson's uses of "time" intended as the course of time, namely, historical time, Spahn's study covers a wider range of topics, including Jefferson's ideas of scientific time.

36. On "this march of civilization," see TJ to William Ludlow, 6 September 1824, *Writings of TJ*, 16:75. On "the immense advance in science," see TJ to Benjamin Waterhouse, 3 March 1818, *Works of TJ*, 12:89.

37. On good sense and reason, see TJ to Diodati, 3 August 1789, *PTJ*, 15:326.

38. See Paine, *Common Sense*, 82, 120.

39. TJ to Lafayette, 9 October 1824, *Works of TJ*, 12:379. A younger Jefferson also used to say that "Every thing in nature decays." TJ to Charles Thomson, 20 September 1787, *PTJ*, 12:160. Eran Shalev demonstrates that there is something typically southern in Jefferson's Epicurean doctrine that "everything has its beginning, its growth, and end." The southern "prevailing" understanding of time, as Shalev argues, envisioned time as "corruptive and baneful to political, as it was to organic, entities." See Shalev, *Rome Reborn*, especially chapter 3.

40. Contemporary psychology widely supports the suggestion that persons have mul-

tiple and often incompatible discourses and allegiances. A person may employ a variety of discourses and "construction subsystems" that, as the psychologist George Kelly says, "are inferentially incompatible with each other." Kelly, *Psychology of Personal Constructs,* 5. "We have curious mixtures of allegiances," the psychologist Anthony Cohen agrees. "The issue is not that we belong to many different kinds of group and association, although of course we do. Rather, the curiosity lies in their incompatibility. Many are positively antagonistic to each other." A. P. Cohen, *Self Consciousness,* 8. Arnold Epstein put the same idea in these slightly different terms: "Identity . . . is essentially a concept of synthesis. It represents the process by which the person seeks to integrate his various statutes and roles, as well as his diverse experiences, into a coherent image of self." Epstein, *Ethos and Identity,* 101.

41. R. W. B. Lewis, *American Adam,* 5.

42. "The characteristic of Bancroft's *History* that most obviously links it to early modern modes of historical perception is its retention of Providence as an active, shaping force in history. Bancroft's work was pre-eminently a history of the millennial American republic, and in it the divine end required divine power." Ross, "Historical Consciousness," 915. For an excellent description of the romantic pattern of historical explanation, see Wierich, "Struggling through History."

43. R. W. B. Lewis, *American Adam,* 5; TJ to Lafayette, 9 October 1824, *Works of TJ,* 12:379. On the American "legend of providential intervention," including its use during the Revolution, see Hay, "Providence and the American Past." On Jefferson's use of providence, see TJ, "First Inaugural Address," 4 March 1801, *PTJ,* 33:150.

44. TJ, "Report of the Commissioners for the University of Virginia" (Rockfish Report), 4 August 1818, in Jefferson, *Writings,* 461. On the prevalence of this natural cyclical pattern in the period, see Meek, *Social Science,* and McCoy, *Elusive Republic,* 18–19. On progress as a mode of necessity, see Bury, *Idea of Progress,* 1–7. In his well-known study of the French *philosophes,* Carl Becker acknowledged that they subscribed to the idea of progress as a secularization of the Christian millennialist interpretation of history. They were substantially incapable of dismissing the traditional religious milieu. See Becker, *Heavenly City.* On the novel idea of progress as depending on the human heart, see Ekirch, *Idea of Progress in America,* 11.

45. Persons, "Cyclical Theory of History," 152, 156; McCoy, *Elusive Republic,* 34. See also Ross, "Historical Consciousness"; Nisbet, *History of the Idea;* and Morley, "Decadence as a Theory." On the Enlightenment view of progress as "circumscribed and impermanent," see Gay, *Enlightenment,* 98–108.

46. Howe, "Republican Thought," 161. On the notion that "Revolutionary thinkers in particular assumed the certainty of declension, holding that all political institutions grew corrupt; . . . even after Independence," see Lienesch, "Constitutional Tradition," 22.

47. Machiavelli, *Discourses,* in *Historical, Political, and Diplomatic Writings,* 2:319; Bolingbroke, *Letters on the Spirit of Patriotism,* 128. Jefferson's advocacy of frequent elections (see, for instance, TJ to James Sullivan, 9 February 1797, *PTJ,* 29:289–90; or TJ to John Adams, 28 October 1813, *A-JL,* 2:387–92) brings to mind the Bolingbrokian recipe to prolong youth. On such civic humanist ethos and the idea of escaping the course of history, or at least retarding its unavoidable conclusion, see also Pocock, *Machiavellian Moment,* 545.

48. A. Ferguson, *Essay on History,* 318. On Adam Smith's peculiar idea of progress, see Heilbroner, "Paradox of Progress."

49. On Colden, see Cassara, *Enlightenment in America,* 169–70.

50. Bowdoin cited in Howe, "Republican Thought," 161–62.

51. "Thoughts on the Decline of States," 408; Barton, *New Views*, v. Other interesting examples are provided by Persons, *American Minds*, 123. On Thomas Cole and cyclical history, see Wierich, "Struggling through History," 58. See also Larkin, *Art and Life in America*, 202, and Richardson, *Painting in America*, 167. Both Larkin and Richardson have suggested that Cole may have been inspired by Volney's *Ruines*.

52. Rush, *Autobiography*, 71; John Quincy Adams quoted in Van Tassel, *Recording America's Past*, 45; Webster, *American Selection of Lessons*, 214, 215.

53. On Jefferson's "heroic failure," see Henry Adams, *History of the United States*, 1:334, 9:226. See also Curti, *Human Nature in American Historical Thought*, 86.

54. TJ to Lafayette, 9 October 1824, *Works of TJ*, 12:379; TJ to Henry Dearborn, 17 August 1821, *Works of TJ*, 12:205; TJ to Benjamin Rush, 17 August 1811, *PTJ, Retirement Series*, 4:88. On Jefferson's use of the trope "ripeness of time," see also TJ to John Adams, 1 August 1816, *A-JL*, 2:484.

55. TJ to James Madison, 6 September 1789, *PTJ*, 15:392–97, passim. For arguments identical to that of the letter to Madison, see also TJ to John Wayles Eppes, 24 June 1813, *Works of TJ*, 11:297–306, and TJ to Samuel Kercheval, 12 July 1816, *Works of TJ*, 12:3–15. On Jefferson's use of the term "generation," see Sloan, "Earth Belongs," 297. And see Morgan, *Inventing the People*, 82–83, 153–54, 267.

56. McCoy, *Elusive Republic*, 16.

57. TJ to Samuel Kercheval, 12 July 1816, *Works of TJ*, 12:14.

58. TJ to Washington, 15 March 1784, *PTJ*, 7:26; TJ, *Notes*, Query 17, *Works of TJ*, 4:81; Kelsall, *Jefferson and the Iconography*, 18. Jefferson was well acquainted with the idea of fate. Douglas Wilson writes that "the theme of bearing whatever the fates or fortune may bestow . . . is one that occurs frequently in the LCB and is closely allied to the Stoic attitude toward death and misfortune." Wilson in Jefferson, *Jefferson's Literary Commonplace Book*, 18. Wilson also notes that in the LCB runs a "counter-theme of defiance and rebellion" (18). This is the typical Jefferson's dualism. See also TJ to John Page, 15 July 1763, *PTJ*, 1:9–11.

59. Persons, "Cyclical Theory of History," 158. On Jefferson and Adams and the novelty of their noncyclical progress, see 160.

60. On past and future fused in an instantaneous present, see Benjamin, *Illuminations*, 263. On the survival of such a "premodern" time in eighteenth- and nineteenth-century America, see Holland, "Notes on the State," 192.

61. Niebuhr, *Faith and History*, 38. A superb example that the premodern mindset did not disappear from modern consciousness, and from American consciousness in particular, is given in chapter 33, "A Dynamic Theory of History," of Henry Adams's *Education of Henry Adams*. Adams clearly contended that as historical time is concerned, "the forces of nature capture man." According to Adams, the mind has no intrinsic importance in deciding the course of events, humans are merely pawns in the cosmic chess game, and the only freedom they really have is the freedom to submit to overpowerful forces or to be wrecked by them. See Henry Adams, *Henry Adams and His Friends*, 121–22. On the founders' acknowledgment of the Stoics, see Richard, *Founders and the Classics*, 169–95.

62. TJ, *Autobiography*, *Works of TJ*, 1:156.

63. Wirt, "Eulogy on Jefferson," *Writings of TJ*, 13:xlvii. On Jefferson as a natural historian and naturalist, see C. A. Miller, *Jefferson and Nature*, 40–44. See also Thomson, *Passion for Nature*.

64. TJ to George Wythe, 16 January 1796, *PTJ,* 28:583–84. The image of time as a destroyer is also conveyed in TJ to Ebenezer Hazard, 18 February 1791, *PTJ,* 19:287–89, and TJ to William Green Munford, 18 June 1799, *PTJ,* 31:126–28. On Jefferson's effort and strategies to preserve the national memory from the loss, see Cogliano, *Thomas Jefferson,* 28–34.

65. McCoy, *Elusive Republic,* 105.

66. John Adams to Mercy Warren, 14 May 1786, in *Warren-Adams Letters,* 2:275–76. On the fact that his sojourn in Europe confirmed Adams in the conviction that Europe seemed to represent what America was fast becoming, see Wood, *Creation of the American Republic,* 571. On Adams's pessimism, see 574–75. On Adams making the point that only force could retard the destiny of the republic, see John Adams to TJ, 9 October 1787, *A-JL,* 1:202–3. See also McCoy, *Elusive Republic,* 114, 115, 259.

67. Ross, "Historical Consciousness," 912. See also Levin, *History as Romantic Art.*

68. Wilson, "Jefferson vs. Hume," 50. Merrill Peterson has given a particularly concise and well-rendered characterization of the Saxon myth, as it was understood by Jefferson and his generation. See Peterson, *Jefferson and the New Nation,* 56–58.

69. A strong analogy exists between the doctrine of progress à la Bancroft, which was completely foreign to Jefferson, and the cyclical view, which Jefferson tried to curb. They both are different in nature from historicism. Historicism believes that past events are fundamentally shaped by past contexts, that these contexts are continually changing, that all events in historical time can be explained by prior events in historical time—without the intercession of extra-historical events—and in particular that contingencies have a real causative role. In contrast, both Bancroft's doctrine and the cyclical view considered history through the exclusive lens of necessity. While historicism, as Pocock writes, is "an attempt to depict history as generating new norms and values," both Bancroft's doctrine of progress and the cyclical view maintain a preformistic view. "Realization" rather than "change," "fulfillment" rather than "process," are the best categories to portray the historical course as a plan written and decided from the outset. See Pocock, *Machiavellian Moment,* 551.

70. Persons, "Cyclical Theory of History," 157; Looby, "Constitution of Nature," 264; TJ to James Madison, 20 December 1787, version printed as an enclosure to TJ's letter to Uriah Forrest, 31 December 1787, *PTJ,* 12:478. See also McCoy, *Elusive Republic,* 13–47.

71. Looby, "Constitution of Nature," 265; TJ to Benjamin Rush, 17 August 1811, *PTJ, Retirement Series,* 4:87. On the Enlightenment's penchant for reducing the problems posed by life and history to mathematical form, see Wills, *Inventing America,* 132–48. On the dream that Louisiana's space would preserve the nation's agrarian character and, together with republican institutions, ensure its progress virtually in perpetuity, see Ross, "Historical Consciousness," 912.

5. IMPOSSIBILITY AND DESPONDENCY

1. John Adams to TJ, 3 May 1816, *A-JL,* 2:469; Colbourn, *Lamp of Experience,* 87. See also May, *Enlightenment in America,* 279. Adams's letter to Jefferson of 3 May 1816 is an answer to Jefferson's abiding optimism as it appears in TJ to John Adams, 8 April 1816, *A-JL,* 2:466–69. On Adams's mental health, see Ferling and Braverman, "Adams's Health Reconsidered." On Adams as a "conservative revolutionist" and the complexities and contradictions of his character, see Kurtz, "Political Science of Adams," 613. See also Miroff, "John Adams." On Adams's "tension between hope and pessimism," see Schulz, "John Adams." Schulz does not intend to downplay Adams's pessimism. That would be impossible. But by

putting emphasis on "an equally important strain of optimism and liberality within Adams's thought" (561), Schulz portrays Adams as a tragic character stretching his mind over two mutually inconsistent (or complementary) categories, namely, hope and pessimism. Moreover, Schulz provides a list of historians who have made Adams's conservatism dependent on a pessimistic outlook upon human history.

2. Lehman, *Jefferson American Humanist*, 106–7. On Jefferson's enduring effort to organize his papers for posterity, see Cogliano, *Thomas Jefferson*, 74–105.

3. Wood, "Trials and Tribulations of Jefferson," 410–13 passim. On the optimist Jefferson yielding in the 1820s to a despondent Jefferson, see also Peterson, *Jefferson and the New Nation*, 980–1009.

4. TJ to Nathaniel Macon, 12 January 1819, *Works of TJ*, 12:110–11; TJ to John Adams, 22 January 1821, *A-JL*, 2:570.

5. Wood, "Trials and Tribulations of Jefferson," 412–13.

6. On Jefferson's radical disillusionment, see Onuf, *Jefferson's Empire*, 117, italics added. On Jefferson and the Missouri question, see *J and His Time*, 6:328–61.

7. TJ to John Holmes, 22 April 1820, *Works of TJ*, 12:159–60. See also TJ to Albert Gallatin, 26 December 1820, *Works of TJ*, 12:185–89; TJ to William Short, 13 April 1820, *Writings of TJ*, 15:243–48; TJ to Charles Pinckney, 30 September 1820, *Works of TJ*, 12:164–66; and TJ to Mark Langdon Hill, 5 April 1820, *Writings of TJ*, 15:242–43.

8. TJ to John Adams, 1 June 1822, *A-JL*, 2:577–78, italics added.

9. TJ to Francis Adrian van der Kemp, 11 January 1825, *Works of TJ*, 12:400.

10. TJ to William Branch Giles, 26 December 1825, *Works of TJ*, 12:427.

11. TJ to John Adams, 11 January 1816, *A-JL*, 2:458–61.

12. TJ to Benjamin Austin, 9 January 1816, *Works of TJ*, 11:502–4. On "our work-shops," see TJ, *Notes*, Query 19, *Works of TJ*, 4:84–86.

13. TJ to William Short, 28 November 1814, *Writings of TJ*, 14:214, italics added.

14. TJ to John Page, 25 June 1804, *Writings of TJ*, 11:31.

15. TJ to James Madison, 1 January 1797, *PTJ*, 29:248.

16. TJ to Samuel Kercheval, 12 July 1816, *Works of TJ*, 12:11.

17. Rush quoted in D'Elia, "Benjamin Rush," 45; Crèvecoeur, *Letters from an American Farmer*, 241–42. Rush made a very similar statement in his autobiography: "It would seem from this fact, that man is naturally a wild animal, and that when taken from the woods, he is never happy in his natural state, 'till he returns to them again." Rush, *Autobiography*, 72. See also Kunitz, "Rush on Savagism and Progress," in particular 38–39.

18. TJ to George Washington, 15 March 1784, *PTJ*, 7:26. While Jefferson was minister of the United States to France, in 1785, a correspondent asked his opinion "on the expediency of encouraging our States to be commercial." Jefferson's reply is revealing. "Were I to indulge my own theory," he said, "I should wish them to practice neither commerce nor navigation." TJ to G. K. van Hogendorp, 13 October 1785, *PTJ*, 8:633.

19. TJ to Albert Gallatin, 26 December 1820, *Works of TJ*, 12:185; Slotkin, *Fatal Environment*, 73. See also Valsania, "'Our Original Barbarism.'"

20. On Jefferson's actual support of capitalism, see Hofstadter, "Parrington and the Jeffersonian Tradition," 400; Appleby, *Capitalism and a New Social Order*, 49–50; and Slotkin, *Fatal Environment*, 69. For further details, see also note 23 above in chapter 2.

21. Simpson, *Lives of Washington and Jefferson*, 189.

22. Pocock, *Machiavellian Moment*, 538. Alexander Hamilton and Andrew Jackson were very far apart, historically and in their deeds and thoughts. Each of the two leaders, however, promoted his particular version of the "American System" fostering a system of mutual dependence and "subservience." President Jackson, for instance, authorized some $10 million in federal improvement bills, aimed at supporting a nationwide transportation network. He fully embraced a strong nationalistic interpretation of the Constitution up to the point that his zeal occasioned the South's growing resistance to the perceived "federal tyranny." (Ironically, he entered the scene of politics as a strong advocate of the state's rights doctrine, in sharp contrast with President John Quincy Adams's program of governmental aid for national economic development.) Jefferson, of course, did not live to see Andrew Jackson's version of the "American System."

23. Wood, "Trials and Tribulations of Jefferson," 410.

24. T. D. Clark, Editor's Note, in Clark, *Travels in the Old South*, 2:73–74.

25. See Kulikoff, "Transition to Capitalism," 136–37.

26. McCoy, *Elusive Republic*, 239.

27. Wood, "Significance of the Early Republic," 19.

28. On Jefferson's favorable attitude toward "coarse" manufactures produced "in our families," see TJ to David Humphreys, 20 January 1809, *Writings of TJ*, 12:235–36; TJ to Du Pont de Nemours, 15 April 1811, *PTJ, Retirement Series*, 3:559–60; and TJ to John Adams, 21 January 1812, *A-JL*, 2:290–92. And see McCoy, *Elusive Republic*, 226–33. Jefferson's advocacy of "coarse" production centered in "our families" appears to be a desperate defense of eighteenth-century Virginian social hierarchies. It seems a defense of the status quo and a bulwark against ordinary people making business and spreading uncontrolled in all directions. In 1794, Jefferson himself added a nail-making operation to the blacksmith shop in an effort to provide a source of income for his own personal "industry," Monticello.

29. Schlesinger, "History and National Stupidity," 16.

30. Dudden, "Nostalgia and the American," 517.

31. C. A. Miller, *Ship of State*, 32. On Jefferson as a mere passenger, see TJ to Francis Hopkinson, 13 June 1790, *PTJ*, 16:490; TJ to Samuel Kercheval, 12 July 1816, *Works of TJ*, 12:3; TJ to John Holmes, 22 April 1820, *Works of TJ*, 12:158; TJ to Thomas Ritchie, 25 December 1820, *Works of TJ*, 12:179; and TJ to Edward Livingston, 4 April 1824, *Works of TJ*, 12:348–49.

32. TJ to Martha Jefferson, 17 May 1798, *PTJ*, 30:354.

33. TJ to George Gilmer, 12 August 1787, *PTJ*, 12:26.

34. For the expression "asylum from grief," see TJ to Maria Cosway, 12 October 1786, *PTJ*, 10:447. On Jefferson's acceptance of both Epicureanism and Stoicism, which he did not interpret as sharply distinguished, see Koch, *Philosophy of Jefferson*, 4. Epicureanism and Stoicism, Koch contended, taught Jefferson the priority of building an "independent morality" and an "autonomous ethics of prudence." Independence and autonomy were Jefferson's ingredients for his recipe to forestall the course of history going toward dependence.

35. TJ to James Madison, 8 December 1784, *PTJ*, 7:559, italics added; TJ to James Madison, 20 February 1784, *PTJ*, 6:550, italics added. See also TJ to James Monroe, 18 December 1786, *PTJ*, 10:611–13.

36. TJ, *Notes*, Query 19, *Works of TJ*, 4:85. On Jefferson's alleged refusal of production, see Marx, *Machine in the Garden*, 126–27.

6. DREAM, IMAGINATION, AND EXPEDIENCY

1. TJ to John Taylor, 28 May 1816, *Works of TJ*, 11:529–30. See also Shoemaker, "'Democracy' and 'Republic.'"

2. TJ to John Taylor, 28 May 1816, *Works of TJ*, 11:533. Jefferson expresses his wish to see the "republican element of popular control pushed to the maximum of its practicable exercise" in a letter to Isaac H. Tiffany, 26 August 1816, *Writings of TJ*, 15:66. On the famous dictum "I am not among those who fear the people," see TJ to Samuel Kercheval, 12 July 1816, *Works of TJ*, 12:10. But compare Jefferson's claim that "a choice by the people themselves is not generally distinguished for it's wisdom." TJ to Edward Pendleton, 26 August 1776, *PTJ*, 1:503.

3. TJ to Jeremiah Moore, 14 August 1800, *PTJ*, 32:103; TJ to William Johnson, 12 June 1823, *Writings of TJ*, 15:441.

4. Montesquieu, *Spirit of Laws*, 12. On the widespread view, particularly in Virginia, that politics should be left in the hands of the gentleman-masters and the men of property, see Wilentz, *Rise of American Democracy*, 200.

5. For Jefferson's praise of the House of Representatives, see TJ to John Taylor, 28 May 1816, *Works of TJ*, 11:530.

6. James Madison to TJ, 6 September 1787, *PTJ*, 12:103.

7. TJ to William Stephens Smith, 13 November 1787, *PTJ*, 12:356. On the Shaysites and their "feminine" attitude, see Smith-Rosenberg, "Dis-Covering the Subject," 856. On the Federalist theory of the mob in America as "thoroughly unrealistic," see Hartz, "Whig Tradition," 1002.

8. David Humphreys to TJ, 5 June 1786, *PTJ*, 9:609.

9. On the allegation that postrevolutionary Americans aimed at the extraordinary and at a reform of character, see Wood, *Creation of the American Republic*, 395.

10. Harrison, *Forests*, 114.

11. For the notion that Americans fought to preserve past liberties at least as much as the imagination of future freedoms, I am indebted to Michael Zuckerman.

12. TJ to J. Correa De Serra, 25 November 1817, *Writings of TJ*, 15:157. For Adams's motto, see John Adams to TJ, 3 May 1816, *A-JL*, 2:469. The "utopian dream" that Jefferson referred to in his letter to Correa was his general plan for education. Jefferson was disappointed by what he perceived as legislators' insufficient trust in knowledge. But I cannot help thinking that in this case Jefferson's reflection had a broader scope. "Utopian" and "imaginative" are the distinctive features of Jefferson's most renowned discourses. In his educational crusade, as Malone also acknowledges, Jefferson "was battling for more than Central College." *J and His Time*, 6:276.

13. TJ to Caspar Wistar, 21 June 1807, *Works of TJ*, 10:429.

14. TJ to John Adams, 8 April 1816, *A-JL*, 2:467.

15. John Adams to TJ, 3 May 1816, *A-JL*, 2:469–71.

16. TJ to John Adams, 1 August 1816, *A-JL*, 2:485.

17. TJ to Barré de Marbois, 14 June 1817, *Writings of TJ*, 15:130–31.

18. TJ to William Short, 4 August 1820, *Writings of TJ*, 15:262–63.

19. John Adams to TJ, 19 May 1821, *A-JL*, 2:572; TJ to John Adams, 12 September 1821, *A-JL*, 2:575.

20. A further example of Jefferson's penchant for lions and lambs, this time dating back to his youth, is discussed in Burstein, *Sentimental Democracy,* 94–95. In the summer of 1775, Jefferson communicated to John Randolph an almost surreal fantasy of reconciliation with the British. See TJ to John Randolph, 25 August 1775, *PTJ,* 1:241–42.

21. TJ, "Death-bed Adieu," in Randolph, *Domestic Life of Jefferson,* 429.

22. *J and His Time,* 5:472. On the struggle between principles and the practice of Jefferson's statecraft and the conflation between a vaulting idealism and the willingness to employ any means to promote American interests, see Tucker and Hendrickson, *Empire of Liberty.* Tim Matthewson argues that Jefferson was far from sympathetic toward Haitian rebels in their war against France. His philosophical love of a universal human freedom did not prevent him from adopting policies aimed at suppressing the Haitian republic. In that case, Jefferson wanted neither to oppose the power of the southern planters nor to put the interests of the United States in jeopardy. See Matthewson, "Jefferson and Haiti." Roger Kennedy shows that Jefferson was fully aware that by acquiring West Florida and other territories of the Old Southwest, planters would have totally displaced Native Americans and replaced them with slaves forced to cultivate cotton. A member of the slaveholding class, Jefferson did not even try to dispute southern hierarchical society, where wealth depended on slavery, cotton cultivation, and the consequent depletion of the soil. Jefferson "lost" his cause, according to Kennedy, because he recoiled from turning the new land into the seedbed for family farmers. See Kennedy, *Mr. Jefferson's Lost Cause.* A further example of Jefferson's expediency is discussed in Wills, *Negro President.* According to Wills, Jefferson favored slavery in the new western territories as a very effective means to apportion greater political power to his Virginian peers. Jefferson tried opportunistically to maximize the advantage deriving from the "three-fifths clause" of the Constitution. On Jefferson not just as a ruthless operator but as a hypocritical ideologue who prosecuted his opponents by illegal means, see Levy, *Jefferson and Civil Liberties.*

23. TJ to James Monroe, 18 June 1813, *Writings of TJ,* 13:261. On Jefferson's Spartan republicanism, see also TJ to James Monroe, 16 October 1814, *Works of TJ,* 11:436–38, and TJ to William H. Crawford, 11 February 1815, *Works of TJ,* 11:450–54. On Jefferson's republicanism as the vision of that "government to be the strongest of which every man feels himself a part," see TJ to Governor Tiffin, 2 February 1807, *Works of TJ,* 10:358. On Jefferson's complete acceptance of war as an effective means to be employed in achieving diplomatic ends, see Stuart, *Half-Way Pacifist.*

24. TJ to Governor Claiborne, 3 February 1807, *Writings of TJ,* 11:151.

25. TJ to John B. Colvin, 20 September 1810, *PTJ, Retirement Series,* 3:99–100. On Jefferson's acknowledgment of self-preservation as the first law of nature, see also TJ to Edmond Charles Genet, 17 June 1793, *PTJ,* 26:297–300. Dumas Malone presented the opinion of Walter F. McCaleb, a scholar sympathetic to Burr. In his book *Aaron Burr Conspiracy* (128), McCaleb described Jefferson's letter to Colvin as highly reprehensible, showing him at his worst. McCaleb was evidently not a Jefferson admirer, but his negative judgment of Jefferson's ruthless pragmatism was quite understandable. See *J and His Time,* 5:278, note 22.

26. TJ to John Wayles Eppes, 9 September 1814, *Works of TJ,* 11:425–26.

27. The argument that Jefferson "never thought he had to live up to some idealized abstraction of 'Jeffersonian democracy' in the real political world" is endorsed by Wilentz, *Rise of American Democracy,* 136.

28. TJ to Richard Rush, 20 October 1820, *Writings of TJ*, 15:284.

29. TJ to John Page, 15 July 1763, *PTJ*, 1:10, italics added.

30. Pocock, *Machiavellian Moment*, 9; TJ to John Adams, 28 February 1796, *A-JL*, 1:260, italics added.

31. Benjamin Rush to Elias Boudinot, 9 July 1788, in Butterfield, ed., *Letters of Rush*, 1:475.

32. Nelson, "Reason and Compromise," 483.

33. Wilson, "Jefferson vs. Hume," 69. To Whig seventeenth- and eighteenth-century historians such as William Petyt, William Atwood, and Sir Edward Coke in particular, feudalism, introduced into England by William the Conqueror in 1066, replaced the original republicanism (based on the principle of the superiority of the common law over the feudal law) with tyranny and a merely effectual power. In his *Second Part of the Institutes of the Laws of England* (1662, later published in London, 7 vols., under *The Reports of Sir Edward Coke*—this edition was owned by Jefferson), Coke harbored the more radical idea of an original constitution precedent to both the Normans and the Saxons, the principle of right belonging to human beings as such. On Jefferson's dissatisfaction with Hume as a historian, see, for instance, TJ to John Norvell, 14 June 1807, *Works of TJ*, 10:415–19; TJ to William Duane, 12 August 1810, *PTJ, Retirement Series*, 3:4–7; TJ to Horatio G. Spafford, 17 March 1814, *Writings of TJ*, 14:118–20; TJ to John Adams, 25 November 1816, *A-JL*, 2:495–99; and TJ to George Washington Lewis, 25 October 1825, *Writings of TJ*, 16:124–29.

34. TJ, *Notes*, Query 6, *Works of TJ*, 3:440–41. On the founders' bad opinion of Julius Caesar, see Richard, *Founders and the Classics*, 91–95.

35. Abigail Adams to John Adams, 31 March 1776, in A. Adams and J. Adams, *Book of Abigail and John*, 121. On women as a "tribe," see John Adams to Abigail Adams, 14 April 1776, 123.

36. Moral deference is the ability "to respond in the morally appropriate way to those who have been wronged." Thomas, "Moral Deference," 233.

37. Tenskwatawa quoted in R. A. Ferguson, "American Enlightenment," 512. On Tenskwatawa, see Edmunds, *Shawnee Prophet*.

38. The episode of the slave is recorded by Sutcliff, *Travels*, 50.

39. TJ to Caesar A. Rodney, 10 February 1810, *PTJ, Retirement Series*, 2:209–10. On the enormities of France and England, see also TJ to Madame de Staël, 24 May 1813, *Writings of TJ*, 13:237–45.

40. On Jefferson's condemnation of the principle that power is right, see TJ to John Adams, 11 January 1816, *A-JL*, 2:459. On Jefferson's refusal of the idea that force is law, see TJ, *Notes*, Query 6, *Works of TJ*, 3:440–41.

41. TJ to John B. Colvin, 20 September 1810, *PTJ, Retirement Series*, 3:99–100. On the "cocks of henyard," see TJ to John Adams, 1 June 1822, *A-JL*, 2:578–79.

42. TJ to John Holmes, 22 April 1820, *Works of TJ*, 12:158–60. See also TJ to John Adams, 22 January 1821, *A-JL*, 2:570: "Are our slaves to be presented with freedom and a dagger?" Similar is TJ to Albert Gallatin, 26 December 1820, *Works of TJ*, 12:185–89.

43. Onuf, *Jefferson's Empire*, 118.

44. TJ, "Summary View," *PTJ*, 1:122; Kelsall, *Jefferson and the Iconography*, 56.

45. See TJ to James Madison, 6 September 1789, *PTJ*, 15:392–97, and TJ, *Notes*, Query 11, *Works of TJ*, 3:496. For argument identical to that of the letter to Madison, see TJ to John

Wayles Eppes, 24 June 1813, *Works of TJ*, 11:297–306, and TJ to Samuel Kercheval, 12 July 1816, *Works of TJ*, 12:3–15.

46. For the "Darwinian" interpretation of Jefferson's doctrine that the earth belongs to the living, I am indebted to Spahn, *Thomas Jefferson, Time, and History*, in particular chapter 5, section 5. See Tenskwatawa quoted in R. A. Ferguson, "American Enlightenment," 512, and TJ to the "Brothers of the Choctaw nation," 17 December 1803, *Writings of TJ*, 16:403.

47. *J and His Time*, 3:39.

48. C. A. Miller, *Jefferson and Nature*, 262. Ari Helo and Peter Onuf maintain that Jefferson never agreed with the idea that all human beings, as simple persons, are equal. Jefferson's conception of the moral sense did not make people morally equal regardless of their actual behavior. See Helo and Onuf, "Jefferson, Morality, and the Problem of Slavery," in particular 611. The belief in the moral sense was not tantamount to praise of the intrinsic worth of the human being, before human beings developed themselves and their faculties. "The central tenet of modern moral thinking, that there is an intrinsic, irreducible value in each individual, was inconceivable to Jefferson" (612). "All men are created equal" would not entail authentic universalism and equalitarianism, that all persons were de facto equals. Correct though Helo and Onuf undoubtedly are, a version of the intrinsic value of all persons seems nonetheless to ensue from Jefferson's philosophy as long as adequate emphasis is put on education. Education allots everyone the *chance* to attain full moral development and equality. As far as I am aware, Jefferson did not put any limit on the right to education, and educability was seen as a general characteristic of the entire humanity. Jefferson the educator allowed that human beings—including those who are still un-equal and "children," like black slaves and Indians—were de facto equal in their right to be raised to understand the requirements of a free society and to behave in a morally valuable way. At least to some extent, Jefferson was committed to the central idea of modern moral thinking, that there is an intrinsic and irreducible value (in this case, educability) in each individual.

49. Smith-Rosenberg, "Dis-Covering the Subject," 848. See also Liss, *Atlantic Empires*, and Egnal, *Mighty Empire*.

50. Onuf, "Scholars' Jefferson," 682–83.

51. Burch, *Elites in American History*, 48, 68. For details about intermarriages and "continuities" between Hamiltonians and the Adams administration, see 65–66. On "the dense network of in-laws and cousinhood" that shaped the early republic, see Wills, *Inventing America*, 35.

52. John Adams to TJ, 2 September 1813, *A-JL*, 2:371. Jefferson's hope in a natural aristocracy of "virtue and talents" is expressed in TJ to John Adams, 28 October 1813, *A-JL*, 2:387–92, in particular 388. On the "Richmond Junto," see Burch, *Elites in American History*, 85. On Jefferson as a member of the "informal oligarchic body," see 86. On the fact that Jefferson must have had more than some loose acquaintance with the yawning gap between poor farmers of the backcountry and the wealthy slaveocracy of the coastal low country, see G. Nash, *Unknown American Revolution*, 387–91. Richard Beeman upholds the thesis that during the eighteenth century "popular awareness of policy issues was developing and that elite control of the political arena was declining." Beeman, "Deference, Republicanism," 424. However, Beeman's thesis of the decline of deference and the increase of popular control can be quite correct as a depiction of what happened on the local level, in Philadelphia particularly. By the mid-eighteenth century, after two decades of German and Scots-Irish

immigration that differentiated and stratified the economic order, the Philadelphia elite began to feel powerless. But on the national level, and especially in the South, decisions kept on being taken by the old economic elites. Elites might have felt they were besieged by the new Jacksonian social order, but they were still firmly at the helm. Not that there was unity and harmony within the household. But the brutal fact of a top-down, exclusive control did hardly change. I am persuaded that the "Revolution of 1800" did not signal the rise of mass participatory democracy and that Jefferson's victory did not help the cause of workers, blacks, Indians, and women. See, for instance, Ben-Atar and Oberg, *Federalists Reconsidered,* and Horn, Lewis, and Onuf, *Revolution of 1800.* On the explosion of "popular participation in politics" during the 1790s, see Wilentz, *Rise of American Democracy,* 138. However, on politics and party affairs continuing to operate at the national level "largely from the top down," see 139.

53. On the Missouri Crisis as the unleashing of real democratic forces and the vision of democracy "privileging persons over property," see Wilentz, *Rise of American Democracy,* 226. On Jefferson and his tentative idea of person, see also note 48 above.

Bibliography

Adams, Abigail, and John Adams. *The Book of Abigail and John: Selected Letters of the Adams Family, 1762–1784.* Ed. Lyman H. Butterfield, Marc Friedlaender, and Mary-Jo Kline. 1975; rpt., Boston, 2002.

Adams, Henry. *Henry Adams and His Friends: A Collection of His Unpublished Letters.* Ed. Harold Dean Cater. 1947; rpt., New York, 1970.

———. *History of the United States of America.* 9 vols. New York, 1889–91.

Adams, Herbert B. *The Life and Writings of Jared Sparks.* 2 vols. Boston, 1893.

Adams, John. *The Adams-Jefferson Letters.* Ed. Lester J. Cappon. 2 vols. Chapel Hill, N.C., 1959.

———. Ed. Charles Francis Adams. *The Works of John Adams.* 10 vols. Boston, 1850–56.

Appleby, Joyce. *Capitalism and a New Social Order: The Republican Vision of the 1790s.* New York, 1984.

———. "Commercial Farming and the 'Agrarian Myth' in the Early Republic." *Journal of American History* 68 (1982): 833–49.

———. *Liberalism and Republicanism in the Historical Imagination.* Cambridge, Mass., 1992.

Bailyn, Bernard. *The Ideological Origins of the American Revolution.* 1967; rpt., Cambridge, Mass., 1992.

———. *The Peopling of the British North America: An Introduction.* New York, 1986.

Banning, Lance. *The Jeffersonian Persuasion: Evolution of a Party Ideology.* Ithaca, N.Y., 1978.

———. "Republican Ideology and the Triumph of the Constitution, 1789 to 1793." *William and Mary Quarterly* 31 (1974): 168–88.

Barton, Benjamin Smith. *New Views of the Origin of the Tribes and Nations of America.* Philadelphia, 1797.

Beard, Charles A. "Thomas Jefferson: A Civilized Man." *Mississippi Valley Historical Review* 30 (1943): 159–70.

Becker, Carl L. *The Declaration of Independence: A Study in the History of Political Ideas.* 1922; rpt., New York, 1942.

———. *The Heavenly City of the Eighteenth-Century Philosophers.* 1932; rpt., New Haven, Conn., 2003.

Bedini, Silvio A. *Jefferson and Science.* Chapel Hill, N.C., 2002.

Beeman, Richard R. "Deference, Republicanism, and the Emergence of Popular Politics in Eighteenth-Century America." *William and Mary Quarterly* 49 (1992): 401–30.

————. *The Varieties of Political Experience in Eighteenth-Century America.* Philadelphia, 2004.

Ben-Atar, Doron, and Barbara B. Oberg, eds. *Federalists Reconsidered.* Charlottesville, Va., 1998.

Bender, Thomas. *Toward an Urban Vision: Ideas and Institutions in Nineteenth Century America.* Lexington, Ky., 1975.

Benet, Francisco. "Sociology Uncertain: The Ideology of the Rural-Urban Continuum." *Comparative Studies in Society and History* 6 (1963): 1–23.

Benjamin, Walter. *Illuminations.* Ed. Hannah Arendt. New York, 1969.

Beran, Michael Knox. *Jefferson's Demons: Portrait of a Restless Mind.* New York, 2003.

Bercovitch, Sacvan. *The American Jeremiad.* Madison, Wis., 1978.

Blum, John Morton. *The Promise of America: An Historical Enquiry.* Boston, 1966.

Bolingbroke, Henry Saint-John. *Letters on the Spirit of Patriotism, on the Idea of a Patriot King, and on the State of Parties, at the Accession of King George the First.* London, 1775.

————. *Philosophical Works.* 5 vols. Ed. David Mallet. London, 1754.

Boorstin, Daniel J. *The Lost World of Thomas Jefferson.* 1948; rpt., Chicago, 1993.

Brodie, Fawn M. *Thomas Jefferson: An Intimate History.* New York, 1974.

Browers, Michaelle L. "Jefferson's Land Ethic: Environmentalist Ideas in *Notes on the State of Virginia.*" *Environmental Ethics* 21 (1999): 43–57.

Brown, Theodore. "From Mechanism to Vitalism in Eighteenth-Century English Physiology." *Journal of the History of Biology* 7 (1974): 179–216.

Buel, Richard. *America on the Brink: How the Political struggle over the War of 1812 Almost Destroyed the Young Republic.* New York, 2005.

Buffon, George-Louis Leclerc, comte de. *Histoire naturelle générale et particulière.* 44 vols. Paris, 1749–1804.

Burch, Philip H., Jr. *Elites in American History.* Vol. 1: *The Federalist Years to the Civil War.* New York, 1980–81.

Burrows, Edwin G., and Michael Wallace. "The American Revolution: The Ideology and Psychology of National Liberation." *Perspectives in American History* 6 (1972): 167–306.

Burstein, Andrew. *The Inner Jefferson: Portrait of a Grieving Optimist.* Charlottesville, Va., 1995.

————. *Jefferson's Secrets: Death and Desire at Monticello.* New York, 2005.

————. *Sentimental Democracy: The Evolution of America's Romantic Self-Image.* New York, 1999.

Bury, J. B. *The Idea of Progress: An Inquiry into Its Origin and Growth.* 1920; rpt., New York, 1932.

Butterfield, Lyman H., ed. *Adams Family Correspondence.* 8 vols. Cambridge, Mass., 1963.

Cassara, Ernest. *The Enlightenment in America.* 1975; rpt., Lanham, Md., 1988.

Cherry, Conrad, ed. *God's New Israel: Religious Interpretations of American Destiny.* 1971; rpt., Chapel Hill, N.C., 1998.

Chinard, Gilbert. *Jefferson et les ideologues.* Baltimore, 1925.

Clark, Jennifer. "The American Image of Technology from the Revolution to 1840." *American Quarterly* 39 (1987): 431–49.

Clark, Thomas D., ed. *Travels in the Old South: A Bibliography.* 3 vols. Norman, Okla., 1956.

Clarke, Dora Mae. *British Opinion and the American Revolution.* New Haven, Conn. 1930.

Cogliano, Francis D. *Thomas Jefferson: Reputation and Legacy.* Charlottesville, Va., 2006.

Cohen, Anthony P. *Self Consciousness: An Alternative Anthropology of Identity.* London, 1994.

Cohen, Lester H. "The American Revolution and Natural Law Theory." *Journal of the History of Ideas* 39 (1978): 491–502.

Colbourn, Trevor. *The Lamp of Experience: Whig History and the Intellectual Origins of the American Revolution.* 1965; rpt., Indianapolis, 1998.

———. "Thomas Jefferson's Use of the Past." *William and Mary Quarterly* 15 (1958): 56–70.

Commager, Henry Steele. *The Empire of Reason: How Europe Imagined and America Realized the Enlightenment.* Garden City, N.Y., 1977.

———. *Jefferson, Nationalism, and the Enlightenment.* New York, 1975.

Crèvecoeur, Hector St. John. *Letters from an American Farmer.* 1782; rpt., with prefatory note by W. P. Trent and introduction by Ludwig Lewisohn. New York, 1904.

Cunningham, Noble. *In Pursuit of Reason: The Life of Thomas Jefferson.* Baton Rouge, La., 1987.

Curti, Merle. *Human Nature in American Historical Thought.* Columbia, S.C., 1968.

———. *Human Nature in American Thought: A History.* Madison, Wis., 1980.

Darwin, Erasmus. *The Temple of Nature; or, The Origin of Society: A Poem, with Philosophical Notes.* 1803. London, 1825.

D'Elia, Donald J. "Benjamin Rush: Philosopher of the American Revolution." *Transactions of the American Philosophical Society* 64 (1974): 1–113.

Destutt de Tracy, Antoine Louis Claude, comte. *Project d'éléments d'idéologie.* Paris, 1801.

Diggins, John. *The Lost Soul of American Politics: Virtue, Self-interest, and the Foundations of Liberalism.* New York, 1984.

Dudden, Arthur P. "Nostalgia and the American." *Journal of the History of Ideas* 22 (1961): 515–30.

Dworetz, Steven M. *The Unvarnished Doctrine: Locke, Liberalism, and the American Revolution.* Durham, N.C., 1990.

Edmunds, David R. *The Shawnee Prophet.* Lincoln, Neb., 1983.

Egnal, Marc. *A Mighty Empire: The Origins of the American Revolution.* Ithaca, N.Y., 1988.

Ekirch, Arthur A., Jr. *The Idea of Progress in America: 1815–1860.* New York, 1944.

Ellis, Joseph J. *American Sphinx: The Character of Thomas Jefferson.* New York, 1997.

————. *Passionate Sage: The Character and Legacy of John Adams*. New York, 1993.

Epstein, Arnold L. *Ethos and Identity: Three Studies in Ethnicity*. London, 1978.

Ferguson, Adam. *An Essay on History of Civil Society*. Edinburgh: 1767.

Ferguson, Robert A. "The American Enlightenment, 1750–1820." In *The Cambridge History of American Literature*, vol. 1: *1590–1820*, 345–537. Cambridge, 1994.

————. "The Commonalities of Common Sense." *William and Mary Quarterly* 57 (2000): 465–504.

Ferling, John, and Lewis E. Braverman. "John Adams's Health Reconsidered." *William and Mary Quarterly* 55 (1998): 83–104.

Fiering, Norman S. "Irresistible Compassion: An Aspect of Eighteenth-Century Sympathy and Humanitarianism." *Journal of the History of Ideas* 37 (1976): 195–218.

Fliegelman, Jay. *Declaring Independence: Jefferson, Natural Language and the Culture of Performance*. Stanford, Calif., 1993.

Foucault, Michel. "What Is Enlightenment?" In *The Foucault Reader*, ed. Paul Rabinow, 32–50. New York, 1984.

Fowler, Robert Booth. "Mythologies of a Founder." In *Thomas Jefferson and the Politics of Nature*, ed. Thomas S. Engeman, 123–41. Notre Dame, Ind., 2000.

Franklin, Benjamin. "The Art of Procuring Pleasant Dreams." In *The Writings of Benjamin Franklin*, ed. Albert H. Smyth, 10:131–37. New York, 1905–7.

Freneau, Philip. "The Philosopher of the Forest," no. 10. *Prose of Philip Freneau*, ed. Philip M. Marsh. New Brunswick, N.J., 1955.

Fresia, Jerry. *Toward an American Revolution: Exposing the Constitution and Other Illusions*. Boston, 1988.

Fries, Horace S. "Varieties of Freedom: An Effort toward Orchestration." In *Freedom and Experience: Essays Presented to Horace M. Kallen*, ed. Sidney Hook and Milton R. Konwitz, 3–24. Ithaca, N.Y., 1947.

Gannon, Kevin M. "Escaping 'Mr. Jefferson's Plan of Destruction': New England Federalists and the Idea of a Northern Confederacy, 1803–1804." *Journal of the Early Republic* 21 (2001): 413–43.

Gay, Peter. *The Enlightenment: An Interpretation*. Vol. 2: *The Science of Freedom*. 1966; rpt., New York, 1977.

Gilreath, James A., and Douglas L. Wilson, eds. *Thomas Jefferson's Library: A Catalog with Entries in His Own Order*. Washington, D.C., 1989.

Goodman, Russell B. *American Philosophy and the Romantic Tradition*. Cambridge, 1990.

Grabo, Norman S. "Crevecoeur's American: Beginning the World Anew." *William and Mary Quarterly* 48 (1991): 159–72.

Gray, John. *Enlightenment's Wake: Politics and Culture at the Close of the Modern Age*. London, 1995.

Greven, Philip. *The Protestant Temperament: Patterns of Child-Rearing, Religious Experience, and the Self in Early America*. 1977; rpt., Chicago, 1988.

Gross, Jonathan, ed. *Thomas Jefferson's Scrapbooks: Poems of Nation, Family and Romantic Love*. Hanover, N.H., 2006.

Harrison, Robert Pogue. *Forests: The Shadow of Civilization*. Chicago, 1992.

Hartz, Louis. *The Liberal Tradition in America: An Interpretation of American Political Thought since the Revolution.* New York, 1955.

———. "The Whig Tradition in America and Europe." *American Political Science Review* 46 (1952): 989–1002.

Hatch, Nathan O. "The Origins of Civil Millennialism in America: New England Clergymen, War with France, and the Revolution." *William and Mary Quarterly* 31 (1974): 407–30.

Hay, Robert P. "Providence and the American Past." *Indiana Magazine of History* 65 (1969): 79–101.

Hayes, Kevin J. *The Road to Monticello: The Life and Mind of Thomas Jefferson.* Oxford, 2008.

Heilbroner, Robert L. "The Paradox of Progress: Decline and Decay in *The Wealth of Nations.*" *Journal of the History of Ideas* 34 (1973): 243–62.

Hellenbrand, Harold. "Roads to Happiness: Rhetorical and Philosophical Design in Jefferson's *Notes on the State of Virginia.*" *Early American Literature* 20 (1985): 3–23.

Helo, Ari, and Peter S. Onuf. "Jefferson, Morality, and the Problem of Slavery." *William and Mary Quarterly* 60 (2003): 583–614.

Helvétius, Claude-Adrien. *Lettre à Montesquieu.* 1789. In Antoine Louis Claude Destutt de Tracy, comte, *A Commentary and Review of Montesquieu's Spirit of Laws . . . to which Are Annexed . . . Two Letters of Helvetius. . . .* Philadelphia, 1811.

Henretta, James. "Families and Farms: Mentalité in Pre-Industrial America." *William and Mary Quarterly* 35 (1978): 3–32.

Himmelfarb, Gertrude. *The Roads to Modernity: The British, French, and American Enlightenment.* New York, 2004.

Hodin, Stephen B. "The Mechanisms of Monticello: Saving Labor in Jefferson's America." *Journal of the Early Republic* 26 (2006): 377–418.

Hofstadter, Richard. *The Age of Reform: From Bryan to F.D.R.* New York, 1955.

———. *The Paranoid Style in American Politics and Other Essays.* 1965; rpt., New York, 2008.

———. "Parrington and the Jeffersonian Tradition." *Journal of the History of Ideas* 4 (1941): 391–400.

Holland, Catherine A. "Notes on the State of America: Jeffersonian Democracy and the Production of a National Past." *Political Theory* 29 (2001): 190–216.

Horn, James, Jan Ellen Lewis, and Peter S. Onuf, eds. *The Revolution of 1800: Democracy, Race, and the New Republic.* Charlottesville, Va., 2002.

Howe, Daniel Walker. *Making the American Self: Jonathan Edwards to Abraham Lincoln.* Cambridge, Mass., 1997.

Howe, John R., Jr. "Republican Thought and the Political Violence of the 1790s." *American Quarterly* 19 (1967): 147–65.

Jackson, Donald. *Thomas Jefferson and the Stony Mountains: Exploring the West from Monticello.* 1981; rpt., Norman, Okla., 1993.

Jayne, Allen. *Jefferson's Declaration of Independence: Origins, Philosophy and Theology.* Lexington, Ky., 1998.

Jefferson, Thomas. *The Commonplace Book of Thomas Jefferson: A Repertory of His Ideas on Government.* Ed. Gilbert Chinard. Baltimore, 1926.

————. *Jefferson's Literary Commonplace Book.* Ed. Douglas L. Wilson. Princeton, N.J., 1989.

————. *Jefferson's Memorandum Books: Accounts, with Legal Records and Miscellany, 1767–1826.* Ed. James A. Bear Jr. and Lucia C. Stanton. Papers of Thomas Jefferson, 2nd series. 2 vols. Princeton, N.J., 1997.

————. *The Papers of Thomas Jefferson.* Ed. Julian Boyd et al. 37 vols. to date, plus 7 vols. in the *Retirement Series.* Princeton, N.J., 1950–.

————. *Thomas Jefferson: Writings.* Ed. Merrill D. Peterson. New York, 1984.

————. *The Works of Thomas Jefferson.* Ed. Paul Leicester Ford. 12 vols. New York, 1904–5.

————. *The Writings of Thomas Jefferson.* Ed. Andrew A. Lipscomb and Albert Ellery Bergh. 20 vols. Washington, D.C., 1907.

Jordan, Winthrop D. "Familial Politics: Thomas Paine and the Killing of the King, 1776." *Journal of American History* 60 (1973): 294–308.

Jung, Carl Gustav. *Psyche and Symbol: A Selection from the Writings of C. G. Jung.* Ed. Violet S. de Laszlo. Princeton, N.J., 1991.

Kammen, Michael. *People of Paradox.* Ithaca, N.Y., 1972.

Kelley, Robert. "Ideology and Political Culture from Jefferson to Nixon." *American Historical Review* 82 (1977): 531–62.

Kelly, George A. *The Psychology of Personal Constructs.* Vol. 2: *Clinical Diagnosis and Psychotherapy.* London, 2001.

Kelsall, Malcolm. *Jefferson and the Iconography of Romanticism: Folk, Land, Culture, and the Romantic Nation.* Houndmills, Eng., 1999.

Kennedy, Roger G. *Mr. Jefferson's Lost Cause: Land, Farmers, Slavery, and the Louisiana Purchase.* New York, 2003.

Koch, Adrienne. *The Philosophy of Thomas Jefferson.* 1943; rpt., Chicago, 1964.

Kulikoff, Allan. "The Transition to Capitalism in Rural America." *William and Mary Quarterly* 46 (1989): 120–44.

Kunitz, Stephen J. "Benjamin Rush on Savagism and Progress." *Ethnohistory* 17 (1970): 31–42.

Kurtz, Stephen G. "The Political Science of John Adams: A Guide to His Statecraft." *William and Mary Quarterly* 25 (1968): 605–13.

Larkin, Oliver W. *Art and Life in America.* New York, 1949.

Lehman, Karl. *Thomas Jefferson, American Humanist.* 1947; rpt., Charlottesville, Va., 1985.

Leibniz, Gottfried. *Theodicy: Essays on the Goodness of God, the Freedom of Man, and the Origin of Evil.* 1710. Ed. Austin Farrer. La Salle, Ill., 1985.

Levin, David. *History as Romantic Art: Bancroft, Prescott, Motley, and Parkman.* Stanford, Calif., 1959.

Lévi-Strauss, Claude. *The Savage Mind.* London, 1966.

Levy, Leonard W. *Jefferson and Civil Liberties: The Darker Side.* Cambridge, Mass., 1963.

Lévy-Bruhl, Lucien. *How Natives Think.* Princeton, N.J., 1985.

Lewis, Jan, and Peter S. Onuf. "American Synecdoche: Thomas Jefferson as Image, Icon, Character, and Self." *American Historical Review* 103 (1998): 125–36.

Lewis, Richard Warrington Baldwin. *The American Adam: Innocence, Tragedy, and Tradition in the Nineteenth Century.* Chicago, 1955.

Lienesch, Michael. "The Constitutional Tradition: History, Political Action, and Progress in American Political Thought." *Journal of Politics* 42 (1980): 2–30.

———. *New Order of the Ages: Time, the Constitution, and the Making of Modern American Political Thought.* Princeton, N.J., 1988.

Liss, Peggy K. *Atlantic Empires: The Network of Trade and Revolution, 1713–1826.* Baltimore, 1983.

Loewenberg, James. *American History in American Thought.* New York, 1972.

Looby, Christopher. "The Constitution of Nature: Taxonomy as Politics in Jefferson, Peale, and Bartram." *Early American Literature* 22 (1987): 252–73.

Lovejoy, Arthur, and George Boas, eds. *Primitivism and Related Ideas in Antiquity.* 1935; rpt., Baltimore, 1997.

Lynn, Kenneth S. *A Divided People.* Westport, Conn., 1977.

Machiavelli, Niccolò. *Discourses on the First Ten Books of Titus Livius.* In *The Historical, Political, and Diplomatic Writings of Niccolo Machiavelli.* 4 vols. Boston, 1882.

Madison, James. *The Papers of James Madison.* Ed. William T. Hutchinson, William M. E. Rachal, et al. 17 vols. Chicago and Charlottesville, Va., 1959–91.

Malone, Dumas. *Jefferson and His Time.* 6 vols. Boston, 1948–81.

Manning, Susan, and Francis D. Cogliano. *The Atlantic Enlightenment.* Aldershot, Eng., 2008.

Marmor, Theodore R. "Anti-Industrialism and the Old South: The Agrarian Perspective of John C. Calhoun." *Comparative Studies in Society and History* 9 (1967): 377–406.

Marshall, Peter, and David Manuel. *The Light and the Glory: Did God Have a Plan for America?* Old Tappan, N.J., 1977.

Marx, Leo. *The Machine in the Garden: Technology and the Pastoral Ideal in America.* New York, 1964.

Matthews, Richard K. *The Radical Politics of Thomas Jefferson: A Revisionist View.* Lawrence, Kans., 1984.

Matthewson, Tim. "Jefferson and Haiti." *Journal of Southern History* 61 (1995): 209–48.

May, Henry F. *The Enlightenment in America.* New York, 1976.

Mazlish, Bruce. "Leadership in the American Revolution: The Psychological Dimension." In *Leadership in the American Revolution,* 113–33. Library of Congress Symposia on the American Revolution, 9 and 10 May 1974. Washington, D.C., 1974.

McCaleb, Walter F. *The Aaron Burr Conspiracy; and, A New Light on Aaron Burr.* New York, 1966.

McCoy, Drew R. *The Elusive Republic: Political Economy in Jeffersonian America.* Chapel Hill, N.C., 1980.

McDonald, Forrest. *Novus Ordo Seclorum: The Intellectual Origins of the Constitution.* Lawrence, Kans., 1985.

McLaughlin, Jack. "Jefferson, Poe, and Ossian." *Eighteenth-Century Studies* 26 (1993): 627–34.

Meek, Ronald L. *Social Science and the Ignoble Savage.* Cambridge, 1976.

Mettrie, Julien Offray de La. *Man a Machine.* 1747. Ed. Gertrude C. Bussey. Chicago, 1912.

Miller, Charles A. *Jefferson and Nature: An Interpretation.* Baltimore, 1988.

———. *Ship of State: The Nautical Metaphors of Thomas Jefferson.* Lanham, Md., 2003.

Miller, Ralph N. "American Nationalism as a Theory of Nature." *William and Mary Quarterly* 12 (1955): 74–95.

Miroff, Bruce. "John Adams: Merit, Fame, and Political Leadership." *Journal of Politics* 48 (1986): 116–32.

Montesquieu, Charles Louis de Secondat, Baron de. *The Spirit of Laws.* 1748; rpt., New York, 1984.

Morgan, Edmund S. *Inventing the People: The Rise of Popular Sovereignty in England and America.* New York, 1988.

Morley, Neville. "Decadence as a Theory of History." *New Literary History* 35 (2004): 573–85.

Murrin, John M. "A Roof without Walls: The Dilemma of American National Identity." In *Beyond Confederation: Origins of the Constitution and American National Identity,* ed. Richard R. Beeman, Stephen Botein, and Edward C. Carter II, 333–48. Chapel Hill, N.C., 1987.

Nagel, Paul C. *One Nation Indivisible: The Union in American Thought, 1776–1861.* New York, 1964.

Nash, Gary. *The Unknown American Revolution: The Unruly Birth of Democracy and the Struggle to Create America.* New York, 2005.

Nash, Roderick Frazier. *Wilderness and the American Mind.* 1967; rpt., New Haven, Conn., 2001.

Nelson, William E. "Reason and Compromise in the Establishment of the Federal Constitution, 1787–1801." *William and Mary Quarterly* 44 (1987): 458–84.

Niebuhr, Reinhold. *Faith and History: A Comparison of Christian and Modern Views of History.* New York, 1949.

Nisbet, Robert A. *History of the Idea of Progress.* 1970; rpt., New Brunswick, N.J., 1994.

O'Brien, Conor Cruise. *The Long Affair: Thomas Jefferson and the French Revolution, 1785–1800.* Chicago, 1996.

Onuf, Peter S., ed. *Jeffersonian Legacies.* Charlottesville, Va., 1993.

———. *Jefferson's Empire: The Language of American Nationhood.* Charlottesville, Va., 2000.

———. "The Scholars' Jefferson." *William and Mary Quarterly* 50 (1993): 671–99.

Paine, Thomas. *Common Sense.* 1776. Ed. Isaac Kramnick. Rpt., Harmondsworth, Eng., 1976.

Pangle, Thomas. *The Spirit of Modern Republicanism: The Moral Vision of the American Founders and the Philosophy of Locke.* Chicago, 1988.

Persons, Stow. *American Minds: A History of Ideas.* New York, 1958.

———. "The Cyclical Theory of History in Eighteenth Century America." *American Quarterly* 6 (1954): 147–63.

Peterson, Merrill D. *The Jefferson Image in the American Mind.* New York, 1960.

———. *Thomas Jefferson and the New Nation: A Biography.* New York, 1970.

Pocock, J. G. A. *The Ancient Constitution and the Feudal Law: A Study of English Historical Thought in the Seventeenth Century.* 1957; rpt., Cambridge, 1987.

———. "Civic Humanism and Its Role in Anglo-American Thought." *Politics, Language, and Time: Essays on Political Thought and History,* 80–103. New York, 1971.

———. *The Machiavellian Moment: Florentine Political Thought and the American Republican Tradition.* 1975; rpt., Princeton, N.J., 2003.

Porter, Roy. *The Creation of the Modern World: The Untold Story of the British Enlightenment.* New York, 2000.

Porter, Roy, and Mikuláš Teich, eds. *The Enlightenment in National Context.* Cambridge, 1981.

Primer, Irving. "Erasmus Darwin's *Temple of Nature:* Progress, Evolution, and the Eleusinian Mysteries." *Journal of the History of Ideas* 25 (1964): 58–76.

Racevskis, Karlis. *Postmodernism and the Search for Enlightenment.* Charlottesville, Va., 1993.

Randolph, Sarah N. *The Domestic Life of Thomas Jefferson.* 1871; rpt., Charlottesville, Va., 1978.

Raynal, Abbé. *A Philosophical and Political History of the Settlements and Trade of the Europeans in the East and West Indies.* 1770; rpt., Edinburgh, 1804.

Reinhold, Meyer. "The Classical World." In *Thomas Jefferson: A Reference Biography,* ed. Merrill D. Peterson, 135–56. New York, 1986.

Richard, Carl J. "A Dialogue with the Ancients: Thomas Jefferson and Classical Philosophy and History." *Journal of the Early Republic* 9 (1989): 431–55.

———. *The Founders and the Classics: Greece, Rome, and the American Enlightenment.* Cambridge, Mass., 1994.

Richardson, Edgar P. *Painting in America: From 1502 to the Present.* New York, 1965.

Rodgers, Daniel T. "Republicanism: The Career of a Concept." *Journal of American History* 79 (1992): 11–38.

Roediger, David R. "The Pursuit of Whiteness: Property, Terror, and Expansion, 1790–1860." *Journal of the Early Republic* 19 (1999): 579–600.

Ross, Dorothy. "Historical Consciousness in Nineteenth-Century America." *American Historical Review* 89 (1984): 909–28.

Rush, Benjamin. *The Autobiography of Benjamin Rush: His "Travels through Life" Together with His Commonplace Book for 1789–1813.* Ed. George W. Corner. Princeton, N.J., 1948.

———. *An Inquiry into the Influence of Physical Causes upon the Moral Faculty.* Philadelphia, 1786.

———. *Letters of Benjamin Rush.* Ed. Lyman H. Butterfield. 2 vols. Princeton, N.J., 1951.

Sanford, Charles B. *Thomas Jefferson and His Library: A Study of His Literary Interests and of the Religious Attitudes Revealed by Relevant Titles in His Library.* Hamden, Conn., 1977.

Scheick, William J. "Chaos and Imaginative Order in Thomas Jefferson's *Notes on the State of Virginia.*" In *Essays in Early Virginia Literature Honoring Richard Beale Davis,* ed. J. A. Leo Lemay, 221–34. New York, 1977.

Schlesinger, Arthur. "America: Experiment or Destiny?" *American Historical Review* 82 (1977): 505–22.

———. "History and National Stupidity." *New York Review of Books* 53, no. 7 (27 April 2006): 14–16.

Schofield, Robert E. *Mechanism and Materialism: British Natural Philosophy in an Age of Reason.* Princeton, N.J., 1970.

Schulz, Constance B. "John Adams on 'The Best of All Possible Worlds.'" *Journal of the History of Ideas* 44 (1983): 561–77.

Shaffer, Arthur H. *The Politics of History: Writing the History of the American Revolution, 1783–1815.* Chicago, 1975.

Shalev, Eran. *Rome Reborn on Western Shores: Historical Imagination and the Creation of the American Republic.* Charlottesville, Va., 2009.

Shaw, Peter. *American Patriots and the Rituals of Revolution.* Cambridge, Mass., 1981.

———. *The Character of John Adams.* Chapel Hill, N.C., 1976.

Sheehan, Bernard W. *Seeds of Extinction: Jeffersonian Philanthropy and the American Indian.* Chapel Hill, N.C., 1973.

Sheldon, Garrett Ward. *The Political Philosophy of Thomas Jefferson.* Baltimore, 1991.

Shoemaker, Robert W. "'Democracy' and 'Republic' as Understood in Late Eighteenth-Century America." *American Speech* 41 (1966): 83–95.

Silver, Mildred. "Emerson and the Idea of Progress." *American Literature* 12 (1940): 1–19.

Simpson, Stephen. *The Lives of George Washington and Thomas Jefferson: With a Parallel.* Philadelphia, 1833.

Sinopoli, Richard. *The Foundations of American Citizenship: Liberalism, the Constitution, and Civic Virtue.* New York, 1992.

Sloan, Herbert, "The Earth Belongs in Usufruct to the Living." In Onuf, *Jeffersonian Legacies,* 281–315.

Slotkin, Richard. *The Fatal Environment: The Myth of the Frontier in the Age of Industrialization, 1800–1890.* New York, 1985.

———. *Regeneration through Violence: The Mythology of the American Frontier, 1600–1860.* Middletown, Conn., 1973.

Smith-Rosenberg, Carroll. "Dis-Covering the Subject of the 'Great Constitutional Discussion,' 1786–1789." *Journal of American History* 79 (1992): 841–73.

Spahn, Hannah. *Thomas Jefferson, Time, and History.* Charlottesville, Va., forthcoming.

Spurlin, Paul Merril. *The French Enlightenment in America: Essays on the Times of the Founding Fathers.* Athens, Ga., 1984.

Staloff, Darren. *Hamilton, Adams, Jefferson: The Politics of the Enlightenment and the American Founding.* New York, 2005.

Stampp, Kenneth M. "The Concept of a Perpetual Union." *Journal of American History* 65 (1978): 5–33.

Strout, Cushing. *The American Image of the Old World.* New York, 1963.

Stuart, Reginald C. *The Half-Way Pacifist: Thomas Jefferson's View of War.* Toronto, 1978.

Sutcliff, Robert. *Travels in Some Parts of North America, in the Years 1804, 1805, and 1806.* Philadelphia, 1812.

Thomas, Laurence. "Moral Deference." In *African American Perspectives and Philosophical Traditions,* ed. John P. Pittman, 233–50. New York, 1997.

Thomson, Keith. *A Passion for Nature: Thomas Jefferson and Natural History.* Chapel Hill, N.C., 2008.

"Thoughts on the Decline of States." *Massachusetts Magazine* 3 (July 1791).

Trees, Andy. "John Adams and the Problem of Virtue." *Journal of the Early Republic* 21 (2001): 393–412.

Tucker, Robert W., and David C. Hendrickson. *Empire of Liberty: The Statecraft of Thomas Jefferson.* New York, 1990.

Tuveson, Ernest L. *Redeemer Nation: The Idea of America's Millennial Role.* Chicago, 1968.

Valsania, Maurizio. "'Another and the Same': Nature and Human Beings in Erasmus Darwin's Doctrines of Love and Imagination." In *The Genius of Erasmus Darwin,* ed. C. U. M. Smith and Robert Arnott, 337–55. Aldershot, Eng., 2005.

———. "'Our Original Barbarism': Man vs. Nature in Thomas Jefferson's Moral Experience." *Journal of the History of Ideas* 65 (2004): 627–45.

Van Tassel, David D. *Recording America's Past: An Interpretation of the Development of Historical Studies in America, 1607–1884.* Chicago, 1960.

Vetterli, Richard, and Gary Bryner. *In Search of the Republic: Public Virtue and the Roots of American Government.* 1987; rpt., Lanham, Md., 1996.

Vyverberg, Henry. *Historical Pessimism in the French Enlightenment.* Cambridge, Mass., 1958.

Wagoner, Jennings L., Jr. *Jefferson and Education.* Chapel Hill, N.C., 2004.

Waldstreicher, David. *In the Midst of Perpetual Fetes: The Making of American Nationalism, 1776–1820.* Chapel Hill, N.C., 1997.

Warren-Adams Letters: Being Chiefly a Correspondence among John Adams, Samuel Adams, and James Warren. 2 vols. Boston, 1917–25.

Washington, George. *George Washington: Writings.* Ed. John H. Rhodehamel. New York, 1997.

Waters, John J. "James Otis, Jr.: An Ambivalent Revolutionary." *History of Childhood Quarterly* 1 (1973): 142–50.

Webster, Noah. *An American Selection of Lessons in Reading and Speaking.* 3rd ed. Philadelphia, 1787.

White, Morton. *The Philosophy of the American Revolution.* New York, 1978.

———. *Philosophy, The Federalist, and the Constitution.* New York, 1987.

White, Morton, and Lucia White. *The Intellectual versus the City: From Thomas Jefferson to Frank Lloyd Wright.* Cambridge, Mass., 1962.

Wierich, Jochen. "Struggling through History: Emanuel Leutze, Hegel, and Empire." *American Art* 15 (2001): 52–71.

Wilentz, Sean. *The Rise of American Democracy: Jefferson to Lincoln*. New York, 2005.

Williams, William Appleman. *The Contours of American History*. 1961; rpt., New York, 1988.

Wills, Garry. *Inventing America: Jefferson's Declaration of Independence*. Boston, 1978.

———. *"Negro President": Jefferson and the Slave Power*. Boston, 2003.

Wilson, Douglas L. *Jefferson's Books*. Charlottesville, Va., 1996.

———. "Jefferson vs. Hume." *William and Mary Quarterly* 46 (1989): 49–70.

———. "Thomas Jefferson's Early Notebooks." *William and Mary Quarterly* 42 (1985): 433–52.

Withers, Charles W. J. *Placing the Enlightenment: Thinking Geographically about the Age of Reason*. Chicago, 2007.

Wolff, Larry. "Discovering Cultural Perspective: The Intellectual History of Anthropological Thought in the Age of Enlightenment." In *The Anthropology of the Enlightenment*, ed. Larry Wolff and Marco Cipolloni, 3–32. Stanford, Calif., 2007.

Wood, Gordon S. "Conspiracy and the Paranoid Style: Causality and Deceit in the Eighteenth Century." *William and Mary Quarterly* 39 (1982): 401–41.

———. *The Creation of the American Republic, 1776–1787*. Chapel Hill, N.C., 1969.

———. *Radicalism of the American Revolution*. New York, 1993.

———. "The Significance of the Early Republic." *Journal of the Early Republic* 8 (1988): 1–20.

———. "The Trials and Tribulations of Thomas Jefferson." In Onuf, *Jeffersonian Legacies*, 395–417.

Yarbrough, Jean. "The Constitution and Character: The Missing Critical Principle?" In *To Form a More Perfect Union: The Critical Ideas of the Constitution*, ed. Herman Belz, Ronald Hoffman, and Peter J. Albert, 217–49. Charlottesville, Va., 1992.

Zuckerman, Michael. *Almost Chosen People: Oblique Biographies in the American Grain*. Berkeley, Calif. 1993.

———. "The Fabrication of Identity in Early America." In Zuckerman, *Almost Chosen People*, 21–54.

———. "The Power of Blackness: Thomas Jefferson and the Revolution in St. Domingue." In Zuckerman, *Almost Chosen People*, 175–218.

Zuckert, Michael P. *The Natural Rights Republic: Studies in the Foundation of the American Political Tradition*. Notre Dame, Ind., 1996.

Index

Recent Books in the Jeffersonian America Series

Douglas Bradburn
The Citizenship Revolution: Politics and the Creation of the American Union, 1774–1804

Clarence E. Walker
Mongrel Nation: The America Begotten by Thomas Jefferson and Sally Hemings

Timothy Mason Roberts
Distant Revolutions: 1848 and the Challenge to American Exceptionalism

Peter J. Kastor and François Weil, editors
Empires of the Imagination: Transatlantic Histories of the Louisiana Purchase

Eran Shalev
Rome Reborn on Western Shores: Historical Imagination and the Creation of the American Republic

Leonard J. Sadosky
Revolutionary Negotiations: Indians, Empires, and Diplomats in the Founding of America

Philipp Ziesche
Cosmopolitan Patriots: Americans in Paris in the Age of Revolution

Leonard J. Sadosky, Peter Nicolaisen, Peter S. Onuf, and Andrew J. O'Shaughnessy, editors
Old World, New World: America and Europe in the Age of Jefferson

Sam W. Haynes
Unfinished Revolution: The American Republic in a British World, 1815–1850

Michal Jan Rozbicki
Culture and Liberty in the Age of the American Revolution

Ellen Holmes Pearson
Remaking Custom: Law and Identity in the Early American Republic

Seth Cotlar
Tom Paine's America: The Rise and Fall of Transatlantic Radicalism

John Craig Hammond and Matthew Mason, editors
Contesting Slavery: The Politics of Bondage and Freedom in the New American Nation

Ruma Chopra
Unnatural Rebellion: Loyalists in New York City during the Revolution

Maurizio Valsania
The Limits of Optimism: Thomas Jefferson's Dualistic Enlightenment

CPSIA information can be obtained at www.ICGtesting.com
Printed in the USA
BVOW08s1414150715

408966BV00001B/29/P